After Adorno

Theodor W. Adorno placed music at the centre of his critique of modernity and broached some of the most important questions about the role of music in contemporary society. One of his central arguments was that music, through the manner of its composition, affected consciousness and was a means of social management and control. His work was primarily theoretical, however, and because these issues were never explored empirically his work has become sidelined in current music sociology. This book argues that music sociology can be greatly enriched by a return to Adorno's concerns, in particular his focus on music as a dynamic medium of social life. Intended as a guide to 'how to do music sociology', this book deals with critical topics too often sidelined such as aesthetic ordering, cognition, the emotions and music as a management device, and reworks Adorno's focus through a series of grounded examples.

TIA DENORA is head of department and professer of sociology of music at the University of Exeter. She has published widely on music sociology. Her books include *Beethoven and the Construction of Genius* (1995) and *Music in Everyday Life* (2000).

After Adorno
Rethinking Music Sociology

Tia DeNora

CAMBRIDGE
UNIVERSITY PRESS

CAMBRIDGE UNIVERSITY PRESS
Cambridge, New York, Melbourne, Madrid, Cape Town, Singapore,
São Paulo, Delhi, Dubai, Tokyo

Cambridge University Press
The Edinburgh Building, Cambridge CB2 8RU, UK

Published in the United States of America by Cambridge University Press, New York

www.cambridge.org
Information on this title: www.cambridge.org/9780521537247

First published 2003

A catalogue record for this publication is available from the British Library

Library of Congress Cataloguing in Publication data
DeNora, Tia
After Adorno : rethinking music sociology / Tia DeNora.
    p.   cm.
Includes bibliographical references (p. 159) and index.
Contents: Adorno, 'defended against his devotees' – New methods and classic
concerns – Music as cognition – How does music 'channel' emotion? – Music and
"control" – After Adorno : rethinking music sociology.
ISBN 0-521-83025-7 – ISBN 0-521-53724-X (pb.)
1. Music – Social aspects.   2. Music – Philosophy and aesthetics.
I. Adorno, Theodor W, 1903–1969.   II. Title
ML3795.D3428   2003
780'.1 – dc21   2003051525

ISBN 978-0-521-83025-6 Hardback
ISBN 978-0-521-53724-7 Paperback

Transferred to digital printing 2010

In fond remembrance of the musical séances, Victoria Palace, Winter 1981

New music: new listening. Not an attempt to understand something that is being said, for, if something were being said, the sounds would be given the shapes of words. Just an attention to the activity of sounds.

John Cage

Contents

Figures

Music examples

Preface: A two part invention

In the early 1980s, I attended a public lecture given by a prominent American sociologist now deceased. We were introduced and conversed briefly. He enquired politely about my academic aspirations and I described my interest in Adorno's socio-musical work. (My undergraduate thesis had been on the *Philosophy of Modern Music* (see DeNora 1986a) and I counted myself as one of Adorno's most ardent devotees.) To the best of my recollection, this sociologist said, 'and what will you do when you *finish* with Adorno, *for finish with him you will*?'

His words stung at the time. But, by the mid-1980s, in the second year of the Sociology Ph.D. programme at University of California, San Diego (UCSD) I had – or so I then assumed – 'finished' with Adorno. Tuning in to a curriculum that emphasised socio-linguistics, ethnomethodology, and action theory, and reading Becker's *Art Worlds* (then something of a watershed), I became less interested in what I began to see as 'impossible' questions about music's link to consciousness and domination. I began to work on the question of musical identity and value, viewed through the prism of reputation in-the-making. As a case-in-point I chose to focus on Beethoven and his musical world in late eighteenth-century Vienna. At that point, for me, Adorno came to seem not only remote but – worse – empirically suspect. His books and writings, and the various studies of his works by others over which I had pored during the late 1970s and early 1980s, were pushed further to the back of my bookshelf as I immersed myself in the history of musical institutions.

It has taken me over twenty years working as a music sociologist to return to Adorno. And I realise now that there is no need to have to choose between the role of acolyte or opponent. It is far more interesting to explore the interplay of 'theme' and 'counter theme', between Adorno's perspective and the perspectives of others on socio-musical subjects. It is with such 'invention' in mind, then, that this book addresses Adorno's work on music, with attention to the critique Adorno has received at the hands of current music sociology and cognate areas. I hope to illuminate a few of the places where, at the centenary of Adorno's birth

(11 September 2003), it is possible to build upon Adorno and in grounded ways. In wending my way through Adorno's musical oeuvre and its critique, I shall suggest that, in its inception, Adorno's socio-musical work is undoubtedly brilliant. I shall also suggest that we gain little by regarding it as a finished system. Indeed, in so far as Adorno's life's work was devoted to the critique of objectification, it seems only fitting that we do not attempt to canonise Adorno as a body of work incapable of change or adaptation. Let us instead consider his writings for insights that lend themselves to further development.

It has now been forty years since Adorno first published his *Introduction to the Sociology of Music*, and interest in his work has flourished. Despite the various criticisms that have been directed against Adorno's unique version of music sociology, there is no discounting its seriousness, no question that the questions he posed were profound. For this reason, Adorno remains a figure with whom to reckon.

In what follows, my aim is to connect Adorno with action-oriented, grounded music sociology. In that endeavour I hope also to provide a programme for doing music sociology (one that reflects my own views and approach within the field). In particular, my aim is to discuss the topics that formed the core of Adorno's agenda, in ways that make them amenable to empirical investigation. It is for this reason that I have called the book 'After Adorno' and I hope that readers will appreciate the double meaning here – both in homage to Adorno (for I believe that music sociology can be refreshed through renewed attention to Adorno's concern with musical structures, modes of listening, cognition, and 'control') and, simultaneously, moving beyond (to the side of?) his original methods and levels of theorising.

Chapter 1 offers a strategic summary of Adorno's socio-musical work, drawing out at the end key themes on which Adorno has been criticised by sociologists. In chapter 2, I review sociology of music and the new musicology and critique their respective conceptions of music (in sociology) and society (in musicology). From there, I describe a programme of grounded, actor-oriented research, focused on the concept of the Musical Event and suggest this programme establishes Adorno's concerns at the 'right' level of generality – at a level, that is, concerned with specifiable musical practices. Although this focus involves micro-level analysis, it lends itself, I argue, to traditionally macro-sociological concerns, illuminating these concerns at the level of action. Chapters 3 to 5 employ the programme outlined in chapter 2, to address Adornoian themes – music's relation to consciousness and cognition (chapter 3), subjectivity and emotions (chapter 4), and, drawing these themes together in chapter 5, the idea of ordering and social control. I hope, at the end of chapter 6, to have made a case that music sociology, empirically conceived, can not only be compatible with Adorno's original concerns, but can actually further cultural theory by helping to identify the mechanisms of how culture (music) works in relation to human agency.

Acknowledgements

I would like to thank the following for discussions and comments on aspects of the work developed here: Wayne Bowman, Daniel Cavicchi, Nicholas Cook, Eric Clarke, Tim Day, Tim Dowd, Olle Edström, Nancy Weiss Hanrahan, Antoine Hennion, Mark Jacobs, Patrik Juslin, Richard Leppert, Lars Lilliestam, Jan Marantate, Pete Martin, Arturo Rodriguez Morato, Susan O'Neill, Julian Rushton, John Shepherd, John Sloboda, Ola Stockfelt, Timothy Taylor, Anna Lisa Tota, Bob Witkin, Vera Zolberg, members of the ESA Arts Network, participants in seminars at the National Sound Archive at the British Library, music departments at Leeds, Southampton, Sheffield, and Oxford, the Sociology Departments at Loughborough and Manchester, the Psychology Department at Keele, the Gothenburg Conference on Musicology and Sociology, and three anonymous readers for Cambridge University Press. I would especially like to thank Sarah Caro, my editor at CUP. Sarah seems to have a gift for combining always-practical suggestions with a delicate touch and I am grateful for her wisdom. It has been a pleasure and a privilege to work with her over the course of two book projects. So, too, I should like to think Sally McCann for her eagle-eyed copy-editing, and Paul Watt at CUP, Cambridge, who steered the project through production. Finally, I would like to thank, for help on Adorno more than two decades ago now, Harvey Greisman, Gunter Remmling, and, for their very courteous answers to my student queries, W. V. Blomster and Martin Jay. Finally, I would like to thank my husband, Douglas Tudhope, for twenty-three years of conversation on and around Adornoian themes.

Parts of chapter 2 draw on material developed in Eric Clarke and Nicholas Cook (eds.), *Empirical Musicology* (Oxford University Press, 2003). Parts of chapter 4 draw on material previously published in Patrik Juslin and John Sloboda (eds.), *Music and Emotion* (Oxford University Press, 2001).

A note on background reading

What follows is not an introduction to Adorno nor is it intended to catalogue all of the themes and topics covered in his socio-musical œuvre.
Such an exercise is superfluous: there are many excellent studies of
Adorno to which readers may turn. These include Richard Leppert's
recent study ((2002) – published as a commentary to thirty-odd essays
by Adorno), and my friend and colleague at Exeter, Robert Witkin's
books (1998; 2002). There are also the now classic texts by Susan Buck-
Morss (1979) and Martin Jay (1984), and, within musicology, the exceptional essays by Rose Rosengard Subotnik (Subotnik 1991; 1996),
whose work set the initial agenda of Adorno studies within musicology
and dates back over more than two decades. Also highly useful is W. V.
Blomster's essay on Adorno's music sociology, published in *Telos* (1976).
For more overtly sociological critiques of Adorno, readers are referred in
particular to extended treatments in work by Peter Martin (1995) and
Richard Middleton (1990). And for a recent consideration of Adorno
in relation to late twentieth-century music technology, there is Michael
Bull's account of the practices of personal stereo use (2000), a work that
shares many of the perspectives developed in my own work on music
in everyday life (2000). All of these sources, in company with Adorno's
own writings, can be read before or as companions to what follows here.
(The most comprehensive bibliography of primary, secondary, and ter-
tiary sources in English can be found in Leppert's recent work (Adorno
2002:681–708).)

1 Adorno, 'defended against his devotees'?

Introduction – music matters

Music has power, or so many people believe. Across culture and time it has been linked with persuasion, healing, corruption, and many other transformational matters. The idea behind these linkages is that music *acts* – on consciousness, the body, the emotions. Associated with this idea is another – the idea that music, because of what it can *do*, should be subject to regulation and control.

The history of music in the West is punctuated with attempts to enlist and censure music's powers. Most interesting of these centre on music's tonal properties as distinct from lyrics or libretti. The realm of sacred music offers many examples – Charlemagne's *c.*800AD 'reform' of chant, Pope Gregory XIII's call for 'revising, purging, correcting and reforming' church music (Hoppin 1978:50), the late sixteenth-century Protestant call for plain hymn singing (as opposed to elaborate polyphony), and, slightly later, J. S. Bach's dictum that the purpose of sacred music was 'to organise the congregation' are some of the better known. In the political realm, music has been mobilised or suppressed for its effects. Shostakovich's commission for a symphony to mark the anniversary of the Russian Revolution (and his later censure for writing 'decadent' music), the banishment of atonal music in Nazi Germany, and, in relatively recent times, the furore over national anthem renditions (the Sex Pistols' *God Save the Queen* or Jimi Hendrix's version of the *Star Spangled Banner*) all attest to the idea that music can instigate consensus and/or subversion. If the lens is widened to consider music in a global perspective, even more dramatic examples emerge, most recently the prohibition, as reported in the Western media, of nearly all forms of music in Afghanistan. If there is one thing the world shares, musically speaking, it is probably the recognition, at times the *fear*, of what music may allow.

Today, debates about music, morality, and pedagogy continue with vigour in and outside of the academy – discussions concerning the so-called 'Mozart-effect', worry about heavy metal and its effect upon the young, the disruptive influence of any number of musical styles, and even, more recently a study sponsored by the British Automobile Association on the effects of music on driving safety. While it is true that in some cases music features in these discussions as a scapegoat or convenient marker of otherwise extra-musical concerns (as when music is criticised as a means of criticising its devotees or constituencies and their cultures), it would be hasty to discard the idea that music's *musical* properties may have power. For many people it is a matter of common sense that music has effects: we know this because we have *experienced* these effects, and *because* of music's effects upon us we may both seek out and avoid music. We know, in short, that music matters.

Until relatively recently, there has been a tradition within social theory devoted to the idea of music's power. That tradition can be traced at least to Plato. '[I]t seems that here in music', says the Socrates in Plato's *Republic*, 'the guardians will build their guardhouse . . . Then, from the start, in their earliest play the young will be kept to law and measure through music' (1966:72). What comes through clearly in this famous passage is the idea that social order is fostered by (and ultimately inextricable from) aesthetic, ceremonial, and moral order, and that these in turn are substantiated by ritual and by the arts. This way of conceptualising the bases of social order remained alive throughout the nineteenth century. Its legacy can be found in Durkheim's emphasis on the elementary forms – a work, albeit, in which music's role is neglected (Durkheim 1915).

One might have expected, with the rise of mechanical reproduction, the broadcast media, and the entertainment industry in the twentieth century, that the need for thinking about music's social functions would have intensified. And yet, within social philosophy after Saint-Simon, music's importance waned. As sociologists and social theorists turned to music in the twentieth century, it was typically *not* to take up the topic of music's social power. Instead, music has been posed more remotely, as a medium that 'reflects' or otherwise parallels social structure. This essentially formalist paradigm, characteristic of theorists as diverse as Max Weber, Dilthey, Simmel, and Sorokin, effectively neutralised more overt concerns with music's link to moral conduct. (For discussions of their work see Etzkorn 1973; Zolberg 1990 *passim*; and Martin 1995:75–167.) And with this neutralisation came a very different interrogative thrust: socio-musical studies moved *from a concern with what music 'caused' to what caused music*. In relation to this trend, music sociology began to develop as the sociology *of* music, a linguistic nuance within which some of the most intriguing questions about music and society, or, more precisely, music in and as society, came to be excised. Even in the otherwise fruitful (and grounded) focus of the 'art worlds' and 'production of culture' approaches of the late 1980s and 1990s (Peterson 1978; Becker 1982; DeNora 1995) the question of music's effects remained unanswered.

As a result, within the sociology of music, the medium of music was implicitly downgraded; its status shifted, from active ingredient or animating *force* to inanimate *product* (an object to be explained). Along with this downgrading, music became, during the twentieth century, a scholarly and specialist topic, and, as with most scholarly matters, the *passion* of the subject drained away such that, today, the fissure between ordinary, everyday responses to music and expert accounts of music came to seem both normal and acceptable. In recent years, there have been signs of change (described below) and interdisciplinary studies of music have gone a long way towards redressing music, as it were, 'in action'. There is, nonetheless, still a way to go.

Enter Adorno

It is from within this context that we can begin to appreciate the unique qualities of Theodor W. Adorno and his socio-musical project. For whatever reason – his minor career as a composer, his geographical and cultural displacement, his affiliation with fellow critical theorists – Adorno did, arguably, more to theorise music's powers than any other scholar during the first half of the twentieth century. Because of this – and despite the many faults that, with the benefit of hindsight, can be found with his work and method – Adorno is hailed, rightly, as the 'father' of the sociology of music (Shepherd 2001:605).

Adorno was intimately acquainted with music; for him, music was not a topic to be considered abstractly in terms of the social forces that shaped it or in terms of its structural properties. Music was, by contrast, a living, dynamic medium. And it was, arguably, from the standpoint of his involvement with music that Adorno launched his philosophical and sociological work. As described in the next chapters, Adorno used music *to think with*. He also devoted his thinking to the ways that music could, for better or worse, transform consciousness. It is critical to recognise from the outset that, for Adorno, socio-musical enquiry provided the key to a perspective that encompassed a breathtakingly broad interrogative span – philosophy and sociology of knowledge, cultural history of consciousness, the history of social cohesion, dominance, and submission. To understand Adorno's work on music, therefore, it is necessary to lodge it within these much broader concerns.

The idea of negative dialectics

Adorno could not have been more serious. His work explored the failure of reason that culminated in the catastrophic events of the twentieth century: the rise of fascism, genocide, terror, and mass destruction. More specifically, he sought to understand what he perceived as a transformation of consciousness, one that fostered authoritarian modes of ruling. To this end, Adorno's project begins philosophically with a critique of reason. It ends, one might argue, sociologically with a psycho-cultural study of consciousness and its conditions. Both of these components of his work need to be understood as part of a wider, interdisciplinary project.

Adorno's critique of reason centres on the idea that material reality is more complex than the ideas and concepts available for describing it. Reality – by which Adorno meant not only nature but also the specificity of lived experience – cannot be fully addressed by words, measurements, concepts, and categories, all of which must be understood at best as approximations of reality, as socially constituted ideas or images of phenomena. In this respect, Adorno was, and remained throughout his life, a materialist and a philosopher of the actual. His work highlighted the disjunction between ideas and material reality, a gap within which the former might be useful, indeed, even 'effective', but never be eternally or comprehensively 'true'.

There were, in Adorno's view, grave dangers associated with equating ideas and reality. First, such an association rendered reason conformist. Second, it deprived reason of its critical, reflexive edge. Third, it built into reason an authoritarian tendency, one in which reality was made to fit reason's pre-designed containers rather than reason bespoke to accommodate reality. These dangers were, according to Adorno, compounded by modern commodity exchange and its cultural correlate – the idea of values as 'goods'. The result, in the twentieth century, was an alteration of reason's character. Reason had become both inflated and linked to an over-estimation of itself and to an under-estimation of reality. The tendency to worship science and to accept without question whatever was purveyed under the banner of science exemplified this inflation *par excellence*. The task of modern philosophy, therefore, was to point up reality's *non-identification* with reason. This task was, in essence, criticism, and it was to be advanced through the idea of negative dialectics.

Unlike both Hegel and Marx, Adorno was not interested in contributing positive knowledge 'about' reality. Adorno sought no form of 'synthesis', whether posed in terms of an ideal formulation about reality or as a philosophy of history culminating in a utopian, and thus positive, state. By contrast, Adorno sought to illuminate difference and contradiction – the residual, the ill-fitting, non-sense, in short, anything that did not 'fit' within existing categories of thought. Through this process, Adorno sought to refine thought. This task was in turn oriented to reconfiguring reason as a form of suspended recognition, that is, as continuous moments of non-recognition between reason and reality. These moments of non-recognition in turn provided a means by which greater complexity could be revealed. Adorno's famous aphorism, 'the whole is the untrue', encapsulates this point: the idea of negative dialectics was thus a mandate for reason to engage in self-critique. In this respect, and despite the humanist estimation of reason that permeates his work, Adorno's idea of negative dialectics is ultimately about the humility of knowledge, its inextricably social – and thus moral – character.

The concern with cognition is central to Adorno's thought world. To gain familiarity with that world it is necessary to understand what Adorno meant when he spoke of reason's tendency to objectify and, along with this, to understand objectification as a social process, that is, as a form of praxis, as described in the two next sections. From there, it is possible to contextualise Adorno's views on the degraded role of both science and art as forms of knowledge in the modern world. These topics, which together highlight Adorno's *philosophical* beginnings, in turn provide the groundwork for embarking upon what, from a *sociological* perspective, may be viewed as the *core* of Adorno's work: his focus on the role played by cultural machineries in relation to objectification, the inclusion, within his philosophy, of a theory of the unconscious, and, related to this second feature, his concern with the links between aesthetic structures and styles of consciousness.

What is objectification?

An objectifying mentality led away from dialectical thinking. It posed instead an identity between human ideas (concepts) and material realities in ways that made these realities appear axiomatic – and therefore non-negotiable. It is important to note that, for Adorno, objectification was *activity* (praxis); it was the subject who, through particular habits of mind, accomplished this work. For Adorno, the subject was thus complicit in her own cognitive alienation. It was the cultural basis of this complicity that Adorno-the-sociologist sought to explore.

Objectification was simultaneously cognitive violence. (In this sense, Adorno's focus overlaps with the post-structuralist concern with discourse and its totalising powers.) For, when an objectifying mentality had come to be established as a habit of mind, the impetus to excise what did not 'fit' pre-given assumptions about the nature of reality also became routine – part of the tacit practices of perceiving and responding to material reality. This objectifying form of consciousness – directed away from the perception of discrepancy – was, needless to say, overly, i.e., ritualistically, conservative: it was oriented to the recognition (and thus reproduction) of general categories (as opposed to a constant interrogation of those categories by material reality). As such, it entailed a generic orientation to the world, characterised, for example, by tacit assumptions about classes and categories of people and the treatment of individuals as instances of those categories. It also involved assumptions about the nature of things (aspects of the material environment) as general types, assumptions which, if acted upon, abolished proximate – intimate – experience of things.

In Adorno's view, such a consciousness was not only dehumanised (it failed to search for specific differences that would, in turn, enlarge general categories of thought); it was above all a consciousness amenable to externally imposed relations of ruling. In the identification such consciousness made between ideas and material realities, it generated *belief in* a 'reliable', i.e., *stable*, material and social world, a world that, in the oft-quoted passage from the *Dialectic of Enlightenment*, 'simply exists'. To speak in this way of a *belief* in 'what simply exists' is to speak of what Adorno occasionally calls, the 'ontological ideology' (Adorno 1981:62). As a habit of mind, the ontological ideology was characterised by a taste for certainty, itself a symptom, in Adorno's view, of lax cognitive functioning. And this habit was highly conducive to 'rational' administration in so far as, at the local level, actors reinforce (identify with) general concepts, modelling the particularity of their experience or action upon those concepts so as to 'fit' or make sense of the 'here and now' in terms of the 'there and then', i.e., to ideas of what is *supposed* (by actors) *to be*. To illustrate objectification as praxis (how actors 'fit' the general to the particular and thereby do violence to the latter while simultaneously aligning themselves with ruling authorities), it is worth considering how Adorno's perspective can be compared to other strands of sociology similarly concerned with the ways that 'reality' comes to be produced as an objective fact. Consider, for example, the ethnomethodological perspective on this topic.

Objectification as social practice

One of the most compelling descriptions of this process can be found in Garfinkel's classic study of the inter-sexed person Agnes (Garfinkel 1967). Garfinkel's essay ('Passing and the Managed Achievement of Sexual Status as an Intersexed Person') examines the practices 'Agnes' employed so as to 'pass' as a generic type of human being – a 'woman'. In this work Garfinkel prefigured subsequent perspectives in performance theory (e.g., Butler 1989) with his focus on the situated practices through which cultural 'work' gets done, performances through which the 'reality' of cultural, often institutional categories (here the identity between the categories of biological sex and natural phenomena and their link to social institutions such as the family), is reproduced. To 'fit' herself into the category 'woman', for example, Agnes mobilised skills and material props (1950s pearls and twin-set sweaters, cookery skills); she subjected herself to radical techniques of body modification (hormones and surgery); and took care to avoid situations that threatened to reveal her less feminine characteristics and attributes (she would not wear a swimming costume; she avoided 'dangerous' intimate situations). In this way, and, critically, by *suppressing* aspects of her material reality, Agnes managed to 'pass' ('for all practical purposes') as a woman.

The lessons to be drawn from Garfinkel's study apply to the performance of *all* meanings, of all cultural categories *as if* they are naturally occurring. What Agnes did, so too 'real' women (and men) do – they orient to (and through their praxis attempt to reproduce) assumed features of socially constituted, generic categories. Agnes's more extreme version of this process thus serves to highlight 'normal' praxis; it illuminates how the specific is rendered in general terms; how, in this case, 'femaleness' (one could here substitute any number of other categories of identity) is achieved through interpretive and material practice – both Agnes's practice and also the practices of those who come to perceive and act towards her as 'a woman'. We also see, in this case study, how difference (that which does not fit within a category) is excised as an often-tacit matter of practical experience. Through these practices, that which is assumed to be an axiomatic feature of material reality comes to take on the appearance of what Garfinkel and the ethnomethodologists call a 'for-all-practical purposes', 'natural, normal world'.

In similar vein, the work of Erving Goffman, on self-presentation, shows us actors as they draw upon pre-given modalities, scripts, images, and other externally provided materials (this topic will be discussed in chapter 5 in relation to the theory of cultural repertoires) so as to enact meaningful social scenarios. We see Goffman's actors produce themselves as 'types' of workers, personalities, or subjects. In this respect, Goffman's actors are fundamentally conservative; they are oriented to (as they perceive them) the culture and requirements of organisations and institutions; to what it takes, in other words, to 'get the work done' and thus to perpetuate organisationally and institutionally specific arrangements.

While at first glance Garfinkel and Goffman may seem unduly remote from Adorno's concerns, their work can also be read as highlighting the discrepancy or gap between social categories and material reality. In their reports, we are able to see some of the *work* that actors do, as practical and interpretive agents, to maintain a cognitive-ritual order. And thus we see what *does not fit* as it is fitted into preconceived forms, as cognitive (and in Agnes's case, physical) violence is done to material reality. From Adorno's critical point of view, the work performed by the actors described by Garfinkel and Goffman would consist of nothing less than mistaken identity – i.e., activity that is obeisant to the authority of the object (i.e., an apparently natural category of being such as sex or a stipulated institutional category). This type of obeisance is one that does not impinge upon the shape of that object or the thought system within which it is lodged. That is, the violence done to material so as to make it conform to an idea precludes any need to refashion – recompose – the idea so as to accommodate it to reality.

Adorno was never an interactionist nor did he concern himself with work in that tradition (indeed there are few references to *any* American sociology in his work). His work diverges markedly from interactionist and ethnomethodological perspectives in that he turned away from a concern with *actual* social practice in favour of a focus on more 'macro'-cultural concerns. By this I mean that he lodged the forms of obeisance described by scholars such as Goffman in *historical* perspective and conceptualised them as modes of consciousness and cognitive praxis, that is, as *structures* of consciousness standing outside individuals and thus serving as conditions for, and of, consciousness (on this point, and for an ethnomethodological account of knowledge production that does provide a historical perspective on knowledge as mode of praxis, see Pollner 1987). In particular, Adorno considered that subjective praxis of objectification was historically specific, a hallmark of modern thought. As part of that project, he criticised the formulation of what passed for knowledge under modernity in his and Horkheimer's jointly written *Dialectic of Enlightenment* (to which, it is worth underlining, Adorno's *Philosophy of Modern Music* was intended as an extended appendix). Examining the critique of science put forward by Adorno, and the transformation of science in the post-enlightenment period and beyond, helps to highlight Adorno's views on the 'true' social role of art – as a condition through which consciousness was structured in the modern world. It is, more specifically, in his treatment of the science–art dichotomy that the groundwork is laid for his ideas about art's (music's) cognitive function, that is, music's link to the shape and tendency of consciousness under modernity, to be conjoined to the habits of mind that characterised the ontological ideology.

In the modern world, Adorno considered, art had been stripped of its status as a means for knowing and, with it, the role of the un-conscious (or quasi conscious) in knowledge formation forgotten.

Art 'versus' science

In Adorno's eyes, the post-enlightenment dualism of art 'versus' science (the impoverished role of the former; the ascendancy of the latter) was symptomatic of the debasement of *both* science and art under modernity (capitalism, cultural commodification, and authoritarian political rule). This debasement was, in turn, part of what Adorno perceived as the 'crisis' of modernity, the disconnection of subject and object, or, in Marxian terms, the alienation that is fostered when, in daily life and on a routine basis, one is required to function in a world one has had little part in making or hope of remaking. For Adorno, the post-enlightenment division of art and science led to the modern human subject's double dispossession.

Adorno's argument runs as follows: on the one hand, science, configured as the positivist pursuit of objective facts, 'progressively' accumulated, was hailed as the purveyor of patent truth. (Such formulations left no space for scientific progress to be examined as a social and cultural construction.) As such, science was rendered aloof from ordinary modes of human inquiry, sequestered as an expert realm and thus as an instrument of ruling. (This was exemplified, perhaps most immediately, by 'science' under the Nazis, but was also illustrated at a sometimes more anodyne level in the everyday understanding of expert-mediated knowledge, and today, perhaps, many of the attempts to inculcate a 'scientifically literate' public particularly when these literacy projects are linked to attempts to *persuade* the public to 'accept' particular scientific policies or practices and/or to quell controversy.)

On the other hand, the role of art, as a form of *knowledge* or, as will be described below, a way of activating consciousness, was undercut. As with science, art came to be something remote something that acted *upon* its beholders, either as allied with the subjective (i.e., 'personal' and thus, 'irrational') realm and with the romantic notion of expression (to 'move' listeners, for example), or as it was debased through being used as an agent of rhetorical persuasion. For Adorno (as will be discussed in detail later), art's link to the mobilisation of emotion and/or action was regressive, symptomatic of the same kind of (authoritarian) communicative relationship he sought to critique. In both science and art, then, the exploration of dialectical tension between form and content, concept and material, was sacrificed in favour of the production of 'effects' – sensations, imageries, findings – in short, applications.

For Adorno, nothing was more insidious than this loss of dialectical tension. Indeed, it is here that we may venture to speak of 'true' science (and perhaps also to begin to appreciate why Adorno has recently been rediscovered by feminist and ecological philosophers), namely, an investigative attitude devoted to recursive revision (negation) of itself (as in the almost ethnographic, 'feeling for the organism' of Barbara McClintock (Fox-Keller 1983)) or art's explorations of things outside the frame, the liminal or otherwise neglected aspects of material. For Adorno, these reflexive activities widened attention's span. They heightened consciousness, that is, the ability to perceive the *differences* between things; to fathom, if never contain, reality. The task of reason was to accommodate, and through formulation as knowledge, *arrange* (without suppressing) complexity, diversity, heterogeneity – to hold as much 'material' as is possible within compromised consciousness. Such a task should be the same, whether accomplished through science or art, and it is at this point that Adorno's philosophy begins to modulate into cultural critique, to a focus on how, in any cultural medium, formulation – *composition* – is accomplished. It is also at the point when Adorno becomes a cultural critic that he becomes, also, a sociologist.

That music sociology may be encapsulated as follows: Adorno was concerned with how music's *formal properties* evinced modes of praxis that in turn were related to, and could inculcate modes of, consciousness. This ability to inculcate modes of consciousness was in turn linked to a theory of the listening subject's unconscious (or quasi-conscious) relation to music, i.e., to the way in which music processing involved a sub-rational and sub-liminal dimension, an ability to elide consciousness and yet still have some effect upon consciousness and/or action. Cultural products, in so far as they evinced particular modes of praxis in their formal arrangements, could, for example, heighten or suppress human critical, perceptual, and expressive faculties. And to the extent that they were able to structure these faculties, they also fostered social arrangement. It is from this perspective that Adorno can be seen as seeking to bridge the gap between aesthetic and scientific modes of knowing and, in so doing, to restore aesthetics to its pre-enlightenment role as cognition's matrix. It is here that Adorno's concern with music in modern societies comes to the fore.

Adorno on music

Adorno was musically trained, an acolyte of Alban Berg and author of atonal compositions. Music was, as will be described in chapter 3, nothing less than Adorno's cognitive workspace; his philosophy can be understood

to have sublimated music into philosophy and, simultaneously, sublimated philosophy into music. This point has been discussed by those
most intimate with Adorno's linguistic-compositional practices: Susan
Buck-Morss and, more recently, Susan H. Gillespie have both outlined
this issue with great insight. Gillespie (1995; 2002) has suggested that
Adorno's texts have a strongly performative dimension, and that their
translation requires that special attention be paid to:

the text's rhythms and stresses, its oblique references to other texts and contexts,
its use of rare or poetic words and frequent neologisms, and also certain more per-
vasive differences in mood, for example between the short, scherzo-like sketches
and the longer, more symphonic essays. (Gillespie 2002:xiv)

Thus the written text, modelled upon music, was itself also an exemplar
of how cognition and cognitive representation could proceed. Adorno's
writings can thus be seen as performing *manners* of composition, ways
of holding on to and accommodating material. In this respect, the philosophical text was no different from composition.

For Adorno, music was nothing less than a cultural site within which
social-cognitive tendencies could, through the formal properties of composition, be 'diagnosed'. Musical composition was, in other words, a
potentially exemplary form of praxis. As such, it involved the handling
or *arrangement* of materials or parts – voices and modes of voicing, mo-
tives, and themes, and also tempos and rhythmic figures, timbres (e.g.,
the sound of the saxophone, the use of vibrato), and the architectonics of
harmonic 'progression'. As a mode of arrangement, a way of fashioning
material into 'parts' and 'wholes', musical composition evidenced, for
Adorno, social content; it demonstrated modes of handling, ways of ordering (musical) reality. Musical composition was not merely analogous
to social organisation. It was also a form of political action (e.g., musical
form inevitably simplifies the sonic tendencies of its materials, inevitably
involves compromise, and, thus, does violence to materials that are cur-
tailed in the service of compositional form). These features could in turn
be revealed by an 'immanent method' of critique, namely, an engagement with music's formal properties and with the ways that composers
handled, within specific works, the tensions between material and formal
arrangement.

This point is worth expanding. For Adorno, music performed two cognitive functions, both of which operated at a level beneath conscious
awareness. The first of these was to portray the 'true' state of the subject,
to provide that subject with a mirror of her relation to the social whole.
When the totality of social relations took on the guise of repressive administration, for example, when it did violence to the subject-citizen, music

could document the discrepancy between (socio-political) subject and object, by illuminating the 'homelessness' of the subject, its inability to find a form capable of accommodating it. Music's first cognitive function was thus to remind the subject of what, in other realms, had been lost.

Music's second cognitive function was to exemplify: in and through the abstract procedures of its composition – the arrangement of material – music offered models of how part–whole relationships could be conceived and configured. In so doing it also showed how the subject (being) or material (nature) could stand in relation to the social and cognitive totality. Musical form thus served a didactic function – it could exemplify how material could be organised so as to do minimal violence. The handling of musical material – composition – could provide models of how one might conceive of, and orient to, realities beyond musical ones, how one might 'handle' arrangement elsewhere – in science or in social institutions, for example, so as to preserve, rather than excise, complexity. It was in this sense that musical compositional praxis provided a simulacrum of praxis more generally. Music's second cognitive function was thus critique by example; music was a structure against which other things could be articulated. It was, in this sense, a cognitive resource.

For example, the question of how music fashions 'closure' might be read for what it tells us about how 'closure' in other realms could, potentially, proceed. Does the piece end with a clashing of cymbals or with the fading away of a single note? Does it reassert the tonic or 'home' key repeatedly through a series of closing dominant seventh to tonic cadences (the music equivalent of saying 'the-end, the-end, the-end') or does it end with a harmonically ambiguous passage? Or, as in the music of Phillip Glass or Steve Reich, does it end abruptly, with no foretaste of cessation, no self-referencing sign that an end is soon to be reached?

To take another example, how are voices interwoven? Does one voice, a solo or the melodic line, lead and are others used (subserviently) as harmonic support? Or are all the voices, as in a fugue or polyphonic composition, equally important, equally 'melodic', as in, for example, Thomas Tallis's choral works? As Adorno puts it, '[p]olyphonic music says "we" even when it lives as a conception only in the mind of the composer . . .' (1973:18).

To develop this example, and in a way that highlights compositional praxis, consider the process of learning how to harmonise the melodic line of a Bach chorale. As part of the rudiments of music theory, it is customary to practise this skill by learning how to harmonise a chorale melody. There are various rules that apply – no parallel fourths or fifths, for example. Novice attempts to follow these rules often result in supporting lines (alto, tenor, and bass) that follow distinctly jagged paths and are thus difficult to sing (i.e., they have no logic of their own but only in relation to the melodic line and the global rules). The *material*, in this case the voice lines, is thus made subservient to the need to produce a greater form; the particular is sacrificed to the general. A 'good' harmonisation, by contrast, would be attentive to the needs of *all* the voices so that the 'whole' could be seen to emerge from a judicious arrangement of the parts. In such a composition, then, one might speak of the music as analogous to a collective ideal.

It is possible, from this example, to imagine how musical relations may come to serve as exemplars of social relations, in particular, as 'ideal[s] of collectivity' (Adorno 1974:18). One sees here the deeply intriguing aspect of Adorno's musical work – his concern with composition, with the handling of musical material, as nothing short of moral praxis. This is one of the greatest strengths of Adorno's position – his concern was not with what music (as a medium or an object) 'represented', it was rather with the actual practice of music – its formal arrangement, both as moral praxis and as exemplar, as a model for praxis in other realms. How, then, to account for the process by which musical forms took shape? What, in other words, was the engine of music history?

Music history – how is it made?

For Adorno, the composer (subject) is understood in dialectical relationship to the musical material (object) in a way that, at first glance appears to engender contradiction. On the one hand, he emphasises music's *inherent* logic (the unfolding or developing of musical material over time). On the other, he emphasises the composer as a subject in relation to the congealed history (conventional musical practices) placed at her disposal. This contradiction needs to be addressed full-on if Adorno's work is to be developed, eventually, in an empirical context. It is necessary, in other words, to press Adorno on the question of musical stylistic change and, equally importantly, on the question of musical greatness and its origins.

On the one hand, Adorno often speaks of how the composer is faced with 'problems' posed by music, or the 'questions directed to him by the material in the form of its own immanent problems', as in the case of Schoenberg (Adorno 2002:399). Here the implication is that the best composers will find ways of responding to music, ways of solving the problems *music* poses. And in this case, music's link to society is conceived as isomorphic: each 'develops' according to its respective internal logics and both these logics are generated by an underlying structural dynamic (congealed history). Here, Adorno can be read as a structuralist, as implying that music 'mirrors' or in some way is structurally related to society. The composer's task here is conceived as essentially passive; she is configured as a conduit, one who follows the 'laws' of development implicit in music's material. 'Good' composers are, within this purview, those who are best able to develop the implications of musical material's potential. There is more than a little metaphysics here of *music*'s trajectory, a metaphysics that is often present in the tenor of Adorno's thought. Such a view skews music history towards musicological determinism and, as such, sits uneasily with more recent work in music sociology as I describe below.

At the same time, Adorno posits a second understanding of the music–society nexus. In this second understanding, the composer is a subject within her world, a maker of that world through her compositional praxis, and thus, a maker of music history – a history that does not simply evolve but is the result of agency. ('The idea that the tonal system is exclusively of natural origin is an illusion rooted in history' (1973:11)). As Adorno puts it, '"material" is itself a crystallisation of the creative impulse, an element socially predetermined through the consciousness of man' (1973:33). Here, Adorno reinserts agency to the compositional equation and thus can be seen to correct the sturcturalist tendencies of his work in ways that presage structuration theory, namely, that position creativity within an enabling and constraining matrix of prior creative acts and materials. And it is also here that we can begin to see just how much weight Adorno expected the 'good' composer to carry: she needed not only to grapple with material but also to find a way both of addressing history (i.e., of being thoroughly encultured) while simultaneously working through that history to forge historical materials to the here and now of socio-musical (political, psychological) conditions. It was in this sense that the composer was – to use the old-fashioned term – a 'maker'.

This focus on the dual nature of composition – the human-made quality of musical discourse and the ways in which musical material was pre-formed by history – points up Adorno's dialectical materialism. But – and not intended by Adorno – it also furthers certain of Adorno's assumptions that were characteristic of the culture in which he was steeped – the belief in musical–aesthetic hierarchy ('good' or 'true' music and, by implication, its opposite), an adherence to a romantic and post-romantic conception of the artist and artistic autonomy, the idea of the artist's marginal position in relation to public life. These were the nineteenth-century emblems of bourgeois humanism that Adorno revered. They led on to the image of the composer as hero. And nowhere is this image more striking in Adorno's work than in the essays on Beethoven, who, in his formal compositional procedures, uniquely exemplified the status of the bourgeois subject in the post-enlightenment world.

Adorno's Beethoven hero

As Adorno makes clear, the utopian moment of human history, the time when music was (briefly) allowed to enjoy its role as affirmation and the time when bourgeois humanist ideology seemed like a reality, was long since by-passed. That moment, and its elision, could be perceived, according to Adorno, in the compositional praxis of Beethoven and his shift from middle-to late-period style during the early nineteenth century.

For Adorno, Beethoven was heroic because his compositions both exemplified the procedures of reason and served as a foil against which reason's historical position could be gauged. Beethoven occupied a particular position in history. Beethoven, unlike his contemporaries, according to Adorno, managed to compose in such a way that his work was drawn into exact alignment with his historical situation. Beethoven was able, in other words, to address music's congealed history and in so doing simultaneously address his historical situation.

In his praxis, then, Beethoven both diagnosed and exemplified the 'crisis' of modernity – a rupture or break between subject and object, individual and society. Beethoven's middle-period works, their affirmation as exemplified by Beethoven's willingness to allow material – the musical subject – to subject itself to the good of the whole (because of a belief in the justice of that whole) represented, for Adorno, Beethoven-the-man's fleeting belief in utopian possibility, the justification of part within whole. Such is the view that preserves the composer as (heroic) agent. Adorno described this point as follows:

Beethoven did not accommodate himself to the identity of the often-cited rising bourgeois of the era of 1789 or 1800; he partook of its spirit . . . where the inner coincidence [i.e., partaking of the spirit of a movement] is lacking and is imposed by force or fiat, the result is merely conformity on the part of the composer . . . regularly at the expense of quality, of the music's stature. (2002: 652–3)

At the same time as he identified Beethoven as an agent, Adorno also identified Beethoven's agency as 'coinciding' with the spirit of an age and, in this respect, Adorno's conception of the work of composers exhibits the structuralism with which Adorno is often associated: Beethoven's works mirrrored social forces in this conception but did not mediate these forces or provide resources through which they were elaborated. Whichever of these views one holds (Beethoven as a 'possessor' of agency or as the 'possessed' by music's material tendencies (its congealed history)), when the moment of social equilibrium passed, and when the object claimed priority over the subject in the guise of administration (Napoleon crowning himself emperor), Beethoven's composition became increasingly fragmented, characterised increasingly by dissonance and disintegration. It exemplified the rupture between subject and object and the apparent impossibility of a future union between the two. Beethoven's later music thus 'diagnosed', as Subotnik puts it (1991), the homelessness of the subject under modernity, and the violence perpetuated against the subject that any attempt to accommodate it would produce. In this regard, Beethoven's praxis provided a direct line to be taken up, in the twentieth century by Schoenberg.

Adorno praised Beethoven for refusing to allow the subject (musical material) to capitulate to the object of musical form. In this resistance, Beethoven fulfilled the 'true' function of art, namely to offer a contrast structure against which 'false clarity' could be perceived (1974:15). Formal 'obscurity' could, Adorno argued, be 'held up in opposition to the prevailing neon-light style of the times'. After the utopian moment was lost in the early nineteenth century, affirmation was no longer a valid possibility, the only valid role for art was critique. Art is able to 'aid enlightenment only by relating the clarity of the world consciously to its own darkness' (ibid.). It is here, then, that Adorno's concern with dialectic, his critique of positivism, his theory of negative dialectics, and his concern with the formal properties of composition coalesce. And music, because of its unrepresentative and temporal character and through its formal properties, could preserve the negative function of reason. It was precisely this negativity, or refusal to capitulate to that 'neon-light style' (an epistemological attitude in which things are taken to be self-evident – i.e., the ontological ideology), that Adorno explored in the *Philosophy of Modern Music*, an analysis of the two main tendencies – negative versus positive, progressive versus reactionary – that music followed in the twentieth century.

Music, progress, and administration

A century and a half after that utopian moment captured in middle-period Beethoven, the dual regime of political authoritarianism and commodity capitalism – both as relations of production and as the producer of cultural 'goods' – had triumphed. And in that triumph, according to Adorno, resided the mechanisms of collective stupefaction – the dynamics of the culture industry and their psycho-cultural consequences. For if 'good' art could 'aid enlightenment' by pointing out darkness, the culture industry and its drive towards standardisation militated against enlightenment through repetition and predictability. According to Adorno, the music industry purveyed an endless parade of popular songs that were generically nearly identical. (Recall here, Huxley's *Brave New World* (1932) and Orwell's *1984*. In both these dystopias music is employed as balm, as distraction, and as focusing device to prevent critical reflection – I return to this theme in chapter 5.) Though the superficial details of the songs varied, popular music fostered 'pseudo-individualisaiton' according to Adorno – the presentation, as a staple diet, of a radically narrowed 'menu' packaged and sold to address the full gamut of difference in, as it were, a cardboard box. And composition was entirely given over to the generation of musical effect; musical material was held tightly in reign by the discipline of form and cliché. As a listener, one attended to, and expected, certain effects. Through this cycle of expectation and gratification, according to Adorno, popular music 'train[ed] the unconscious for conditioned reflexes' (1976:29).

In an early essay, Adorno analysed the psycho-cultural effects of such music, referring to the fetishisation of music and the regression of hearing. As he described that work in the preface to the *Philosophy of Modern Music* (1973:xi), Adorno said that he had sought to show how music's function had been altered in the modern world, and that this change was due to the impact of commercialisation on composition (on the 'inner fluctuations suffered by musical phenomena'). As he described it, these changes were linked to a shift in the structure of musical hearing (that is changes in the social construction of aural perception, of how we hear), a point later developed in the opening pages of the *Introduction to the Sociology of Music* (1976). These changes were, importantly in Adorno's view, linked to the fundamental shift in consciousness that was the hallmark of modernity, the emergence of the ontological ideology.

Musically conceived, this shift was characterised in particular by the listener's susceptibility to music's effects on the body and the emotions, and her orientation to music as a source of pleasure, as a token of lifestyle, and as a diversion and a way of coping. Here, then, music loses its status as dialectical praxis and as a resource for the instigation of critical consciousness (the perception of difference). It is reduced to the status of a commodity, a commodity that subverts critical faculties and substitutes for knowledge a kind of compensatory affirmation. To put this bluntly, music's commodity value was, according to Adorno, derived from its *psychological* function, its ability to gratify, to offer (temporarily and for money) pleasure, sensation, and a (false) sense of security. In this sense, music was re-specified as that supreme function of capitalism – a good.

Thus, for Adorno, it was ultimately the music industry, its forces and relations of production, that generated music's increasingly administrative tendency; its standardised products provided the totems that undercut reason. In short, the culture industry produced music that ordered its listening subject by narrowing the horizons of consciousness by invoking desire and then channelling it through stereotypical routes. In this way, the music industry and its wares reconfigured music's listeners and its function.

Adorno develops this thesis through an examination of the tendencies inherent in twentirth-century music – through his comparison of Schoenberg with Stravinsky. Written between 1940 and 1948, the *Philosophy of Modern Music* juxtaposes its two subjects as the greatest representatives of compositional extremes. While Adorno bestows the distinction of 'radical' upon Schoenberg, he sees Stravinsky's compositional practice as ultimately linked to the fetishisation and regression that characterised the twentieth-century shift in music's function.

Adorno launches his critique of Stravinsky on a number of grounds. We can begin to explore these grounds by considering his treatment of *Le Sacre du Printemps*, particularly Stravinsky's handling of musical material. We are treated to a veritable catalogue of how not to compose or, rather, how composition may come to evince the fetishist tendencies and thus inculcate the regression in hearing that Adorno described in his earlier work. In short, Stravinsky installed on the 'high' cultural stage the same, regressive, musical compositional procedures that could be found in the popular realm. 'The assembled rhythmic patterns of exotic dances . . .', Adorno writes about Stravinsky's *Sacre*, 'are an arbitrary game, and, to be sure, their arbitrariness is deeply related to the habit of authenticity throughout Stravinsky's music. *Sacre* already contains those elements which later undermine any claim to authenticity and revert music – because it aspires to power – to impotence' (1973:155).

Because, as Adorno believed, Stravisnky's music invoked the body directly, it disengaged the mind. Stravinksy's music did not deal with the part–whole problem of arrangement but was rather oriented – not unlike the popular songs Adorno disdained – towards *effect*. Moreover, in permitting rhythm to dominate, Stravinsky elevated the collective – the object – over the subject; the potential of his musical materials was made subservient to the music's pulse. And finally (and bearing in mind that *Le Sacre* was a ballet), Stravinsky used music to *depict* topics and scenes and this, Adorno claimed, led him to use music as a 'pseudomorphism of painting' – to reduce music to the role of depictive rendition and thus deny its specifically musical properties, understood as the processual unfolding of musical material, its 'becoming' (1973:162).

By contrast, by retaining the (Beethovenian) concern with music's formal problems (which were simultaneously the problem of how to configure the subject–object relationship), Schoenberg's compositional praxis preserved music's cognitive role – at least up until his adoption of the twelve-tone *system*, after which he was perceived by Adorno as having permitted the object to incorporate the subject (i.e., by abdicating his compositional agency to the dictates of pre-ordained modes of procedure). Schoenberg's 'liberation of dissonance' (recall that he termed his music 'pan-tonal as opposed to a-tonal' (pan-tonal meaning 'inclusive of all tonalities' – note the capaciousness of this strategy in relation to musical material)) was simultaneously viewed as an attempt to accommodate the musical subject within the object of form (rather than forcing musical material into subservience to the composer's intent, and to some external aim, such as when music becomes tone painting or when material is made to conform to pre-ordained form). In so doing, it also purged music of its tendency towards depiction, a tendency evidenced in Stravinsky where music was converted from 'becoming' to 'being', from unfolding process to positive representation. As Adorno puts it, Schoenberg solved 'technical problems' within music that, despite his music's obscurity, were 'socially relevant', that could be applied in non-musical, social realms (2002:399):

Schoenberg . . . never behaved 'expressionistically', superimposing subjective intentions upon heterogenous material in an authoritarian and inconsiderate manner. Instead, every gesture with which he intervenes in the material configuration is at the same time an answer to questions directed to him by the material in the form of its own immanent problems (ibid.)

Moreover, in his refusal to meld material to pre-determined form, Schoenberg deprived the listener of music's 'crutches', as Adorno calls them, of listening – the conventions and clichés that were the stock-in-trade of popular music (the composer Pierre Boulez later (and polemically) termed this task – in reference to his own project – an attempt to 'strip the accumulated dirt' from music). In so doing, Schoenberg elevated the listener to the status of compositional partner, opening up music to the active sense-making (composition) of its hearers. (On this point, see my discussion of Adorno in relation to John Cage (DeNora 1986a), where I suggest that Cage's philosophy of the listener as active participant in the composition process leads to a situation where musical consciousness is re-attuned to observing the situated specificity of musical material. For an ethnomethodological rendering of the 'meaning' problem in music and the listener as compositional partner, see DeNora 1986b.)

In Adorno's view, the listener, like Schoenberg himself, had to *learn* to compose (make sense of) music's parts. And in demanding this cognitive, interpretive work from the listener, in calling her attention to the effectively 'homeless' character of musical material and to the perception of difference, Schoenberg's music did two things. First, it embodied a value orientation in relation to the individual–social relationship through its demonstration, procedurally, of the alienated subject. Second, in and through its tonal breadth, it inculcated a form of advanced cognition, a mode of sense-making that could accommodate more of material – lengthy stretches of tones and attenuated tonal relationships, for example. Thus, through the demands it made, and through the ways that it exemplified the form–content relationship (in particular by demonstrating the material need for new, distorted, forms – for the incorporation into form of the material subject), Schoenberg's music inculcated critical reason. The subject who could listen to Schoenberg, wherein was contained, 'all the darkness and guilt of the world' (1973:133), was thus a subject who had achieved 'true' consciousness.

Atomisation and absorption

It is perhaps unsurprising that Adorno's work is of so much interest to contemporary critical theorists. His idea that one's hearing, if fed on a diet of the predictable, pre-digested material (musical cliché), would 'regress' in the same way that, as is often argued, one's faculties of taste and smell regress in the face of a diet of soda pop and soft-textured McFood. Music's commodification is thus like the commodifaction of anything else involving the senses (and Adorno occasionally makes reference to sexual gratification in these ways) – it inculcated a hollowing out of sensory faculties in ways that made individuals vulnerable to capture by (to pursue the culinary metaphor) whatever was 'served up' to them by their *chefs* (masters) – as long as it was laced with the appropriate seasoning. No wonder, then, that Adorno's work resonates so well with relatively recent theories of McDonaldisation and Disneyfication (e.g., Ritzer). Whereas 'true' music taught its listener how to perceive illogic – contradiction – through its challenge to critical faculties, 'false' music taught the listener how to relax and enjoy, and how to identify with particular representations or forms, and how to take pleasure in reliability, in repetition of – through that process – fetishised objects. Ultimately, these forms of pleasure served a didactic function: they taught the skill of how to adapt to (and enjoy) what was given. The ultimate trick, then, in Adorno's view, was to persuade the subject that the highest pursuit to which she could be called was the pursuit of (her own) happiness.

In this conception we hear also the strains of Goffman (discussed above), particularly his discussion of the inmates in *Asylums*, who, 'trimmed' to fit the requirements of the total institution, can do no more than re-enact institutionally stipulated roles, who cannot, in other words, exert themselves as agents involved in the making of forms that could contain rather than annihilate difference. Goffman's subject is one for whom genuine expression is prohibited but who is expected to engage in the various moral careers built upon institutionally- specified forms of self-presentation. (I return to this concept in chapters 4 and 5). This type of passivity and its inculcation, Adorno believed, provided conditions conducive to authoritarian domination, and it is here that we see clearly music's link to the idea of the 'ontological ideology' and to the concept of social control.

Adorno, 'defended against his devotees'

In the essay 'Bach Defended Against His Devotees', Adorno set out to rescue Bach from the reputation he had gained as an 'antique' composer. Adorno was at pains to establish Bach as the harbinger of musical modernism, 'the first to crystallise the idea of the rationally constructed work, of the aesthetic domination of nature' (1981:139). So too, I suggest, it is possible to defend Adorno against both devotees and detractors, and to re-conceptualise his role in relation to subsequent music sociology in a manner that at least tries to implement Adorno's ideas empirically. It is time to rescue Adorno from the status of 'antique' music sociologist (as his detractors often view him) and also to try to engage with Adorno in a way that moves Adorno scholarship on from the exegesis of his devotees (but without abandoning that focus, for which there is still need).

There is precedent within socio-musicology for this move. As Richard Middleton has aptly put it, 'anyone wanting to argue the importance of studying popular music has to absorb Adorno in order to go beyond him (Middleton 1990:35). Adorno's work, it should be clear at this stage, is far too important to be set aside by music sociologists. At the same time it would benefit greatly from further specification, in particular from a better connection to more recent methodological developments within the human sciences. In the remainder of this chapter I deal with three key themes in Adorno's work and describe how they may be criticised and redeployed at an empirical level of enquiry.

The first of these themes centres on the idea that music is, at least potentially, a means for knowledge formation (a mode of attending to material reality, a mode of posing the relationship between concepts and material detail). In so far as music was a realm of dialectical praxis, it could both exemplify and inculcate such praxis in its listeners, understood as modes of consciousness. It was thus possible to discern in music modes of orientation to 'material' that corresponded to modes and impulses found in other realms. That is, in *how* composition handled its musical materials, it was possible to discern strategies and impulses that corresponded to (and sustained) forms of social arrangement elsewhere in society – modes of political organisation, for example. In particular, it was possible to show how music enhanced or detracted from the dialectics of non-identity, the critical device through which reason could resist a growing administrative tendency in modern societies.

The second theme, as discussed above in relation to Beethoven, concerns the composer, who, because she is a subject, possesses (at least latent) potential to intervene in the shaping of music history. The composer's role is thus as important – if not more important – than that of the social critic. Beethoven's intervention, in particular his (late-style) response to the betrayal of the individual subject in favour of ruling power during the nineteenth century, directed music's so-called 'true' path, according to Adorno, away from affirmation and towards the alienation of subject (motif, harmonic progression) from object (harmonic unity, resolute forms of closure, lyric coherence). Music is thus a medium with which to 'do' things psycho-socially.

The third theme concerns the music industry and the ways in which it both reflected and instigated a shift in music's function and the translation of the listener from active subject to passive recipient of music's effects. It is important to observe that for Adorno, both so-called 'high' and popular music were affected by music's commodity form during the nineteenth and twentieth centuries. For him, in other words, there was little difference, aesthetically and in terms of their psycho-social effects, between the songs of Tin Pan Alley and the music of Tchaikovsky, who, as Adorno so memorably remarked, 'portrays despondency with hit tunes'.

Taken together, these themes give rise to many avenues for further study, some of which are explored below. They have also inspired a good deal of criticism from those engaged in less theoretical, more empirically detailed, research on music and society. In the next section I examine these criticisms, as they have been applied to the three themes outlined above.

In relation to all three themes, sociological criticism of Adorno – that is, the reaction to Adorno by more empirically oriented sociologists of music – can be said to centre on gaps in his investigative technique, all of which relate to Adorno's insufficient attention to musical *practice* as it is conducted within music-producing and music-consuming worlds. This, arguably methodological, deficiency is, I shall suggest in the next chapter, consequential for the character of Adorno's theory and its utility today. I begin with theme number three, Adorno's notorious and oft-misunderstood views on the work of the music industry.

Popular music, but where are the people?

Music sociologists tend to agree that Adorno's conception of the culture industry is over general. In Adorno, the culture industry is too quickly written off as a monolithic force, its products dismissed a priori as undifferentiated, equally worthless (on this point, see Witkin 2002). This is because, as Richard Middleton has observed (1990:37), Adorno began with that which he knew well – Germany during the 1930s – and he projected this model of cultural production inappropriately across time and space. That projection blinded Adorno to the heterogeneity present within the various enclaves of what he referred to, perhaps simplistically, as 'the music industry' – middle-range sectors, networks, individuals, groups, and rivalries through which production occurred. To take but one example, Adorno's conceptual apparatus did not permit him to consider how the record industry was multi-textured, composed of a mixture of small, independent companies and larger conglomerates, and how the interaction between these sectors might have implications for the type of work produced.

This is most assuredly an area upon which subsequent sociologists have improved. The classic study in this respect is by Peterson and Berger (1990 [1975]), well worth considering because it gives a taste of the empirical issues that Adorno ignored but which could have served to develop his theory. Peterson and Berger suggested that 'innovation' (diversity) in pop music arises from competition between large record companies and their smaller rivals, showing that variety of musical forms (and thus epochs of musical innovation and experimentation) is linked to the social structural arrangements of production, in this case, inversely related to market concentration. At the time their article was published, Peterson and Berger were trailblazers for the 'production of culture' perspective, and their study still serves as a model of how to conduct work in this tradition.

Examining number one hit songs over twenty-six years of record production, from 1948 to 1973, and dividing this period into five eras of greater and lesser degrees of market concentration, Peterson and Berger argued that eras of high market concentration were those in which a high proportion of the annual production of hits emanated from one of four leading companies, who, during the era of highest market concentration controlled over 75 per cent of the total record market (in fact just eight companies produced nearly all the hit singles). From here, they considered whether oligopolistic concentration bred homogeneity of product, pursuing this question by examining the sheer number of records and performers who recorded the hits during their five eras (with the idea in

mind that there would be little incentive to introduce 'new' products under conditions of market concentration); they also examined the lyrical
content of hits and traced these variables through the five eras as competition between record companies grew and then diminished over the
26-year period. Simultaneously, they considered indicators of 'unsated
demand', such as changes in record sales and the proliferation of music
disseminated through live performance and backed up by independent
record producers – genres such as jazz, rhythm and blues, country and
western, gospel, trade union songs, and the urban folk revival. From
there, they considered the conditions under which the independent producers were able to establish more secure market positions, as the top
four producers lost control of merchandising their products over the radio. They then traced how the record industry and its degree of market
concentration expanded and contracted cyclically over time.

By tracing conditions of record production and marketing, relating
these conditions to new developments in the communications industry,
and examining trends in record output and product diversity, Peterson
and Berger concluded that changes in concentration lead rather than follow changes in diversity, that they are an effect of how powerful producers
are able to be. Their finding 'contradicts', as they put it, 'the conventional
idea that in a market consumers necessarily get what they want' (1990
[1975]: 156). In short, Peterson and Berger highlighted the impact of
production-organisation on musical trends and styles and showed how
popular music production is characterised by cycles, and they detailed
some of the mechanisms that affect cyclic development.

Peterson and Berger's study set the scene from the 1970s onwards for
the concern, within popular music studies, with the production system –
as examined from the inside out. More recently, Dowd (forthcoming)
has built upon this production-organisation approach to examine the relation between musical diversity and industry concentration in relation
to specific genres and to the output of the industry as a whole. The tradition forged by Peterson and Berger has also been developed by Negus
(1992), for example, who has suggested that working practices within the
popular music industry are linked to an artistic ideology associated with
college-educated white males who came of age in the 'rock generation'
of the 1960s and 1970s. This occupational stratification is consequential for the types of pop that are produced: women and unfamiliar styles
and artists, for example, are marginalised (Steward and Garratt 1984).
(These forms of musical-gender segregation may be seen within musical production in pedagogical settings (Green 1997), particularly with
regard to instrument choice – a topic that overlaps with work by social
psychologists (O'Neill 1997).)

In these works, the music industry is explored from the inside out. In Adorno's work, by contrast, the music industry remains a black box, the contents of which are deduced without need of opening, or an empty screen upon which Adorno projected his assumptions about the music industry. There is a raft of questions that remains unanswered by Adorno. For example, as Middleton has observed, how does stylistic change in popular music come about, and how does it take particular forms (Middleton 1990:38)? This is, according to Middleton, but one of a range of questions about the music industry, its production, and reception that can only be answered by 'a complete "production history" of popular music from 1890 to the present' (1990:38).

In lieu of this history, Adorno deals in abstractly posited social forces (concentrations of power, commodification) and two types of musical worker: on the one hand, those rare, heroic types who confront social tendencies by grappling with the medium of form so as to preserve true expression; and, on the other hand, those musical workers who trade upon musical cliché and thus capitulate to (and serve to reinforce) administration, the 'collective tendency of the times' (1973). In short, Adorno's socio-musical landscape is sparsely populated: it consists of social forces, musical materials, composers, and listeners. And even here, we are not offered a sufficient view of people *doing* things, that is, of actors caught up in the contingencies and practical exigencies of their local spheres of action. All action in Adorno is *ex post facto*; it is primarily seen once it has congealed in musical form, composition. It may be an exaggeration but with a grain of truth to say that the only process to which Adorno actually attends is the process as exemplified in musical *form*. It is because of this – Adorno's undue emphasis upon musical *works* – that in turn leads to what may be considered a major flaw in his music sociology, namely, his tendency to use his own interpretation of form (his immanent method of critique) as a methodology of knowing about social relations and about history. This is made quite clear in relation to the second theme to be discussed, the relation of the composer and her works to socio-musical history.

The imaginary museum of musical 'works'

In her well-known study of the history of musicological ideology, the philosopher Lydia Goehr (1992) describes how and where the modern notion of the self-contained musical work came to emerge as a 'fact' of music history. This 'fact' was not neutral but part of the project of asserting music's autonomy during the nineteenth century. This project was simultaneously a game about status politics, a game that elevated the composer to the role of master (*sic*), genius, and, in the case of Beethoven, hero. To be sure, Adorno was complicit in this project. His conception of music history, like his conception of the music industry and its history, is similarly over-theorised.

There were, arguably, at the time, good reasons for this over-theoretical approach, as Richard Leppert explains:

Adorno's sociology worked from both the outside and the inside of musical works. 'Outside' musical texts, he looked at social practices, but here he upset musico-logical convention by his relative lack of interest in empirical research, though Adorno knew well the 'basic facts' of music history, to be sure. But he insisted on the inadequacy of musical facts as such to the understanding of music – precisely the argument in musicology that emerged in full-blown form only in the mid 1980s, but was nonetheless foreshadowed during the last decade of Adorno's life in his critique of positivism, especially as represented by the British philosopher Karl Popper. 'Inside' the musical text, Adorno committed to what he named 'immanent criticism,' analyzing objective musical details in relation to one an-other, that is, to musically specific compositional procedures, and also interro-gating them as objectively subjective engagements with the reality external to the musical text, a kind of musical hermeneutics that the discipline of musicology only slowly accepted as legitimate, and not without continuing controversy. (Adorno 2002:74)

Leppert's defence of Adorno highlights what is missed, sociologically and phenomenologically, through too strict an adherence to 'the facts' of music history and this argument is critical to the development of any music sociology that wishes to further the direction forged by Adorno. At the same time, such an approach need not be incompatible with his-torical research, in particular with a greater attention to the detailed practices of composing, distributing, and consuming music, and, in re-lation to his study of Beethoven, to the social construction of musical worth.

Scott Burnham has commented on how Beethoven and the idea of the Beethoven-hero in 'the paradigm of Western compositional logic . . . proved so strong that it no longer acts as an overt part of our musical consciousness' (1995:xiii). His work has revealed how, in other words, Beethoven's musical practices, and the Beethoven-ideology has become 'a condition of how we tend to engage the musical experience (ibid.). So, too, work by William Weber (1992) and James Johnson (1995) has shown us how the cultures of listening within European cities came to be transformed, in great part in relation to Beethoven. It is on this point that Adorno's views on Beethoven begin to appear more clearly linked to Adorno's occupation of a particular place and time in musical culture. As Middleton has suggested:

with Beethoven the *potential* of music is so raised that older assumptions are shattered. But this could be seen as simply a more than usually coherent version of a familiar Austro-German interpretation of nineteenth-century music history, which sets an over-privileged Viennese tradition at its normative centre. Adorno's preference for 'immanent method'-analysing and evaluating works in terms of the implications, the immanent tendencies, of their mode of existence rather than approaching them comparatively – means that, having set his criteria for 'autonomous bourgeois music' from his interpretation of Beethoven, he exports those criteria to all music of the period and finds the rest of it wanting. At the same time, Beethoven himself is a less comprehensive representation of the totality of the social struggles of his age than Adorno pretends; in a way he is just as 'partial' as his far more popular contemporary, Rossini. Indeed, at times Adorno's Beethoven comes close to being a fetish: the image objectifies those musical tendencies Adorno wants to privilege. (Middleton (1990:41))

The problem, stated crudely, is this: how do we know that in his analysis of Beethoven he is not merely engaging in musical-ideological work, elaborating a trope of Beethoven reception that is prominent within the field of discourse that he operates? How do we know that Adorno's valuation of Beethoven is not the artefact of historical tropes, of the myths of compositional history? Some might counter 'listen for yourself', the idea being that, if one has ears that have not been corrupted (and perhaps also honed through care and study), the 'truth' of music will be self-evident.

But to suggest that 'just listening' or 'training' is enough is to dismiss the power of music education – the material and linguistic cultures that come to frame musical texts, that help to draw out particular meanings. This is a problem that routinely arises in discussions between musicologists and music sociologists. It has been explored in various studies of value and the attribution of value, such as in my own work on Beethoven (DeNora 1995a) and more recently in Fauquet and Hennion's study of Bach (2000). These studies illustrate some of the objections music sociologists have lodged against the idea that analysis and/or criticism is sufficient as a method of socio-musical analysis.

By no means posed in contradiction to the idea of musical value (which was conceptualised as the outcome of social practice, institutionalised over time), sociological studies treat value as produced through the social and material cultural organisation of perception. During Beethoven's first decade of operation in Vienna, musical life, in particular ideas about music and categories of musical value, changed. They were increasingly transformed in ways that were conducive to the perception of Beethoven's 'greatness' and to the idea of 'great composers'. A niche was being carved, in other words, for the very idea of greatness and, as I have described elsewhere (DeNora 1995a), Beethoven was astute enough to seek to lodge himself within this niche, and, more dynamically, to try to adapt the shape of that niche to fit the specific contours of his talent. In this way he was able to embark upon projects that enabled him to garner increasing cultural weight within the changing cultural terrain. Beethoven was not, in other words, considered the 'best match' to an *already existing* set of musical evaluative criteria. It is not reasonable to suggest that his work took the 'only' or the 'best' musico-logical direction available at the time. On the contrary, his career and work helped to shape the apparently 'logical' direction of music and, simultaneously, the criteria applied to his work. It is precisely this internal shaping of the musical world that Adorno's theory of music history omits. This omission is particularly problematic when we turn to the final theme to be abstracted from Adorno's work – music's role as a constituent ingredient of consciousness and knowledge formation. For, because Adorno's theory of music reception is not fully specified, he cannot describe how, in practice and in context of specific hearings, music comes to 'work' upon consciousness. Indeed, had the world of music reception been populated with specified and socially located hearers and music consumers, a good deal of Adorno's aesthetic hierarchy would have been undermined.

Responding is composing

To speak of framing a musical work and its impact upon that work's perception is to speak of how listening is mediated through one or another cultural schema; how it inevitably takes place from within the confines of particular and selective universes of works, and is often linked to status group affiliation. When scholars have examined musical consumption practices these lessons are repeatedly borne out. To put this differently, music's own discourses come to have meaning inter-textually, in relation to other works, yes, but also to other types of discourse and practice. Music's relation to these other things, moreover, is interactive. In short, music can neither speak 'for itself' nor can other things (including other human speakers or texts) speak entirely for it.

To make this observation, however, is not also to suggest that musical compositions, taken in conjunction with the demands they make of performers and listeners, possess no social significance or force as derived from their musical material. Rather, it is to suggest that these significances should be examined in terms of how they come to be *situated* within particular social contexts, where music will indeed come to possess various types of semiotic force, but that a given music's properties may lend themselves to various significances as its situation changes. In following chapters, I suggest that Adorno's analyses of how music handles its relation to previous music, to musical convention, is necessary to socio-musical analysis. But I shall also argue that socio-history, in the Weberian sense (Weber 1978) of actors operating on and in their social worlds is also necessary. The focus on action is necessary if we are to understand how, within specific social contexts, discourses (including musical discourses) come to be created, stabilised, revised, and received by actors, that is if we are to understand not what music *might* do, but rather what music does and is made to do in actual contexts. And again, in relation to the imaginary museum of musical works and the critique of Adorno's value orientation, sociology of music *after* Adorno has had much to say on this subject, particularly as it has focused on the stratification of composers, styles, and genres.

Historical studies have helped to unveil the strategies by which the musical canon and its hierarchy of 'Master [sic] Works' were constructed and institutionalised during the nineteenth century in Europe (Weber 1978; 1992; Citron 1993) and America (DiMaggio 1982). An aesthetic movement, and also an ideology for the furtherance of music as a profession, the fascination with 'high' music culture during the nineteenth century was simultaneously a vehicle for the construction of class and status group distinction. It was also a device of music marketing and occupational advancement and, as such, illustrates Adorno's point that aspects of 'high'-culture music shared the mass-culture approach (an argument developed by Judith Blau (1989)). More recently, focus on the distinction between 'high' and 'low' musical forms has widened to include investigation of how 'authenticity' is itself constructed and contested (Peterson 1997). These investigations dismiss the concept of the 'work itself' in favour of the idea that 'works' are configured through the ways they are performed and heard (Hennion 1997; see also Clarke and Cook 2003).

Adorno's work dealt only obliquely with these historical issues because he was concerned only obliquely with the social shaping of cultural products, with how particular representations and evaluations (including the ones to which he espoused) gained prominence. His real quarry lay, as described above, in the analysis of the *formal properties* of cultural products, and in particular how these properties were linked to epistemological *styles*. Such a project differs greatly from the 'sociology of knowledge' as practised today, whether as the 'Edinburgh School' focus on interests and the shaping of scientific knowledge (Barnes 1977), feminist focuses on alternative representations (e.g., Martin 1989), or the Latourian 'actor network and beyond' focus on how the production and institutionalisation of scientific 'fact' is akin to political campaigning (Latour 1987; 1989; Law and Hassard 1999). In the sociology of science that developed from the 1970s onwards, focus was directed at the question of how those things that pass as matters of fact are 'composed' and thus bear traces of their compositional milieu. One of the great contributions of these works is their critique, implicit and sometimes explicit, of so-called 'Whig histories' of science, that is, histories that tell the progress of scientific development as a story of how one theory gave rise to the next, histories from which all traces of human agency and exigency are erased. The comparison here to histories of the 'development' of musical material should at this point be obvious.

In the case of both music and science, the failure to focus on the specific details of historical production, that is, on the 'inside' of production and its worlds (and the commensurate concern with the construction of compositional 'choices') courts, at best, hagiography and, at worst, disjunction with music as it actually functions at the ground level of social activity. For example, as we have seen in his treatment of Beethoven, Adorno perceives Beethoven's style periods from a twentieth-century vantage point; his perspective does not permit a deconstrutive focus on periodisation, nor can it consider discrepancies between how Beethoven's contemporaries perceived the significance of his work and how it has come to be framed by music historical and music critical discourses (DeNora 1995b; Webster 1994). Along with this, Adorno does not attempt to distinguish – to search for a non-identity – between his own comprehension of the social meaning of Beethoven's compositional praxis and how Beethoven's praxis may have been embedded in, and perceived by, his *others* (Beethoven himself and his contemporaries, for example, but also Beethoven listeners today or in Adorno's time). Without such an analysis, Adorno has no warrant (apart from his own belief and his ability to persuade others to join him in that belief) to know what Beethoven was 'really' doing when he engaged in the act of composition.

Adorno's avoidance of both a 'comparative' perspective and a contextualising methodology, moreover, allow him a particular form of theoretical luxury – that of letting his examples 'illustrate' (rather than drive) the direction of his theory. For example, Beethoven's incorporation of 'shock' or surprise, his deconstruciton of form, may, if perceived from the point of view of the contemporary responses to his works (and the level of surprise expressed), have been at its strongest during his early period, when, in terms of the reception history of his work, reactions to Beethoven were most extreme. Beethoven was not, moreover, the only composer to experiment with – and thus attenuate – form; indeed, may of the devices he employed were to some extent shared by others in his world. Such matters are held in abeyance by Adorno in favour of particular interpretations of musical works and, via this, their history (the specificity of historical detail) is sacrificed to the immanent method. He begins, in other words, with the figure and from it deduces the ground.

To what extent would this criticism have troubled Adorno? Very little, I suggest, for the following reason.

Earlier in this chapter I quoted Susan Gillespie on how Adorno's texts may be usefully read as types of performances, like music, meant to stand themselves, as forms of exemplary practice. Is it perhaps possible that Adorno was less interested in being empirically correct than making a rhetorical point for which musical analysis was a highly useful resource? To be sure, many have noted Adorno's penchant for textual drama. As one commentator has observed, 'Adorno habitually alternated microscopies of musical detail with sweeping, caricatural indictments of the social whole, with virtually nothing in between . . . his correlation of results with historical trends often has an arbitrary, almost eerie quality about it (Merquior 1986:134, quoted in Martin 1995:115). More recently, Richard Leppert has suggested that the work Adorno co-authored with Max Horkheimer, the *Dialectic of Enlightenment*, is characterised by the 'fundamental rhetorical device [of] . . . exaggeration, embodied in the vast historical sweep from Homer to the movies, in an implicitly unbroken historical thread, as exemplary of domination as it was grist for subsequent criticism' (2002:27).

Adorno does indeed paint history on a large canvas and with a large brush, turning now and again to illuminate the workings of these sweeping forces through minute attention to one or another detail. While this may not be the best recipe for the so-called macro–micro link in sociology, it had perhaps other uses. To be clear here, I am suggesting that the empirical world was perhaps less something that Adorno wished to describe with accuracy (that would have been part of the positivism he so disdained) than to employ as the backdrop for an aesthetic creation, namely, the 'composition', of critical theory. Speculative as this point is, it is in keeping with Adorno's views on the cognitive role of art – his deployment of the immanent method was, in other words, the practising of an art form. Indeed, we perhaps understand Adorno best if we think of him as a sociologically and philosophically inclined composer-in-letters. He was certainly never an ethnographically or empirically oriented researcher. As Brecht once described him, Adorno, 'never took a trip in order to see' (Blomster 1977:200). Peter Martin captures this point well:

Adorno's 'ground position', then, casts him inescapably as a social philosopher or social critic rather than as a sociological analyst. Not that this would have worried him unduly: the sociological work which he encountered during his stay in America, and which he took to be typical, was in his view irredeemably positivistic, not only generating spurious 'facts', but doing so on behalf of the dominant agencies of social control. (Martin 1995:19)

So does Adorno's abstention from empirical enquiry actually matter? Does it tarnish Adorno's contribution to socio-musical study? On one level one could argue that it does not; Adorno's analyses are not meant to *explain* (i.e., to 'tell' the reader) but rather are intended as poetic interventions (to take the reader through a mode of experience, a mode of being conscious of the world). As such, their 'truth value', like the music they describe, becomes exemplary; their role is to call our attention to the social world in a particular manner, to quicken or recall consciousness in a particular way. This may help to explain in part the fascination Adorno's work holds for so many readers. It is, like the work of Alban Berg, 'beautiful' and, in the arrangement of its lines it sought to do in words what 'true' music could do in tones –a form of exemplary praxis.

As Witkin has observed, 'Adorno's formal analyses of musical works are preoccupied with meaning in the context of a hearing of the works' (1998:5). It certainly seems right that Adorno was concerned with music's structure as it came to affect listeners and his focus on how musical material is handled attests to this – the shock value, for example, of a particular chord within the context of an entire movement. Yet, despite Adorno's obvious concern with music's 'effects' upon listeners – effects such as the regression in hearing prompted by false music or the capacity for complex awareness promoted by Schoenberg – the 'audience' is never encountered with any specificity in Adorno's work but is rather deduced from musical structures. Adorno remained fundamentally uninterested in, as Middleton has observed (1990:60), *real* moments of consumption practice. By contrast, Adorno treats music's listener as he treated both music history and the social significance of musical works – he hypostatises listeners and listening. 'The people clamour', he tells us, 'for what they are going to get anyhow' (1976:29, quoted in Middleton 1990:57). He describes listeners as 'identifying . . . with the . . . product' and tells us that such listeners have 'needs' (ibid.). After Beethoven, there is only one correct mode of attention to music – silent contemplation. His typology of listening (1976), with its top-down itemisation of listening modes, from the valued, rational, listener who 'grasps' music's structure to the 'emotional' listener who orients to music in search of sensation, underlines Adorno's adherence to music in only one form – cognition. This adherence itself can be traced to Adorno's value-orientation within the discourse of serious music, itself a product of the nineteenth century.

Given these statements, it is hardly surprising that Adorno fails to consider the way in which listening, as interpretive processing, is itself a part of composition and that, therefore, if we are to understand music's effects we cannot afford the luxury of reading these off from musical works. 'For Adorno', Middleton succinctly puts it, 'the meaning of musical works is immanent; our role is to decipher it' (1970:59). The result of Adorno's avoidance of specific acts of listening is an additional theoretical luxury: it enables Adorno to invoke an *image* of the audience whenever that is expedient as a means for advancing his theory.

An unresolved ending

Richard Middleton summarises the flaws in Adorno's theory as consisting of, first, his use of the immanent method (and thus his depopulation of the musical field) and, second, his own historical location and its link to his 'ontologisation of history'. By this he means that Adorno's focus on individual works allowed him, as I described earlier, certain theoretical luxuries – as a strategy the confinement to what he had to say about composition permitted him to find that to which he was already predisposed. And this bias, coupled with Adorno's personal position – a Jew in 1930s Germany, a member of the educated elite, an acolyte of Alban Berg – led to his establishment of a particular version of music history and history more generally as the 'true' version. This version was, moreover, a 'truth' that Adorno's theory sets itself (and its author) in a privileged position as being able to grasp. There is more than a touch of hauteur in Adorno. And while hauteur may be a matter of style, in this case it is adjunct to what in some circles has been called a 'sociology of error', by which is meant a mode of analysis predicated upon the assumption that its statements will either define 'the world' correctly or that they will, as it were, be in error. We must not, however, dismiss Adorno simply because we think that on points he erred. What is of value in Adorno transcends all of this. It concerns Adorno's vision, his way of perceiving the social world and music's interrelationship with that world. Above all, Adorno bequeathed a perspective. Thus it seems right to subject this perspective to the test of criticism, to interact with it across time and culture.

As Middleton puts it, the problems that we perceive in Adorno today need to be addressed, 'if we are to understand [Adorno] – and to make use of him, rather than simply dismissing him as an embittered elitist pessimist' (1990:61) A dismissal is simply too facile a response (it is also not dialectic); there is much, at least at an intuitive level, that 'rings true' in Adorno's work and, indeed, it is for this reason that there has been so much written about him. But, just as Adorno deserves more than derision, he also deserves more than respectful exegesis. The greatest tribute to Adorno consists of, as Middleton suggests, 'making use' of his work. And if we are to 'make use' of Adorno, I suggest it is necessary to specify ways of grounding his ideas, not necessarily in positivist mode as testable and measurable hypotheses, but to specify their meaning by

trying to consider, at least hypothetically, how we might be able to develop his work at or more closely to the level of action and experience.
As it stands, Adorno's music sociology almost completely by-passes the
need for empirical work, in particular for the micro- and middle-range
modes of investigation pursued by music sociology over the past two or
three decades – in the roughly forty years since the English publication of
Adorno's *Introduction to the Sociology of Music*. As Martin puts it, without
this level of analysis, Adorno's ideas remain unfulfilled:

Yet, for all his theoretical virtuosity, it is far from clear that Adorno did in fact
provide a coherent account of the relationship he claimed between musical and
social structures; indeed, in his unremitting efforts to relate the whole to the parts
he leaves unresolved the familiar problems encountered in any attempt to explain
individual action in terms of macro-sociological structures. (1995:112)

Martin continues by quoting Rose Subotnik, who suggests that the links
between artistic structure and social reality are, in Adorno, 'indirect,
complex, unconscious, undocumented, and rather mysterious' (Subotnik
1976:271, quoted in Martin 1995:115). She is, I would concur, right on
all five counts.

In recent years, empirical sociology of music has begun to illuminate
those links. The enterprise of music sociology since the 1970s has been
anything but abstract (for a recent review, see DeNora in Clarke and Cook
2003; Peterson 2001; Shepherd's entry on music sociology in the revised
Grove (Shepherd 2001)). And yet, there are gaps and omissions. There
are, more to the point, issues that music sociologists have for the most
part dismissed, and many of these are precisely the topics that scholars
within what is often termed, 'the new musicology' have sought to preserve. What, for example, has become of Adorno's concern with music
and consciousness; or music and its link to social 'control'? How, similarly, are we to explore music in terms of its psycho-cultural consequences
in relation to action? There is no doubt that the sub-field would benefit
from re-engagement with these questions. The challenge lies in attempting to recover these issues while maintaining music sociology's concern
with empirical documentation, with a type of constructivism grounded in
things that lie outside the analyst's interpretation of musical texts. And,
as I describe in the next chapter, this project depends upon finding an
appropriate level for socio-musical investigation.

Music sociology, the 'new' musicology, and Adorno

While Adorno has been all but forgotten by music sociologists (though not by social and cultural theorists), his work is alive and well in musicology. Indeed, the vicissitudes of Adorno's reputation within music scholarship highlight just how dramatically that field has changed since the 1970s, when Rose Rosengard Subotnik's uncanny sensitivity to his thought was virtually the only torch to be carried for Adorno there. Subotnik's work has since been vindicated and interest in Adorno's work burgeons. This interest can, I suggest, be read as part of a wider paradigm shift within musicology.

Today – or so it seems looking in from the outside – most musicologists would probably agree with Donald Randel's observation (1992) that musicology's more traditional 'toolbox' had been designed for the work of constructing and maintaining a canon of acceptable topics – works, great works, great composers. In roughly the past fifteen years, and in response to developments in other disciplines such as literary theory, philosophy, history, anthropology, and, to a much smaller extent, sociology, the field of musicology has been thoroughly revised. Today the 'new' musicologists (a term dating to at least to the middle 1980s) have called into question the separation of historical issues (biography and the social contexts of music-making) and musical form. They have focused instead on music's role as a social medium. This move, once controversial, has now, it seems fair to say, been institutionalised within the discipline. It is now 'normal', or at least acceptable, to pursue questions about the interrelation between musical works on the one hand, and categories and hierarchies of social structure – identity, power, and the practices of ruling – on the other. One could argue that the 'new' musicology is now, for all practical purposes, 'musicology' writ large, or, if not, then part of what is officially recognised as part of musicology's forefront. From a sociological perspective this development is welcome. But there is still more work to be done before musicology and sociology can operate in tandem. This work involves rethinking both music sociology and musicology so as to highlight what, within each discipline, has been ignored.

What is missing, then, from music sociology? As alluded to early in chapter 1, work on music by sociologists can be characterised almost entirely as a sociology *of* music, that is, a sociology about how musical activity (composition, performance, distribution, reception) is socially shaped. This work has not correspondingly dealt with the problem of how music 'gets into' social reality; how music is a dynamic medium of social life. In this respect its empirically grounded focus is directed away from Adorno's key concerns. Most sociologists do not bother with the question of music's specifically *musical* properties and how these properties may 'act' upon those who encounter them. Indeed, sociologists tend to infuriate musicologists when they suggest that musical meaning – music's perceived associations, connotations, and values – derive *exclusively* from the ways in which music is framed and appropriated, from what is 'said' about it. Musicologists often assume (and in some cases correctly) that this notion overrides any concept of music's own properties (conventions, physical properties of sound) as active in the process of perceived meanings.

The problem with the new musicology viewed from the perspective of music sociology is that it has been too tightly committed to the interpretation and criticism of musical texts. This commitment in turn has constrained musicology's conception and interrogation of the social. This focus is perhaps hardly surprising, given the traditional concerns of musicology as a discipline. It also helps to explain why Adorno's work is more highly valued by music scholars than by music sociologists. Richard Leppert's and Susan McClary's influential edited collection, *Music and Society: The Politics of Composition, Performance and Reception* (1987), a paradigmatic work in the field of new musicology, helps to clarify these points.

Musicology's society paradigm

As the editors put it in their introduction, the volume was oriented to 'presenting alternative models to the reading of music history and music criticism – models that strive to permit social context and musical discourse to inform one another' (1987:xiii–xiv). Analytically, this aim was addressed in ways that resonated with two aspects of Adorno's methodology.

The first of these resonances was described by Rose Subotnik, whose essay ('On Grounding Chopin') outlined the techniques to be employed for illuminating music's 'mediating role'. 'The problem of trying to relate music to society *is'*, Subotnik wrote, 'fundamentally, a problem of criticism, requiring very much the same sorts of means that one would take to the interpretation of a literary text' (1987:107). The second resonance involved the technique (as described above in chapter 1, in the discussion of Adorno's critics) of juxtaposing 'microscopies of musical detail' (as Merquior put it, quoted in Martin 1995:115) with broad-brush depictions of the social whole. This strategy was the primary strategy within musicology at the time for illuminating music's ideological role. Its usefulness was linked to its ability to point to structural *patterns* between musical and social forms – to make suggestions about how music – in and through its compositional practices – might be related to ideas or social arrangements.

For example, in 'On Talking Politics during Bach Year', Susan McClary wrote, '[t]he values it [functional tonality] articulates are those held most dear by the middle class: beliefs in progress, in expansion, in the ability to attain ultimate goals through rational striving, in the ingenuity of the individual strategist operating both within and in defiance of the norm' (1987:22). Similarly, John Shepherd's discourse (in 'Music and Male Hegemony') also alluded, in a general way, to music's ability to afford social action. He described what he regarded as rare forms of music that manage, 'to subvert, if only partially, the bureaucratised norms of "classical" music. *The structure of many Afro-American and Afro-American influenced "popular" musics reflects the situation of proletarianized peoples* contained by social institutions that they cannot influence or affect in any consequential fashion' (1987:162, emphasis added).

As a strategy, the juxtaposition of micro-musical and macro-social analysis helped reorient scholars to music's social dimension – and it required a good deal of professional courage at the time. But this strategy also constrained the possibilities for theorising society (and with it, available modes of, and rationale for, empirical socio-musical investigation). This constraint can be seen as linked to the tactic of positing social structure as a backdrop or foil for detailed musical analysis – a resource for musical analysis but not a topic of socio-musical analysis. By this I mean that the social was not theorised in a manner that could highlight the mechanisms of its making and remaking. As such, music comes to be seen as reflecting society, a conception that, at least implicitly, forfeits a theory of dynamism between music and society (and within which links between the two can only be stated hypothetically). In short, we never see music *in the act of* articulating social structure or as it is mobilised for this articulation. Instead, through reference to 'middle-class beliefs' or 'proletarianised peoples' social structure is (at least implicitly) posited as extant (objectified).

Society in a pumpkin shell?

In his seminars at the University of California, the sociologist Bruno Latour used to describe how the macro-oriented sociologists critical of his work (theorists of global systems, the various quantitative analysts and statistical modellers) would often ask him where, within his focus on the networks, strategies, and campaigns through which scientific 'facts' were established, was the 'big picture'? Where, for example, were the 'systems' – legal, political, economic? Where were the historical 'eras', 'epochs', and 'regimes'? Sociology, they would argue, had to consider 'the big picture'. When they uttered these words ('the big picture'), Latour recounted, their voices would (reverentially) drop an octave and their arms would sweep upwards to describe a circle. At this point Latour would say (and I paraphrase), 'you see? They make reference to "the big picture" but that picture turns out to be no bigger than a pumpkin [i.e., the size of the arm span used in the gesture]'. By this Latour meant that the 'wider society' to which these scholars alluded (democracy, revolution, norms, criminality, the family, indeed society itself) was an extrapolation of the known, an attribution, in part, of imagination and faith. The 'bigger picture' was, in short, a literary production, one that came to be performed (indexed) through statements 'about' it.

While one might counter this position by pointing to the ways in which these 'fictions' nevertheless manage to produce highly tangible signs of their presence (state-sponsored violence and war; apartheid; purdah; the caste system; systematic forms of discrimination), Latour's point remains, on *methodological* grounds, unchallenged. There, lessons to be drawn from Latour are straightforward: it will not do to 'sociologise' social structure. Instead, all claims about 'structures', social forces, and the like need to be examined in terms of mechanisms of operation, in terms of the agents or (to use the terminology employed by this perspective) 'actor networks' within which social patterns and institutions are performed and, for varying lengths of time, consolidated. These mechanisms include people's day-to-day activities, their meaningful orientation to the things that they understand as 'society', 'law', 'government', the 'economy', 'family life', and many others.

Such questions imply a grounded focus on the connections between culture (including ideas of structure) and agency (activity). Doing science, or music (which includes consuming these things) is simultaneously doing social life, and it was precisely this point that Latour sought to make in *The Pasteurization of France* (1989). It should be clear by now that this paradigm is concerned with how, *at the level of situated activities*, science and society do not 'reflect' each other (as if they are distinct) but are rather 'co-produced'. The term, 'co-production' highlights how it is possible to, as it were, *do things with science* (one could substitute here, music), that is, how the form that scientific knowledge takes has *consequences* for, is part of the ecosystem of, the various worlds within which it is formulated, received, and used. This idea, while linked to a methodological programme fundamentally different from Adorno's, nonetheless resonates with his concern with cultural products as active ingredients in relation to consciousness and to ruling.

In sum, Latour's notion of co-production offers lessons for both the new musicology and for music sociology. For the former, the lesson is that, on its own, the analysis of the discursive properties of texts is not enough. It leaves in shadow the actual workings of 'society', that is, the question of how music and non-musical features of social life can be seen to interact. It also sidesteps issues concerning the construction of musical meaning in actual contexts of reception and thus the issue of *contested* meanings (including resistance to particular musicological interpretations – e.g., disputes within and between 'expert' and 'lay' respondents to music). Music's mechanisms of operation within this model are unspecifiable – that is, there is no methodology for describing music as it 'acts' within actual social settings, eras and spaces, and in real time.

For music sociology, the lesson is that the new musicology's concern with music as a dynamic medium within social life cannot be ignored. Music is not simply 'shaped' by 'social forces' – such a view is not only sociologistic, it also misses music's active properties and thus diminishes the potential of music sociology by ignoring the question of music's discursive and material powers.

In what follows, I attempt to build upon these lessons to develop a programme for socio-musical research that draws together the concerns of musicology and sociology and sets them on an empirical plain. This programme takes to heart Howard Becker's disarmingly clear observation that society (or music) is, 'what a lot of people have done jointly' (1989:282). Its focus is on music as (and in relation to) social *process*, on how musical materials (and the interpretations and evaluations of these materials) are created, revised, and undercut with reference to the social relations and social contexts of this activity. It also is concerned with how music provides constraining and enabling resources for social agents – for the people who perform, listen, compose, or otherwise engage with musical materials.

This focus attends to the question of *how* links between music and agency, music and forms of community, music and ideas, come to be forged. It takes as its first commandment Antoine Hennion's stricture that 'it must be strictly forbidden to create links when this is not done by an identifiable intermediary' (1995:248). By this, Hennion means that while music may be, or may seem to be, interlinked to 'social' matters – patterns of cognition, styles of action, ideologies, institutional arrangements – these links should not be presumed. Rather, they need to be specified (observed and described) at their levels of operation (e.g., in terms of how they are established and come to act). We need, in short, to follow actors in and across situations as they draw music into (and draw on music as) social practice. And *this* is where empirical methods come into their own within the sociology of music. It should be obvious at this point that I am seeking to move the argument on to a level where social life can be portrayed in less general, more socially located, terms. I suggest that this is a theoretical advance for music sociology, a move towards greater nuance in keeping with Adorno's own critique of reason – it is a move towards specificity.

Grand theory and everyday experience

In her novel *The Good Apprentice*, Iris Murdoch has a character exclaim 'the modern world is full of theories which are proliferating at a wrong level of generality, we're so *good* at theorising, and one theory spawns another, there's a whole industry of abstract activity which people mistake for thinking' (1985:150). The argument developed so far has led to this point: too much of socio-musical studies (and too much of sociology as well) has been conducted on this 'wrong level'. By the term 'wrong level', I mean a level of theorising that does not address or attempt to document the *actual* mechanisms through which music plays a mediating role in social life. In this suggestion, I am by no means original.

Olle Edström clarifies this point. Describing how his musicology study group at Gothenburg became frustrated after many months of Adorno Study-Group, Edström says, '. . . we gradually gained a deeper insight into the pointlessness of instituting theoretical discourses on music without a solid ethnomusicological knowledge of the everyday usage, function and meaning of music' (Edström 1997:19).

The focus on 'use' described by Edström entails certain shifts. First, as described already, it involves a shift away from a sole preoccupation with 'works' and towards, instead, the ways that works are incorporated into practice. There is most assuredly a place for 'readings' here, but they are used either as heuristic aids or as topics in their own right, as I describe below. Second it involves a shift from 'what' to 'how' questions – that is a shift from a concern with 'what' musical works might 'tell' us to a concern with 'how', as they are incorporated into practice (whether through the ways they are consumed or performed or through the ways that they may provide resources for the composition and/or interpretation of new or other works) they may come to have 'causal' or structuring powers, effects. In short, to understand music as a constitutive ingredient of social ordering (and this is ultimately Adorno's concern), it is necessary to gain distance from the prevailing models of music's relation to 'society', common within musicology, cultural studies, and socio-cultural theory. By contrast, what is required is a focus on actual musical *practice*, on how specific agents use and interact with music. Such an approach makes no assumptions about 'what' music can do but examines music's social 'content' as it is constituted through musical practices in real time and in particular social and material spaces. Only through observation of these practices is it possible to document music's mechanisms of operation, to follow agents as they *do things with music*. It is only through this empirical work that theories can be extended beyond the 'wrong level' of generality. Some examples are in order.

Example 1: criticism is constitution

'Doing things with music' includes music critical analysis itself. As the ethnomusicologist Henry Kingsbury once put it, 'musicological discourse is not simply talk and writing "about music", but is also constitutive of music' (1991:201). Think about, in terms of activities, what is being done (Becker 1982). Someone, a type of social actor – a musically trained scholar or professional – has been selective. She has 'decided' to engage in communicative action – in this case, talking about a piece of music, usually as the topic of a published piece or public talk (i.e., as part of an already highly framed and visible mode of action). She has selected *this* work as opposed to others. (She may or may not also tell us about the criteria that governed her selection.) She then calls our attention to that work in particular ways. She may describe it in terms of its harmonic progressions, its handling of themes, or some other formal aspect which, again, she selects. She then goes on to tell us – if she is concerned with socio-musical analysis – what this signifies (e.g., its ideological content). Her conclusions may make reference to how this music stands in relation to patterns of musical activity – genre, conventions, styles.

For example, the new musicology may suggest that, to return to the essay I quoted earlier, the duets between the soul and Jesus in Bach's Cantata *Wachet auf* and his 'casting the individual believer as female, in-complete and longing for satisfaction and fulfilment from the divine male' (McClary 1987:53) recast the presumably gender-free soul (as McClary observes, 'male souls are also supposed to long in this manner . . .' (ibid.)) as feminine, as, 'a nagging, passive-aggressive wife, insecurely whining for

Example 1. J.S. Bach, *Wachet auf*

repeated assurances of love and not hearing them when they are proffered' (ibid.). In offering these words (and drawing upon particular linguistic discourses), McClary *frames* this music; she shows us how to perceive *it in a particular way*. And if we do, in turn, perceive Bach's 'sexism' – not as an individual but as 'a product of his time' – we simultaneously engage in at least two further acts, both of which are affected by this music analytical appropriation of the 'object'. First, this new way of seeing/hearing Bach may come to affect our future perception of Bach's music (and thus his status in relation to the rest of musical culture – e.g., our perceived 'need' for a 'feminine' and/or 'feminist' musical aesthetic); and second, our perception of the analyst herself and her status in relation to other musicologists may change. In relation to this second point, if we accept this radical rereading of Bach, then, implicitly, we have simultaneously endorsed the analyst's claim to interpretive power, as someone able to 'reveal' the object of Bach's music to us, to help the scales drop from our eyes (the wax from our ears?). Simultaneously, we reaffirm the role of the musical expert as one who has the power to 'reveal' things about music to us. In this example, then, a simple critical comment about one work by one composer effects several things at once. It reconfigures the music by repositioning attention and reframing that music (showing how it is 'like' other things). It repositions that music in relation to other music and it positions the analyst in relation to other analysts (previous analysis that failed to see Bach's 'sexism' were insufficient) and to ourselves as readers (the analyst has authority) and, in this last respect, it maintains the cultural authority of music criticism as an enterprise. Finally, it is active in the game of doing society through doing (responding to) music, in a way that converts the analyst into an intermediary, rather than maintaining her as the observer of links made by others. As J. M. Fauquet and A. Hennion have observed in their own study of Bach and the history of his 'glory', the point is to

follow the archaeology of [Bach's] greatness . . . Aesthetic, historic or social interpretations 'about' music in general have superseded interpretations 'of' the music, itself, yet they tackle Bach in exactly the same terms: could there be yet another, unexplored approach to deciphering him differently? By contrast, it is this relationship that we wish to reveal, rather than exploit by proposing yet another in a long line of Bach interpretations. (Hennion and Fauquet 2001:77–8)

Thus, to offer a feminist reading of Bach presents 'another in a long line of Bach interpretations'. This is not to say that such an interpretation is not *useful*; on the contrary, as I have just observed, it 'accomplishes' a good deal (it shifts our perception of this music) and at the least, through example, how music may be used or come to act ideologically. In suggesting that Bach's musical representations have consequences for how we conceptualise gender relations today, it draws upon something that the music affords and so reorients readers to new values within the community of musicology and beyond.

But to what extent do these claims satisfy Hennion's criteria, that one must not state a link without also identifying a mediator? Later in the essay, McClary considers the question of how actual listeners (students in her classes) 'tend to situate themselves differently with respect to its [the aria's] dialectic'. (There is no adjacent methodological account of just how their listening may have been previously framed.) Male listeners, 'unselfconsciously identify with the male character (with Christ!) and sneer at the Bride's tiresomeness. And the women realize that they are supposed to identify with the Bride but resent the pleading insecurity with which she is portrayed' (p. 55). This is one place where more overly sociological analysis could assist musicology, by pursuing the theme of how music is heard and how it is identified, *linked* to other matters as part of world-making activity.

To repeat the underlying theme here – musicology and music sociology are both necessary to the enterprise of socio-musical study of how music's properties may offer their recipients materials for types of response, for building role relationships and their adjunct subject positions (i.e., the feeling forms associated with these roles). Music does function discursively – the new musicologists are right. Music's recipients may, in other words, identify with particular aspects of music or see themselves in particular features of compositions. When they do this, music can be said to 'do' things, in this case, to 'get into' (inform, lend form to, structure) subjectivity. Musicological readings of works may thus help us to see how musical structures give rise to subjective orientations (subject positions) and their relations; may help us to see how cultural artefacts may serve as object lessons in social relations and may be associated with particular patterns of reception. In the case of the Bach, different types of people (men/women) may relate themselves to the representations of social relations in different ways, taking the role of one or another of the 'voices'/characters depicted within an aesthetic form. If they do, then the music may be understood as an object of gender socialisation.

But this question – how music orients its listeners to particular notions about gender – is too important not to explore in grounded, methodologically rigorous ways. The question arises, then, how should this be done? Is it sufficient, for example, to use the traditional methods of reception study, simply to ask people to 'talk about' what this music means? I have been suggesting that these traditional methods are insufficient to the task, that we need to explore music as it functions *in situ*, not as it is 'interpreted' but rather as it is *used*. Such a focus, I argue in what follows, helps to situate socio-musical study at the 'right' level of generality – it preserves a concern with the fine-grained texture of, on the one hand, social practices of musical appropriation and, on the other, music's musical features as they are relevant to this process.

What can music afford?

Reception and media studies have been useful. They have taught us how the meanings of cultural media (including their perceived 'value') – come to be articulated through the ways people (media consumers) interact with media products (for sociological discussions of this point see, for example, Van Rees 1987; Moores 1990; Tota 2001c). Among these 'consumers' are music scholars, analysts, and critics who are just one sub-set (albeit perhaps a prominent and often influential sub-set) of music consumers and music users. This *emergent* aspect of cultural-textual meaning includes both the meanings found 'in' texts by amateur or lay consumers, and the meanings divined by 'expert' analysts and readers.

At the same time, as the new musicologists have sought to demonstrate, it is wrong to suggest that texts make no contribution to the ways they are received. Musical texts, or, more broadly, musical materials, are by no means neutral. They are created and distributed in ways that employ and reinforce meanings. There are many aspects of music that can serve as examples here: music's physical features, such as volume and pace; the physical requirements of performance (e.g., solo violin or massed strings); conventions such as genres, styles, melodic devices, or topoi; and, in the case of repeated hearings, accumulated connotations, institutionalised interpretations. While no musical unit, passage, or work may guarantee its reception under all circumstances (even the most conventional of materials can still be, in Eco's term (1992), 'over-interpreted'), musical materials are nonetheless part of, and contribute to, their circumstances of hearing (see DeNora 2000:21–45 for a more detailed discussion of these points). To take a very basic example, it is unlikely that any listener will hear a march tune as 'dreamy' or Debussy's *Prélude à l'après-midi d'un faune* as suitable music for marching.

Particular musical materials may thus be perceived, often with regularity, as commensurate with a variety of 'other things'. These 'things' may be other works (how we come to recognise the 'style' of an era, composer, region, for example) but, more interesting for socio-musical analysis, they may be some extra-musical phenomenon, such as values, ideas, images, social relations, or styles of activity. The *sociological* significance of this last point is intensified when music's social 'content' is not merely hailed (as a representation of a reality or imagined reality) but is rather acted upon, when music comes to serve in some way as an organising material for action, motivation, thought, imagination, and so forth. It is here that we can begin to speak of music as it 'gets into' action. And it is here that socio-musical study can be extended beyond notions (derived from textual analysis) of music's symbolic character, its interpretations and perceived *meaning(s)*.

There are precedents here in the work of scholars – prominent in the American context here is Robert Wuthnow – who have been concerned with the *interrelationships between* (rather than *meanings of*) cultural elements, an emphasis that seeks to retain the sociological impetus within cultural studies by redirecting our focus on culture's organising properties and away from the individualistic focus on meaning and its reception. As Wuthnow has observed, meanings emerge from cultural systems and fields that provide 'categories in which formal thinking about ourselves' may be conducted. This is, again, a focus on how meanings and forms 'get into' action – how they provide, in the words of other theorists, *repertoires* for action – and I discuss this perspective in some detail in chapter 5. The focus on meaning systems leads, at least implicitly, to a focus upon actors as they engage with and mobilise cultural materials, as they move through particular cultural fields and so configure themselves as conscious agents. Such a perspective is in line, I believe, with the focus, within organisational studies, on structuration and agency – work such as DiMaggio's (1982) that has consisted of an abiding focus on agents as they mobilise cultural structures to produce and reproduce organisations. Here, then, music can be understood as a resource for getting things done and, in this sense, the sociology of music can not only learn from existing theoretical and empirical work on institutions, it can also advance that work through its potential to reveal the aesthetic and non-cognitive dimensions of social agency.

In short, the 'right level' of generality in socio-musical studies consists of a focus on music-as-practice, and music as providing a basis for practice. It deals with music as a formative medium in relation to consciousness and action, as a resource for – rather than medium about – world building. Within this dynamic conception of music's social character, focus shifts from *what* music depicts, or what it can be 'read' as saying 'about' society, to what it *makes possible*. And to speak of 'what music makes possible' is to speak of what music 'affords'.

Adapted from social psychology, the concept of 'affordance' captures music's role as, to use Antoine Hennion's term, a 'mediator' of the social (Hennion 2001). And, depending upon how it is conceptualised, the concept of 'affordance' highlights music's potential as an organising medium, as something that helps to structure such things as styles of consciousness, ideas, or modes of embodiment. To speak of music as affording things is to suggest that it is a material against which things are shaped up, elaborated through practical and sometimes non-conscious, action. Some examples will help to clarify this point.

Example 1, embodied action: Different types of rhythm may afford particular types of bodily movement (music can 'cause listeners to experience their bodies in new ways' (McClary 1991:25)). Indeed, this is the point of many 'work songs', traditional and, via time-and-motion study, modern (Lanza 1994). Rhythm may be said to 'afford' movement to the extent that it is perceived as profiling specific types of movement (e.g., tempos, energy levels, styles of movement) and these are acted upon to the extent that actors entrain their bodily movements to its properties. While dance may be the most obvious example of how bodies come to be entrained to rhythms, dance is simply one of the more formalised activities where this entrainment occurs. Music may be linked to a retinue of more subtle bodily features that characterise movement and comportment in daily life – posture, pace, and movement style. It may also be linked to more fundamental bodily processes, such as heart rate or blood pressure. These things in turn may be associated with forms (and images) of social agency as types of being, and with, when certain individual attributes are associated with those forms, hierarchies of individuals in relation to those forms. In this we can begin to see the topic I shall consider in chapters 4 and 5: the connections between music, embodiment, emotional state, and conduct. Music may also afford the imaginative projection of bodily movement, as when one 'pictures' a type of movement when hearing a type of music. The example of marching music serves to illustrate these points. On hearing march music one *may* (but not automatically – see below) be reminded of or begin to imagine – to 'picture' – marching. One may, in other words, become motivated or aroused in relation to a type of agency – marching – to a particular movement style, and one associated with a particular set of institutional practices and their particular agent-states, such as bodily regulation, coordination, and entrainment. One may 'become' (produce one's self as) a 'marcher' – that is, on the occasion of music heard, one may adapt one's self to its perceived properties and so become, via the music, a type of agent, in this case, one imbued with march-like, militaristic agency. (On marching music, see McNeill 1995.)

Example 2, recognition and cognition: There is a style of collective singing that consists of a kind of droning in which the voices
produce more notes than the sum of singers (harmonics or 'over-
tones' emerge). This droning produces 'extra' notes, that is, notes
that are not being sung by any individual singer. One *could* imagine how this type of music 'affords' or provides, a model for
thinking about the concept of community (e.g., 'the whole is
greater than the sum of its parts'). (Compare this to the example
of marching music and the bodies who march to it – there each
individual enacts or incorporates into his/her action an external
source of entrainment – the pulse or beat which is externally provided, rather than emerging out of what is produced by 'all' in
concert.)

Here, we see how music can serve as a resource for: (a) reconfiguring
bodily conduct; or (b) providing a model for thinking about, elaborating
some concept (e.g., community). Things found 'in' music (even highly
abstract aspects of music's texture or structure) thus come to serve as
resources for elaborating knowledge and its categories, and, in this case,
music may be understood to provide patterns against which that knowledge takes shape. Thus, even at its most abstract (e.g., textless music,
experimental or unconventional music), music can provide resources for
thinking, resources in the form of object lessons, analogies, exemplars,
models. I shall return to this point in the following chapter.

In both these examples, music 'causes' nothing; it 'makes nothing happen', as Auden said of poetry, and certainly it does not 'give rise', in and
of itself, to either marching or ideas about social organisation. That is, to
speak of music as an affordance structure is by no means the same as to
speak of music as 'cause' or 'stimulus' of action, thought, or emotional
response. It also does not imply that there is some 'set' of things that a
particular music may afford, since what comes to count as the musical
'object' emerges in relation to how that object is handled by its recipients.

By contrast, the concept of affordance extends developments within reception theory, emphasising music's effects as dependent upon the ways
that those who hear it respond to it; how they incorporate it into their action; an how they may adapt their action (not necessarily or in most cases
consciously) to its parameters and qualities. It posits music as something
acted with and acted upon. It is only through this appropriation that
music comes to 'afford' things, which is to say that music's affordances,
while they might be anticipated, cannot be pre-determined but rather
depend upon how music's 'users' connect music to other things; how
they interact with and in turn act upon music as they have activated it.

TIME 1 – Before the Event (all prior history as meaningful to A. Actor(s))

1. Preconditions
Conventions, biographical associations, previous programming practices

---

TIME 2 – During the Event (the event may be of any duration, seconds to years)

2. Features of the Event

> **A** **Actor(s)** Who is engaging with music? (e.g., analyst, audience, listener, performer, composer, programmer)

> **B** **Music** What music, and with what significance as imputed by Actor(s)?

> **C** **Act of Engagement with music** What is being done? (e.g., individual act of listening, responding to music, performing, composing)

> **D** **Local conditions of C.** (e.g., how came to engage with music in *this* way, at *this* time (i.e., at Time 2 – 'During the Event'))

> **E** **Environment** In what setting does engagement with music take place? (material cultural features, interpretive frames provided on site (e.g., programme notes, comments of other listeners))

TIME 3 – After the Event

3. Outcome Has engagement with music afforded anything? What if anything was changed or achieved or made possible by this engagement? And has this process altered any aspect of item 1 above?

Fig. 1. The Musical Event and its conditions.

It is here, then, that we can sustain socio-music analysis at a 'right' level of generality. This level focuses upon what shall be called from here on *The Musical Event*, an indicative scheme for how we might begin to situate music as it is mobilised in action and as it is associated with social effects.

The Musical Event consists of a specific act of engagement with music. The core of the concept can be found in the five components, items **A** to **E**, listed in the centre of figure 1. These events consist of an actor or actors (**A**), composers, listeners, performers, music analysts, and others, who engage with or 'do things with' (**C**) music (**B**) within specific environments (**E**) and under local conditions (**D**). Music (**B**) can mean whole 'works' or any aspect or feature of musical material (e.g., a fragment of a work, a bit of improvised music (even something like whistling or humming to one's self)), whether being made/heard live or on record or imagined. What is key here is how the music is, or comes to be, meaningful *to the actors who engage with it*, including such matters as whether the relevant actors notice it (as in the case of background music in public places).

The Swedish musicologist Ola Stockfelt has developed this last issue (Stockfelt 1997). Stockfelt describes different 'modes' of listening in a way that takes us further from Adorno's original hierarchy of *listeners* and towards an empirical concern with *listening*. Stockfelt describes several modes of engaging with music, modes that are related in turn to types of social situation and which are posited as 'possible' modes of listening – i.e., the typology is open to future elaboration. One of the key features of listening modes to which Stockfelt draws our attention is the issue of how we, as listeners, shift between different forms of attentive and disattentive listening. At times, music is positioned, by the listener, in the foreground, at times the background (Stockfelt 1997:140–1).

This engagement may also involve interaction between types of actors, such as between one listener and another, as they engage with some music, or between a performer and her audience, such as between a popular musician and her fans. These events are in turn connected temporally to the past (**1** 'Preconditions') and the future (**3** 'Outcome[s]'). Preconditions include such things as prior patterns of musical engagement (recognisable conventions of composing or style, biographical associations that particular music may hold for actors); any previously determined or practised patterns of programming, e.g., when actors engage with particular types of music for specific reasons, such as to alter mood (of self or other) or to sell merchandise or to demonstrate some analytical point. Outcomes (**3**) are whatever the music comes to afford or make possible, the 'work' that it may do as indicated in the actor's/actors' orientations to it and in their behaviour in relation to it. For example, if the 'act of engagement' (**C**) is music criticism, of the kind that Adorno himself engaged in, then the music can be said to afford the ideas that are fashioned in relation to it (e.g., ideas about the music, what it signifies, or ideas about other things that engaging with the music facilitates, exemplifies, or otherwise helps to make possible). To take another example, if the 'act of engagement' is, by contrast, listening to music at home, then what the music affords may be mood change, or motivational change or pleasure, or a shifting of ambience, energy levels, or a way of signalling taste/lifestyle issues.

It is in how music is drawn into connection with other things, how it is acted upon, that it comes to serve as an affordance structure. And it is the features that are accessed in this process that may be said to afford what is accomplished. Thus, just as one may come to use the concept of speech-act to capture the *constitutive* power of language in use, so too, we may wish to speak of music-acts, so as to capture the ways in which things are accomplished through musical events and their appropriations through words and deeds. And, as with speech acts, music-acts function according to how, retrospectively, they are acted upon – there is, in other words, no point in drawing up a taxonomy of music-acts in advance and in the abstract. How, then, might Adorno's own music-sociological questions be pursued through this scheme? It is time for an extended example.

The conductor, his orchestra, their audience

Adorno's essay 'Conductor and Orchestra: Aspects of Social Psychology' (Adorno 1976) provides a useful starting point. First, it alludes to the study of music as a performative medium, a focus that is now current within socio-musical studies. Second, it points to themes in the social psychology of music as physical practice and as involving social relations of production that are also now current, particularly within the social psychology of music and in the sociological study of music education. Third, and most significantly, the 'social psychological' treatment Adorno gives to this topic illuminates modern orchestral music and its 'multimedia' performance (visual plus aural) as a means of domination. The psycho-cultural process of consuming the event of conducted music provided, according to Adorno, a mechanism for 'taming' the audience, for subduing that audience and converting them from an active public into a passive 'mass' (Adorno refers in passing to Elias Canetti's *Crowds and Power* in this context). We see here quite clearly Adorno's notion that music served as a form of exemplary praxis.

Two interrelated issues are explored by Adorno to develop these points. The first of these issues is the idea that the orchestra is a '[m]icroscosm in which social tensions recur and can be concretely studied' (Adorno 1976:104). The second issue centres on the conductor's embodied presence, *his* (I use the male pronoun here for reasons that will be clear below) 'figure and striking gestures', which embody and provide an 'imago of power' (ibid.). This imago in turn provides a focal point for the audience, who may identify with it and so 'act out with impunity' certain 'fantasies of power'. And the audience's indulgence in this fantasy is, ultimately, the means by which the audience is subdued: '[t]he conductor acts as through he were taming the orchestra, but his real target is the audience – a trick not unknown to political demagogues' (p. 105).

Adorno elaborates this thesis by describing how the conductor's costume and his prop (the baton) generate associations with three quite different social figures: the 'whip-wielding ringmaster in a circus' (the instrument of dominance, the baton here equated with the whip); a member of the master class (in 'posh' tailcoat); or, a head waiter, i.e., a servant. (Note here the Chesterton detective story in which the theft of valuable cutlery is accomplished because the thief manages to pass himself off at different times in the evening as both a guest and a waiter.) Adorno suggests that the conductor turns his back on the audience as if 'unconcerned' or 'detached' (p. 106), again a means of demonstrating 'that loveless detachment from his devotees which Freud, in *Mass Psychology and Ego Analysis*, named among the constituents of the leader imago' (ibid.). Simultaneously, the relation between conductor and orchestra is ambivalent. The ideological justification of the conductor, 'of needing one to unify all' (p. 107) is both justified and unjustified.

It is unjustified (the conductor's actions can 'easily degenerate into charlatanism' (p. 108)) because an orchestra can manage without the conductor (and can ignore a poor conductor). The conductor is, to some extent, superfluous:

[t]he orchestra's attitude toward the conductor is ambivalent . . . [they] want him to hold them on a tight rein, but at the same time they distrust him as a parasite who need not bow or blow and instrument and gives himself airs at the expense of those who do play. The Hegelian dialectic of master and servant is here repeated in miniature. (Adorno 1976:110)

It is justified because the large orchestra (with its complex division of labour and the spatial distance between parts of that division) may create a condition in which the 'orchestra apparatus is as much alienated from itself . . . as from the unity of the music due to be played. This is conjured up by the alienated institution of the conductor whose relation to the orchestra, the musical as well as the social relation, prolongs the estrangement' (p. 108). This estrangement is 'reinforced' by the class antagonism between conductor and orchestra: '[t]he orchestra musician's social background . . . serves to reinforce the psychological ambivalence, but its roots extend to the objective situation also' (p. 108). In short, the conductor–orchestra relation represents in miniature, according to Adorno, the relation between individuals and their political leaders in the modern social world. It is here that Adorno's primary concern reasserts itself – the interrelation of subject and object. The conductor is seen to embody a form of domination that curtails individual subjects in favour of the whole and is yet not fully justified; the conductor is, as Adorno suggests, 'the opposite of what seeks to be polyphonous' (ibid.).

Adorno's analysis of the psycho-cultural effects of the spectacle of conductor–orchestra is undeniably intriguing. He suggests nothing less than that the 'sight of sound', to use Richard Leppert's phrase (1993), in tandem with the particular ambivalence of the conductor–orchestra production relation, provides a means of socialisation for the audience. In particular, it provides a means for rendering listening subjects amenable to authoritarian rule. The 'microscosm' of the orchestra–conductor thus serves to normalise the macrocosm ('bigger picture') of the public/mass and leader.

TIME 1 – Before the Event

1. Preconditions Adorno's prior experience: e.g., his previous experience of: (a) conductor and other types of actors (e.g., the circus ringmaster (baton/whip); head waiter; member of the 'master class' [dinner jacket]); (b) other social relations of work (e.g., labourers and manager) and theories about this; (c) previous understandings of conductor's role and justification; (d) information about *this* conductor

TIME 2 – the time of writing the essay

    A Actor(s) Adorno
    B Music Embodied acts/gestures of the conductor; his displayed relation to the orchestra/audience *as imagined* by Adorno who draws upon 1. Preconditions (prior experience in this case) – no 'real' (time/space) event is described
    C Act of Engagement with music The imagined music scenario is 'read' as simulacrum of power relationship and experienced/identified with as vicarious scenario of dominance
    D Local conditions of C. unknown
    E Environment unknown; some (unspecified) concert hall

TIME 3 – After the Event

    3. Outcome ideas/psychological imagery is provided about the meaning of the conductor/orchestra relationship ('leadership'; emotional/physiological state (e.g., listener/audience member engages in fantasy of power))

Fig. 2. The conductor and the orchestra.

The idea here is that Adorno seeks to 'unmask' the ideological content of orchestral labour as it is displayed. But has he actually accomplished this task in full? Or has he offered a poetic description, a set of images or frames within which to 'see' both orchestral performance and society writ large? Consider his analysis within the scheme for the analysis of Musical Events discussed above. If we attempt to specify the various components, it soon becomes clear that there are gaps in Adorno's analysis, points at which it cannot be fixed to actual social practice and to the situated experience of music.

Adorno's analysis does not relate to any performance or set of performances. There is no specific conductor or group of conductors, no particular orchestra or groups of ensembles, no consideration of which pieces, nor of the material culture of the listening setting. And there are, as usual, no listeners. There is also no sense of which, if any, political and/or historical regimes Adorno has in mind. Instead, at every level of his analysis, Adorno describes *general* tendencies – ideal types. In every respect, we must 'take Adorno's word' for what he has managed to reveal to us. And his essay thus becomes a prescription, a means through which to 'see' the orchestra–conductor relationship 'with new eyes'. This is not to say that Adorno's comments have no merit, nor that they cannot be useful. Rather it is to point out how Adorno's style of presentation risks being labelled 'authoritarian'; to suggest that he did not provide the basis for his knowledge claims. Indeed, we, like the orchestral labourers Adorno describes, are expected to 'follow' the gestures made by the master (conductor/scholar) and interpret material (music/social reality) in accordance with these gestures. But just who is superfluous, here, the theorist or those who seek to test the theory?

There is only one way to answer this question. We need to lay Adorno's analysis alongside empirical studies, to convert his assertions into researchable questions so as to see, at the level of real musical events, how Adorno's ideas might be investigated and assessed. To borrow Bruno Latour's titular phrase (*Science in Action*), we need to view this aspect of music-making 'in action' in terms of how and whether it does, in practice, afford the things that Adorno suggests. Just what, from within particular contexts, might the spectacle of the conductor afford?

This question can in turn be subsumed under a more general heading – does the visual display of music-as-performed provide any 'object lessons' for its audience? This question has been pursued in recent years by scholars with interests in music and gender formation, for example in work by Lucy Green (1997) and Susan O'Neill (1997), and work-in-progress by myself (DeNora 2002a). While the more specific direction of their work differs from Adorno's (it is concerned with the articulation and justification of gender difference, not with more general political arrangmenets), it is nonetheless related. Both Green and O'Neill are interested in how gender stereotypes are constituted and reinforced through musical performance, in particular how ideas about gender relations are formulated through reference to musical arrangements. This is indeed part of Adorno's concern with the *display* of performed music, a topic Green has developed at length in her 1997 book *Music, Gender, Education*.

There, Green develops a theory of *delineated* meaning in music, by which she means a concern with how music may be taken to signify a range of contextual ('social') meaning; how it may be referred to as embodying a metaphor for things external to it. Although Green does not deal in detail with *conducting* as a type of musical activity, she nonetheless shows how music activities – for example, different types of performance and compositional activities – come to be associated with ideas about what is appropriate and inappropriate for male and female musicians. It is Green's methodology that is of interest here, for she has found useful techniques for illuminating the interpretive work done by different types of actors (music professionals, teachers, pupils) that draw connections between musical and social structures and, in so doing, legitimates particular social forms (e.g., in this case gender stereotypes). The point here is that Green engages in two types of work that Adorno left undone. First,

TIME 1 – Before the Event

1. Preconditions Prior associations made by audience members (e.g., what they already know about the conductor/orchestra, the work; conventions of conducting and conducting styles)

TIME 2 – The time of witnessing the performance

    A Actor(s) Audience member(s)
    B Music music plus visual display
    C Act of Engagement with music Any evidence that A. Actor(s) respond to
    B (e.g., through their talk during/afterward, their emotional states)
    D Local conditions of C. Programme notes; social relations of event
    E Environment Concert Hall? Television?

TIME 3 – After the Event

3. Outcome Any delineated meanings (Green 1997) imputed to the music (and its visual display) as made by particular audience member(s) (e.g., ideas about the conductor as 'powerful', ideas about links between conducting and 'how' other forms of social organisation should/should not be arranged (e.g., the 'need' for effective leaders who can 'hold it all together')); any changes in the emotional/physiological 'state' of audience member(s) (e.g., pulse rate; reported emotional change)

Fig. 3. The conductor and orchestra as a Musical Event.

she elaborates a theory of how music may come to provide resources for the ideological work of justifying gender conventions – her theory of delineated meaning. Second, she engages in empirical work. She listens to (and serves as participant observer with) socially situated individuals (students and teachers), follows them as they deploy interpretive strategies, as they describe how music 'reflects' society. Unlike Adorno, in other words, Green shows how, in describing music, her respondents are simultaneously constituting aspects of the social world; when pupils or teachers are 'outraged' at the idea of a girl playing the drums, they are simultaneously engaged in classificatory activity. The act of musical engagement – expressing ideas about what seems musically 'correct' – is simultaneously the act of reinforcing particular social relations. Thus, Green's interrogative focus is useful as a means for re-establishing Adorno's focus on a more empirical footing and in ways that are capable of addressing items A to D in figure 1. Adorno's initial concern with the conductor can now be conceived as in figure 3.

In short, if we want to discover whether the reception of performed music may afford particular attitudes, assumptions, ideas, or feeling states, it is useful to set this question in context of specific Musical Events, specific instances of musical engagement, and then to work backwards, following actors as they refer to the Musical Event in the course of some other action, movement, feeling, or utterance. At that more specific level of analysis, it is possible to see how music comes to afford particular things and thus, *how* music 'gets into' social life. Green's work thus transforms criticism into empirical enquiry. This transformation not only produces the warrant for criticism, it also reveals the mechanisms and points upon which critical praxis might dwell so as to effect social change. The importance of this point is heightened when analysis is overtly critical of a particular style or genre of music or of a particular composer's works. There, where actual livelihoods are at stake, immanent method, the analysis of texts, is not sufficient. Alone, it is in danger of degenerating into a matter of personal or status group taste. This can be seen most clearly in Adorno's critique of jazz.

'Why did Adorno hate jazz?'

Robert Witkin has written extensively on the question of 'why Adorno hated' jazz (Witkin 1998). His exegesis of Adorno's critique is thorough and needs no duplication here. Two points are worth developing from it. First, Witkin observes that Adorno believed jazz rhythms to be pseudo-liberatory because these rhythms elided the beat while simultaneously observing it. As Witkin puts it, 'jazz is seen as constituting, in its distinctive sound, an amalgam of deviation and excess on the one hand and utter rigidity on the other' (1998:163). In this respect, jazz was just one type of music produced by the mass culture industry.

Second, as Witkin puts it, 'the division into "couplet" and "refrain" (verse and chorus) . . . represents . . . the contingency of the individual in everyday life [and] . . . the constraint of the society or collectivity. Adorno argues that the individual in the audience experiences him or herself as a couplet-ego and then feels transformed in the refrain, merges with it in the dance and finds sexual fulfilment. The production process, he argues, realises the primacy of the refrain over the couplet in that the refrain is written first and as the principal component' (1998:169). Here, as in Stravinsky, then, 'the objective sound is embellished by a subjective expression' (quoted in Witkin, ibid.).

Again, the problem with Adorno's analysis is its dislocation. Adorno does not specify which jazz he has in mind (and his knowledge of jazz was, though perhaps not as limited as suggested by Jay, still restricted to the recordings he heard while in England (see Leppert 2002:357)). Nor is there any attempt to document just how the psychological effects claimed for jazz are achieved in relation to real listeners. Again, Adorno's theory is located at the wrong level of generality. And again, it could be relocated in terms of actual jazz production and consumption.

In ongoing work on the production and consumption of avant-garde jazz, for example, the French music sociologist Olivier Roueff shows how aficionados of experimental jazz forms 'see in' those forms models for alternative social structures. Like Adorno, Roueff takes as his starting point the idea that jazz may be linked to, and inculcate, political inclinations. But, unlike Adorno, Roueff relocates his enquiry; he directs it to the discourses used by jazz aficionados and participants (focusing on how they 'translate' jazz structures into political structures and vice versa). This is in turn combined with an ethnography of jazz activity. In other words, to find out what jazz may afford, Roueff examines specific actors as *they* make links between jazz and other things, as they engage and interact with jazz so as to construct, simultaneously, jazz and the things to which jazz is said to refer, represent, and afford. This empirical focus on music-users, then, allows for Adornoian questions – such as the links between music and politics – to be pursued. No analyst should be permitted to get away with not specifying just what they have in mind and just how they can document their ideas at the actual level of lived musical experience.

Music as a resource for agency

The notion of musical affordance that I have sought to develop in this chapter is dynamic; it points to a conception of music as resource for doing, thinking, and feeling 'other things'. Contra Adorno, however, music's affordances cannot be regarded as residing 'in' musical texts, and it is for this reason that socio-musical analysis cannot proceed on a general level. Rather, what music 'does' is dependent upon the ways in which music is heard and perceived; how its meanings are, to use Lucy Green's phrase, delineated. It is the job of the socio-musical analyst, therefore, to examine this process of delineation, to follow the terms of musical engagement. Music comes to afford things when it is perceived as incorporating into itself and/or its performance some property of the extra-musical, so as to be perceived as 'doing' the thing to which it points. Music is active, in other words, as and when its perception is acted upon, and this circularity is precisely the topic for socio-musical research into music's power. Thus, music is much more than a structural 'reflection' of the social. Music is constitutive of the social in so far as it may be seen to enter action and/or conception when 'things' take shape in relation to music; when actors move in ways that are oriented to music's rhythms (e.g., making the body move 'like' marching rhythm); or when actors employ musical structures as models or analogies for elaborating conceptual awareness. And, by contrast, action may be said to 'get into' music when music takes shape in relation to things outside itself, as when music incorporates aspects of the physical, conceptual, or imaginative world. It is here that socio-musical analysis can develop Adornoian questions. How, for example, does music enter into fantasy life, as in the case of Adorno's essay on the conductor and the orchestra? How does music facilitate cognition, as in the case of Adorno's analysis of Schoenberg? How does other music come to pacify its listeners, to inculcate modes of consciousness that are amenable to particular regimes – political or social – as in the case, according to Adorno, of popular music?

The answers to these questions need to be framed in specific terms. If they are, it is possible to see acts of musical engagement simultaneously constituting both music's power and extra-musical modes of sociality. And it is here that *both* earlier music sociology and the new musicology erred. The one focused on how society shaped music; the other on how musical discourse could shape or reflect society. By contrast, I suggest that we consider both questions at once, melding them together as a theory of musical affordance and a practice of ethnographic investigation, historically informed, devoted to the study of how music's affordances are accessed and deployed. If, on the other hand, we are willing to observe actors as they engage in the acts of drawing music into extra-musical realms and vice versa (and not always with deliberation), as music is employed for world-building, and as aspects of non-musical realms and materials are employed for building and responding to music, we arrive at a 'right' level of generality. This level calls for new methodologies, particularly qualitative techniques that focus on music production and consumption in specific spaces and over time. And this in turn suggests case studies.

Case studies are useful, I suggest, not simply because they are empirically rich and as such make for good history (their usual rationale) but also because close attention to the details of musical practice makes good theory, that is, provides a means for describing the mechanisms of culture (music) in-action, for specifying *how* music works. This focus on practice leads us further away from a concern with musical textual objects and towards the materiality of music as event, its relations, circumstances and technologies of production/reception, its uses. From here it is possible to consider how music 'performs' social life, in the sense that its performance and appropriation provide resources for the production of social life, that it affords modes of thinking and feeling, topics to be examined in the next two chapters.

3 Music as cognition

Just as Adorno was not a sociologist 'of' music, so too, his focus on the history of consciousness transcended what is typically termed the sociology 'of' knowledge. Knowledge, in the sense of propositions (as in 'what' is to be known) was never Adorno's primary quarry. He was concerned rather with historical styles of cognition – habits and attitudes of mind and modes of attention to the world. Within this focus, knowledge formation in the sense of the production of 'facts' was conceived as a ceaseless process. One could never *rest* upon formulations because, in so far as all cognition was an attempt to accommodate (as opposed to approximate) reality, it was, inevitably, always moral. And, within that activity, aesthetic forms provided exemplars, structures of attention and thus ways of 'handling' awareness of the material world. For Adorno, aesthetic experience was part of the matrix from which consciousness was formulated and his admiration for Schoenberg makes this clear: if we pursue his line of thinking, music emerges as nothing less than a medium through which modes of attention are formed. It was in this sense that music was an active ingredient in the formation of consciousness and thus of knowledge formation.

This idea is nothing if not intriguing. But to what extent is it possible to specify this issue in terms of actual modes of consciousness in particular locations? Is it possible to reveal the processes by which music comes to inform knowledge production? Can they be observed in cognitive praxis? To ask these questions is to ask whether it is possible to identify particular instances when music structures or in some way informs the production of knowledge. And for this task it is necessary to turn our attention to specific social actors as they draw upon music during their activity of knowledge production or, as they can be seen, in the act of engaging with music, to produce knowledge in a way that makes reference to the music with which they are engaged. It is only through such highly focused examinations that it is possible to speak, at the 'right level' of generality about how attention to the world is structured and how particular instances of cognition are actually produced.

To introduce these issues, some examples are in order. I begin with two sets of examples. Both deal with the topic of how knowledge is articulated, that is, with how some types of phenomena come to be identified and thus, made known, to self or other(s). This 'making known' includes acts of remembering, recognising, and more generally becoming aware of some phenomena. The first set of examples draws on data collected for *Music and Everyday Life* (DeNora 2000). It centres on the act of *remembering*, conceived as a form of knowledge production and, simultaneously, as an orientation of consciousness (i.e., to particular aspects of 'the past'). The second set deals with the formation of formal knowledge in the realm of philosophy, in particular, with the question of how consciousness is itself produced in relation to the world. In both examples, it is possible to follow, in the knowledge-producing activities of *individuals*, certain uses of, and appeals to, music. The individuals involved will be called, Elaine, Lucy, and Ted.

Two daughters – 'Elaine' and 'Lucy'

In 1997–8, I conducted a series of interviews with women in the USA and the UK about music in their daily lives. The results of this research are described in *Music in Everyday Life* (DeNora 2000). The focus of each interview was to explore music as it entered daily experience, 'from the moment you woke up in the morning to the moment you fell asleep that night, whether it was music you chose to listen to or play, or music that you overheard, such as in a shop or on the radio', as one of the interview questions put it. Respondents were asked to describe music's presence in 'a typical day'. In some cases, the music respondents heard (whether because overheard or intentionally programmed) was associated with shifts of consciousness and with changes of orientation (for example, shifts in mood or in the topic of thought). In these cases, it was possible to speak of consciousness as emerging *in interaction with* musically configured environments.

Some respondents were able to reflect with a good deal of insight on how this process worked for them. In particular, respondents with musical performance skills (for example, early piano lessons, or choral singing, or participation in an amateur group) and those who were older and able to reflect upon themselves at different life stages (and who had experienced rich and often difficult life events and passages) offered highly reflexive commentaries on music's active role in their lives. One example of this reflexivity concerned their reflections on how music 'brought back' memories.

Within this category of response, music was often described as a medium that reminded respondents of their relation to loved ones. Music was described as something that could draw consciousness into closer association with (thinking about) parents, partners, children, or special friends, both living and deceased. It was a medium that 'put them in mind of' people and social relationships, which simultaneously involved emotional reorientation. I have written (DeNora 2000:67) of how this 'pairing' of music and people, music and memory, is about something greater than that music 'accompanied' previous times shared with the re-membered other(s). Music does more than this: it penetrates experience: it is part of the material from which initial experience is formed such that, to quote the title of a popular song, 'the song is you'. By this I mean that one's very perception and experience of other(s) takes shape through and with reference to music. It is for this reason, I suggested, that music can so powerfully 'bring it all back':

to the extent that, first time through, a past event was constructed and came to be meaningful with reference to music, musical structures may provide a grid or grammar for the temporal structures of emotional and embodied patterns as they were originally experienced. Music is implicated in the ways that, as Urry observes with poignant reference to Proust's famous phrase, 'our arms and legs . . . [are] full of torpid memories' (Urry 1996:49); it is a mediation of, in Proust's sense, the aesthetic, memory-encrusted unconscious (Lash and Urry 1994:43). (DeNora 2000:67–8)

Consider 'Elaine' (described in DeNora 2000:171–3), who, in the course of the interview, described how her father would call her attention to music when she was growing up:

My father, though he was really untutored in all these things, I think he had just a natural bent, that caused him to have an interest in music, and he used to play on the radio and call my attention to 'listen, isn't this beautiful', all that kind of thing. Classical music.

When she was 30 years old, Elaine received a phone call from her mother to say that her father had been taken ill:

he'd had a heart attack and was in the hospital and I was afraid he was going to die and I put on Brahms and I . . . played it very loud and just let it sweep around me and just prayed for my father. So whenever I hear that I am always taken back to that day, that time, when I feared for him . . .

Here music serves as a medium for remembering in two ways. First, when Elaine chose to listen to the Brahms, she was choosing to listen to music that had been shared with her father during her formative years.

Sharing this music was a medium through which their relationship was initially forged (. . .'he used to play on the radio and call my attention to, "listen" . . .'). Second, when she learned the distressing news that he was seriously ill, she turned to that music, the music of her relationship with her father, to, as it were, keep vigil and pray for his recovery. After he recovered, as Elaine describes it, that music became paired with the intense experience of that vigil ('. . . whenever I hear that I am always taken back to that day, that time, when I feared for him . . .').

Here, then, we have a glimpse of music's role as a medium of consciousness. Music has the capacity to reorient awareness, to direct consciousness back to past times and experiences. When Elaine described how she is 'taken back' when she hears the music of that vigil, she is describing how that music has the power to shift her awareness from the flux of present-centred activity to a more emotionally charged mode of consciousness, namely, the remembering of an important time in her past, a time that remains significant to her present relationship with her father. Here then, albeit briefly, it is possible to speak of music as implicated in the reorienting of consciousness.

A second example, and again one involving the father–daughter relationship, helps to elaborate this theme. It involves Lucy, who was one of the key informants described in *Music in Everyday Life* (The same example is discussed briefly in DeNora 2000:63):

As I've got older I've realised how important music must have been to [my father] . . . there were certain records that he took away with him when he was away during the [second world] war . . . the Schubert *Impromptus*, the Brahms *Double Concerto*, *Finlandia*, and he played those records while he was separated from my mum . . . they were obviously very important to him and then I remember those records being played when *I* was little, I can see myself sitting in my dressing gown in front of the fire . . .

And so they were extremely important to me, and when he died, [. . .] years ago, um, I remember I was coming home from Choir practice one evening, out at [names place], and I had the car radio on, switched it on as soon as I got going and it was playing the Double Concerto and I just had to stop, and some friends were coming behind, you know, and I was just in floods of tears, and they said, 'why don't you turn it off?' and I said, 'I can't' and that, it was ages before I could listen to that, or anything like it without thinking of him.

It's only in the last year or so, because I know now that it meant so much to him and it means so much to me and I realise *now* how much like him I am.

Here in this extraordinary musical event, one which, unplanned, happened upon her and took her by surprise, music not only 'reminded' Lucy of her relationship with her father, it was, beyond this, a catalyst for profound emotion, emotion that forced her to curtail an ongoing action course (driving home) and pull off the road to listen the music through (work through the spasm of grief).

In this case, music not only instigated a moment of intense emotion and thus a shift in how Lucy oriented to her surroundings (and, with it, a shift in the 'contents' of her thoughts); it also provided an opportunity for reflection and for knowledge production and it is for this latter reason that it is of especial interest here. It provided, I suggest, a matrix within which Lucy came to 'realise' (as she puts it) one aspect of her self-identity, namely, in relation to the music, her consciousness of her father and her own relation to him was posited in terms of similarity. Lucy realised, in thinking about music, 'how much like' her father she was.

This case provides a useful beginning for thinking about music as cognition, because it shows us music as it provides a medium through which (Lucy's) reflection and knowledge-formation is accomplished. It is, I suggest, a resource for *modelling* activity, for the realising of one thing (self) *as like* another thing (father). To put this another way, the music provided an impetus for Lucy to engage herself in self-modelling, projecting onto her self-conception a remembered set of characteristics of her father. Music was, on this occasion, a place within which to reflect; it provided a 'workspace' for meaning making (DeNora 1986b). In this case, the Musical Event was linked to the production of knowledge – about self and other. Within and upon hearing the Brahms, Lucy 'saw' her relationship with her father.

To speak of music as a 'workspace' is to suggest that music provides material for the reorientation of consciousness (Lucy's sudden remembrance of her father) and simultaneously, a device that may prompt some form of knowledge production. Here, the Brahms created an aesthetic climate conducive to the formation of knowledge about self-identity. To develop this issue it is useful to return to the diagram of the musical event, see figure 4.

Consider the various aspects of this event:

A The actor and B the music: the actor here is Lucy; the music, Brahms *Double Concerto*. The occasion in question (**Time 2**) consists, in fact, of two, rather than one, engagements with music, at two different times, the time of the event she is describing, and the time of the interview when she is remembering an engagement with music and re-engaging with that in order to 'tell' (at the time of the interview) about music's 'effect' (at the time of hearing it in the car. This 'double' engagement highlights just how complex any Musical Event may be, and just how layered are the associations and other factors that make up the preconditions to any Musical Event. (Imagine, for example, an event where the preconditions (**Time 1**) contained memories of many other times of engaging with this

TIME 1 – Before the Event (2 temporal/spatial events: (1) Lucy in car (2) Lucy's account during interview)

1. **Preconditions Prior associations made by actor(s)**
   (1) 'I remember those records being played when I was little' 'see myself sitting in my dressing gown in front of the fire . . .' 'extremely important to me' 'he died, x years ago'
   (2) Lucy's memories of the preconditions that were relevant at time one plus any further issues that she was aware of during the interview, perhaps prompted by her involvement in the interview

---

TIME 2 – (2 temporal/spatial events: (1) Lucy in car (2) Lucy's account during interview)

A **Actor(s)** Lucy

B **Music** Brahms Double Concerto
   (1) as heard on radio
   (2) as remembered hearing on radio

C **Act of Engagement with music**
   (1) Lucy stops car to listen
   (2) Lucy formulates retrospective account of (1)

D **Local conditions of C**
   (1) Lucy's bereavement; on her own in car
   (2) interview about music in her life, music and memory

E **Environment**
   (1) alone in car at night, pulled off road
   (2) formulating the experience (and her relationship to her father) for interviewer

---

TIME 3 – After the Event

3. **Outcome** In relation to (1) – powerful memory of her father and grief. In relation to (2) knowledge offered to other 'about' her father (e.g., *'how important music must have been to [father]'*) and her relation to him; about herself, what she is 'like'

Fig. 4. Remembering through Brahms.

music and Lucy only glancingly refers to these in her account – though later in the same interview she elaborates on that topic.)

Thus the first act of these two acts of engagement (**B1**), which is also one to which the researcher (myself) had no access (I had only a historical account of it from Lucy), was the real-time event described in the interview, the night in the car after choir practice. At *that* time, Lucy would have drawn upon various preconditions (**Time 1** in the diagram) as she heard the music – memories of her father, for example. The act of engagement occurred at the time of the interview when Lucy 'told' about a previous musical event. At *this* time, the memory of that event is itself a precondition for re-experiencing the music, for engaging further with music, through the memory of that music and its previous effects. Because of this temporal layering of the experience Lucy describes, it is necessary to distinguish between at least two strands of items **B** to **E**, that is, the other 'features' of the musical event(s): music, engagement, local conditions, and the environment as illustrated in figure 4.

Part 3. The 'outcome' of the Event(s): there are, as stated, two outcomes here, the first, associated with **B1**, the event she describes as having occurred, namely her grief (the 'floods of tears'). The second outcome is associated with **B2**. It is Lucy's 'realisation' (her formulation) of her similarity to her father, how she is 'like him'. (It is important to note here that the only outcome to which the interviewer has genuine access is outcome 2 – Lucy's engagement with remembered music (i.e., the memory of **B1**) and the interpretive work she does *during* the interview that produces knowledge about how 'like' her father Lucy is. Indeed, this example highlights how what we count as 'music' needs to be broadened well beyond music heard in real time, for people may replay music in their heads, they may call upon not only musical fragments or entire works in memory but also more diffuse memories of music heard before.

In both **B1** and **B2** music provided a resource for Lucy's knowledge formulation. It was a resource that afforded her conclusions about her relationship with her father, and about his and her qualities, their identities, separately and in relation to each other. In this sense, music was a material that helped to position Lucy's consciousness such that she was able to imagine and thus establish social relation and thus a definition of social reality. Here, then, music was active in calling Lucy's attention to aspects of reality – it served as a device that reminded her of these aspects in ways that resulted in her extreme response. In particular, music helped Lucy to recast her understanding of her role as a daughter. For these reasons, and in this case study, it is possible to speak of music as a material through which a particular mode of consciousness and its attendant social relations was established/re-established. This example shows – at the 'right level' of theorising, congruent with the argument developed in chapter 2 – music as a medium with and in which to think about, experience, and re-experience social reality.

While this example helps to show how music may provide a structure against which knowledge formation occurs (and how, in turn, making knowledge is inevitably making social relations), it has *not* also illustrated how music's specific *properties* may come to inform that process. The issue of how music's specific properties imbricate cognition is one of the most intriguing of all for socio-musical analysis. To take the most obvious example, did Lucy orient to the 'father–daughter' voicing of the instruments, both from the same 'family – the string family – and in dialogue? (Recall here McClary's analysis of *Wachet auf*, discussed in chapter 2.) With what we know, we cannot say and this gap highlights one very useful point of collaboration between music analysts and music

Example 2. J. Brahms, *Double Concerto*

sociologists – why it would be wrong to omit music's specific materials from consideration in the socio-musical equation.)

Another brief example from Lucy helps to illuminate just how such a question might be pursued. At one stage in the interview, Lucy spoke of how she especially liked music's 'lower sonorities' (e.g., alto rather than soprano voice, cello rather than violin) because they are, 'part of the background . . . the basses and the altos . . . fill out [the music] . . . I think maybe that characterises me in life, that I don't like being in the limelight . . . [be] part of a group . . . seeing what needs doing and doing it but not being spotlighted and being "out front" sort of thing' (DeNora 2000:69).

In making this statement, Lucy was alluding to how she found, as she put it, 'the me *in* music'. That 'me' could be found particularly in the middle voice parts of, as she called them, 'juicy' chords (of which, incidentally, she said, a lot could be found in Brahms). In the 'inner voices' of certain musical passages, she was able to find exemplars of her nature and identity, her habit of, as she put it, 'doing what needed doing' (like middle voices) while 'being in the background and avoiding the limelight'. Here, for Lucy, music provided a template or model against which self-knowledge could be fleshed out or mapped. And it is here that we can see how an individual's conception of some particular musical structure or set of musical properties comes to be projected by that individual as a grid or guide for the work of tracing out (articulating) awareness of some other realm. To speak of this process is to speak of how music may at times provide metaphors for the construction of other, extra-musical phenomena. Here, the Musical Event involves (Lucy's) modelling activity, for which music provides the referent and it is in this sense that we can see it actually entering into cognition.

Music provides, in other words, a medium that 'is like' some other thing (Lucy's self-identity in this case). Lucy draws, in other words, a connection between a type of music, a concept of self-identity, and a kind of social ideal. This work is accomplished as she 'finds herself' or locates her identity 'in' musical structures, as she finds, as she puts it, 'the me in life' within musical structures. These structures she reads as a map or model of who she is and also of who she wishes to be, and in *her* reading (i.e., not *our* hypothetical reading of what that music might help her to accomplish) it is possible to see music as it takes the lead in cognitive formation, as its structures are projected ahead of the formulations that take shape against its reference. In short, Lucy shapes up a form of understanding, produces knowledge (about herself in this case) against the structures that she finds in music. In this way, music permeates Lucy's personal knowledge formulation. In so doing, it provides a basis for self-knowledge and self conduct. It provides a model of who she is (how she knows herself) and a map for how, therefore, she should proceed.

It would be misleading to overstate music's role in relation to cognition. Music is certainly not the *only* cultural medium that may serve as a referent for knowledge formulation, nor is it equally significant as a resource for all people or at all times. Other cultural materials – metaphors, analogies, narrative and poetic structures, aspects of the natural world, technologies, and artefacts may all provide structures against which realities are mapped. This point has been well illustrated in science and technology studies where knowledge, iterated over time, can be seen to appropriate a range of resources for formulation. Emily Martin's study, for example, of the metaphors employed to build knowledge about the female body and its physiology (1991); my own work on the representation of physiology as a resource for 'feminist' knowledge production (DeNora 1996); Nancy Nersessian's study (1984) of how paradigm 'change' (as opposed to shift) occurs in scientific knowledge formation – all of these follow the process by which things extrinsic to scientific knowledge are appropriated as resources for its making, ways of seeing, conventions for telling about, and so forth. The point here is that cultural materials, of which music is one, enter into and therefore mediate knowledge formation. This mediation may occur in the realm of personal and self-knowledge and its formulation as just discussed. It may also occur in the realms where more 'public' forms of knowledge are wrought as in the next example of philosophical knowledge and its formulation in relation to music.

'Ted'

The son of a middle-class merchant and a professional singer, 'Ted' was a well-known academic during the 1930s–1960s. A prominent figure in an equally prominent group of social philosophers, Ted's work is today studied internationally and, if anything, has undergone a recent resurgence. Ted is generally recognised for his innovations in philosophy (and for the ways his work critiques conventional philosophical procedures). Viewed from the perspective of the sociology of knowledge, Ted is thus interesting: how and from what bases, in other words, did Ted's innovatory work proceed? What sustained it? What provided the resources for its articulation? To ask these questions about the production of philosophical knowledge is to enquire about how cultural production changes. This question is characterised by more nuance than is the classical Kuhnian question concerning paradigm *shift* (of knowledge-producing enterprises); it is, by contrast, a specific question about how new forms take shape, how creative work proceeds, and how it comes to be lodged within and fostered by the cultural environments within which it is produced and distributed. It is a question directed to the 'inside' of knowledge-producing world.

These questions about knowledge formulation are not, I venture, fundamentally different from questions of how ordinary people (such as 'Elaine' and 'Lucy' above) produce the knowledge that they live by; in both cases, we may look for the resources with which knowledge is articulated, such as, in Lucy's case, how particular cultural materials are mobilised so as to shape up and frame knowledge. As just described, this sort of question has been pursued to effect by recent work on concept formation in science and on the study of change in knowledge formation; how materials for the production of knowledge are mobilised, tapped, or otherwise drawn into the vortex of knowledge production. But it has not been pursued in relation to how music may provide materials for this formation.

While we cannot now interview 'Ted' (he died in the late 1960s), there are nonetheless ample documents in which, like Lucy, he appeals to music as a tool for accomplishing his 'new' philosophy. Using Ted's engagement with music as an example, moreover, is nice for two reasons. First, in the case study of Ted's work, we can locate one of the most extensive examples of how music has been employed as a resource for the production of public knowledge. Second, and as readers will no doubt have recognised, 'Ted' is none other than Theodor W. Adorno (who incidentally seems to have been called 'Teddy' by his closer friends).

There is a good deal of work devoted to tracing the articulation of Adorno's work over time, indeed, most of the classic studies of Adorno are explicit about the cross-fertilisation between music and philosophy as found in his work. One of the best introductions to this topic can be found in Susan Buck-Morss's 1979 book, *The Origin of Negative Dialectics*. The study was, as Buck-Morss put it, concerned with finding the 'key' to Adorno's 'esoteric language', a study of 'the historical origins of Adorno's philosophy'. Buck-Morss suggests that Adorno's understanding of dialectics was 'modelled more on aesthetic experience than, as with Marx, on the experience of economic production' (1979:xiii). Adorno's description of his resources makes this clear. Indeed, his very understanding of the history of philosophy was constructed through the prism of music. 'Beethoven's music', he said:

is Hegelian philosophy: but at the same time it is truer than that philosophy. That is to say, it is informed by the conviction that the self-reproduction of society as a self-identical entity is not enough, indeed that it is false. Logical identity as immanent to form – as an entity at the same time fabricated and aesthetic – is both constituted and criticized by Beethoven. Its seal of truth in Beethoven's music lies in its suspension: through transcending it, form takes on its true meaning. This formal transcendence in Beethoven's music is a representation – not an expression – of hope (1999:14)

Adorno not only trained as a philosopher. He also studied composition in Vienna with Alban Berg and this work provided resources for the articulation of his theory. Adorno himself made this clear in the parallels he drew between atonal music and the negative philosophy he came to articulate. Both were involved in the overthrow of bourgeois, affirmative systems – functional tonality in music, bourgeois idealism (in which an identity was posited between mind and social reality) in philosophy. For Adorno, Schoenberg was a 'dialectical composer' (Buck-Morss 1978:15) and a model for how to proceed. Early in the development of his work, in a 1934 letter to Ernst Krenek he wrote:

It is . . . the task of a true theory not to conceal and 'mediate' reality ruptures by means of harmonious thought-forms, but precisely to expose them and through knowledge of them to contribute to overcoming them. And I indeed believe that Schoenberg distinguishes himself from other music in that through the conception and resolution of its antinomies he goes as far beyond the structure of present society as the most progressive social theory. (quoted in Buck-Morss 1979:130)

Adorno's language is, as many have observed, difficult to comprehend. His sentences are lengthy and convoluted, perhaps even more difficult to parse in German where the verb comes at the end (see Samuel and Shierry Weber's preface to *Prisms* (1967), 'Translating the Untranslatable'). As described in chapter 1, however, this was probably less a matter of obtuseness and more one of communicative orientation. As Adorno himself put it, 'defiance of society includes defiance of its language' (1981:225). There seems little doubt that, as Jay has observed (1976:176; see also Martin 1995:87), Adorno's writing style was intended as 'a direct challenge to the reader to respond with commensurate seriousness'.

In Schoenberg, Adorno saw a 'liberation' of tones from functional tonality (the hierarchy of tones as 'tonic' and 'dominant', 'sub-dominant' and 'leading tone') as analogous to the utopian 'association of free men', as he put it in a 1934 letter to Ernst Krenek (Buck-Morss 1979). The association Adorno made between this music and philosophy was more than analogous, however. In Schoenberg's method – the 'abandonment of tonal dominance' and the 'aversion to harmonious totalities', as Buck-Morss puts it – Adorno found something that he could appropriate for philosophy, 'transposing' it, 'from musical to the philosophical mode' (Buck-Morss 1979:131). As Adorno himself put it even earlier in his own development, in the 1932 essay, 'On the Social Situation of Music' (Adorno 2002:399):

Schoenberg's really central achievement . . . is that he . . . never behaved 'expressionistically', superimposing subjective intentions upon heterogenous material in an authoritarian and inconsiderate manner. Every gesture with which he intervenes in the material configuration is at the same time an answer to questions directed to him by the material in the form of its own immanent problems.

The music Adorno most respected included Schoenberg's *Book of Hanging Gardens* and Schoenberg's pre-twelve-tone music more generally. Adorno's devotion to Berg is well known and it is in works by these composers (and others admired by Adorno, such as Mahler) that Adorno 'sees' the situation of post-enlightenment history. Berg's Violin Concerto, for example, is seen by Adorno to survey all that which was lost of the bourgeois ideal, in its sweep from the drama of Beethoven (a time when agency was still empowered and outer-directed, directed to interacting with, transforming reality) to the psychological specificity of Mahler ('even what takes delight in limitation seeks to be rid of its own limits' (Adorno 1992:49)). For Adorno, this music exemplified a way of 'arranging' that did not 'impose' affirmation but rather found a space for the contradictions and tensions of material reality. As he emphasised in his more mature work, while music and philosophy were not identical enterprises, there were similarities between critical consciousness and musical composition (see Buck-Morss 1979:133; and Paddison 1982:18, who describes Adorno's desire to 'shock' readers into more active modes of textual engagement). Richard Leppert explains this connection as follows:

Adorno's writing intentionally thwarts effortless reception by passive readers – which not coincidentally parallels his understanding of the resistant quality of socially 'pure' music. In particular, it resists the 'logic' of systematized argument, defined by the expectation that point A leads directly and inevitably to point B . . . The result, as Susan H. Gillespie aptly explains, 'is a grammatical trope that, like the "broken-off parables" [in Kafka], creates a kind of disjunction and nonspecificity that undermine logical clarity and causality, leaving room for a certain vagueness, and for interpretation'. (Leppert 2002:62–3)

Key here, as Leppert and Gillespie enunciate, is the idea that conventional cognitive forms can be defied or undermined through unconventional aesthetic forms, namely, through forms that deliberately introduce ambiguity, that confuse, and thus, that require active interpretation on the part of the reader/beholder. Thus, what Schoenberg achieved in musical form, Adorno wished to achieve in literary form, in the format of social philosophy and its 'logic of disintegration' as he called it, during the early 1930s (see Buck-Morss 1979:63, 63–95; Adorno and Horkheimer 1972:145).

The compositional procedures of the 'logic', its building blocks, are similarly modelled upon procedures employed by Schoenberg. Susan Buck-Morss, for example, has traced Adorno's work as it appropriates from Benjamin the organising principle of the 'constellation', by which Adorno meant, as he put it in his inaugural lecture in 1931 ('The Actuality of Philosophy'), 'the juxtaposition of elements isolated by analysis and the illumination of reality by the power of such interpretation' (quoted in Buck-Morss 1979:93).

This 'juxtaposition', as Martin Jay has described it, resists reduction (Jay 1984:14; and Leppert 2002:63–4). It featured disparity; the constellation – a complex – permitted the elements of material reality (social experience, nature, musical pitch) to be explored rather than rounded off into pre-given, metaphysical forms. It is in this sense that Adorno sought to 'actualise' philosophy. Adorno's literary form of choice– the essay – furthers the musical analogy. As described in chapter 1, Susan Gillespie points to how Adorno's essays vary from 'the short, scherzo-like sketches and the longer, more symphonic . . .', a point Adorno himself underlines at times by his choice of titles ('Impromptus'; 'Kompositioner'; 'Moments musicaux'; 'Quasi una fantasia'). Again, Richard Leppert explicates this point:

As a structure for philosophical thought, the essay is not predetermined by a philosophical first principle; the thought it reflects arises more directly from the material it studies and less from the concepts that precede the material and which always threaten to overwhelm it . . . The essay – in a sense ideally unsystematic, spontaneous, fragmented – formally constitutes itself less as a magnifying glass, more as a splinter in the eye [refers to Adorno's aphorism, 'the splinter in your eye is the best magnifying-glass']. Its tendency is critical, its purpose, 'to move culture to become mindful of its own untruth'. (Leppert 2002:65)

In short, music served Adorno as an exemplar – a resource from which to extrapolate something non-musical, namely philosophy. Thus, not unlike 'Lucy' described above, Adorno turned to – appropriated – music to formulate knowledge, a task accomplished through the identification of the latter with structures and aspects of the former. Music served as a referent for this task. In this sense, Adorno's personal response to Schoenberg – his identification of particular characteristics in Schoenberg – came to provide an origin for the articulation of his (musical) philosophy. For Adorno, involved in articulating a different type of philosophy of negativity, one that required the reader to 'compose' rather than receive meaning, Schoenberg's music afforded a mode of consciousness capable of producing a complex type of knowledge, a mode of knowing that was inclusive, *analogous*, in other words, to Schoenberg's 'pan'-tonality. In this sense, Adorno can be seen to have 'done things [made philosophy] with [reference to] music'. Thus, in this example from Adorno's writings, we see music serving as a medium for the extra-musical activity of thought and its articulation as, in this case, philosophy. Like Lucy, then, Adorno used (or made recourse to) music to do something, to achieve cognition. Unlike Lucy, who turned to music and through reference to it achieved identification work, Adorno used music as a model for how thinking about how thought itself should proceed.

Music has consequences for cognition and cognitive practice

These two examples serve, albeit in indicative form, to highlight actual examples of music as it informs cognition. This topic has been almost entirely neglected by musicology and music sociology. It is possible that music can be seen to provide cognitive resources for many forms of creative, interpretive, and cognitive endeavour. To speak of this issue is to speak of how some aspect of music (the ways it formulates endings, for example) comes to provide a referent for the doing of some non-musical activity.

Music may, in short, inform all types of cultural production; the examples discussed so far relate to the creative effort of articulating knowledge or imagery. So, too, music may provide a resource for the development of other artistic enterprises. The author Anthony Burgess has spoken on this issue. In a BBC Radio 4 interview he described how, 'Beethoven let me' fashion a particular plot resolution. By this, Burgess meant that he 'saw' in Beethoven's music a particular way of handling material, one that he could translate into textual practice. Beethoven showed Burgess that a particular strategy of arranging material, a particular way of making transition and closing, was possible at a literary level. In this sense, Burgess, like Lucy, like Adorno, borrowed from music's formal procedures to produce procedures for doing something else – literature.

For Adorno, however, the empirical project of identifying music as it gets into cognition would have been insufficient as a music sociological task. Adorno's concerns extended well beyond this issue. He was not, in other words, merely concerned with 'what' music might afford. He was equally concerned with styles of consciousness, with epochs of awareness, musically afforded. This issue can be seen perhaps most clearly in relation to Adorno's focus on Schoenberg versus Stravinsky, in particular in relation to the different modes of consciousness their music inspired. In chapter 1 this issue was broached. It is now time to develop it, and at the 'right level' of theorising. Just how, in short, can the idea of music as working upon (or working with) styles of consciousness be theorised at the level of the Musical Event, i.e., in relation to grounded situations, in real time and space?

To recapitulate his position, Adorno emphasised Schoenberg's antipathy to affirmation, his disdain of musical formulas, and, simultaneously, his non-violent handling of musical material, its ability to contain material without harming (imposing form upon) it. Schoenberg's music was unfamiliar and did not attempt tone-painting (making itself subservient to external images or ideas – a process that would be the reverse of the process so far discussed of music serving as model for the extra-musical activity of knowledge production). Because of this strangeness, Schoenberg's music did not afford stock responses, did not 'remind' listeners of existing phenomena but rather challenged listeners to attend to the world in new ways, to search for difference, non-identity, contradiction, dissonance, rather than similarity, harmony, repetition, and identity and the psychological comfort afforded by these properties. It was in this respect that Adorno believed that Schoenberg's music was progressive; it could, like Adorno's own negative philosophy with its convoluted sentence structure, instigate new and liberating modes of consciousness. Its sense, in other words, had to be constituted, as opposed to received.

By contrast, popular music, and the music of Stravinksy, with its 'pseudomorphism of painting' (1973:191) and its stock patterns of presentation geared for effect, reinforced the known. Music in this sense drew upon conventions, tropes, and familiar evocative figures, and, in doing so, *reminded listeners of things* (for 'things' here read 'givens'). Through this reminding, music provided, at least hypothetically, a device that reinforced an idea of a world 'of things', of pre-given entities and thus, a world characterised by stasis rather than critique and interrogation. For this reason, such music instilled a form of certainty and, ontological security in its listener. One would feel reassured by this musical representation of musical reality. It was this that Adorno meant when he referred to music's affirmative function. This issue has special salience to, and helps to develop, the sociology of memory, both collective memory and the individual activity of remembering. Consideration of recent sociological work on memory in turn helps to illuminate Adorno's initial (and critical) focus on music and its link to consciousness.

Memory studies and their lapses

Memories are cultural constructs. They are located in and elaborated with reference to specific media and materials – symbols, material culture, talk, literature, film, and, of course, music. All memory involves *identification,* the fleshing out of 'what happened' – of experience – through reference to some marker of that experience. In this sense, recall is knowledge production, activity; it is a representation of historical events. As Robin Wagner-Pacifici has put it:

Memories . . . come to us as narratives, pictorial images, textbooks, pamphlets, legal charters, wills, diaries and statues. And the forms do more than simply present the collective memory in each case. (1996:302)

Wagner-Pacifici describes how memory, contra to the common-sense depiction of remembering and recall, is much more than a 'log' of events, of what happened. Memory is *dynamically* involved with the modes and materials available for representing the past. In this respect, Wagner-Pacifici's work exemplifies one of the most interesting developments within cultural sociology in recent years, namely, the study of how publicly available categories and genres of memory mediate our memories of what has passed. Memory is, in other words, itself a cultural product, an aesthetic creation. Memory thus is fabricated by drawing upon available resources for its production. It is a cultural and socially constituted product.

As Alan Radley puts it, 'artefacts . . . become evidence on which other interpretations of the past can be reconstructed' (1990:58). There are, in other words, media and genre of memory, a point that can be seen perhaps most clearly in the study of commemoration and its forms, in particular how this process is inevitably shot through with political tensions. Anna Lisa Tota's work on communities of memory highlights just this issue. In her study of memory disputes that surround a terrorist bombing of the Bologna train station, Tota highlights just how fraught is the struggle to remember at a public level (Tota 2001b), the machinations over what is to count and what forms are to be used to contain/represent memory.

In short, the research on social memory has dealt predominantly with commemoration, and with the analysis of representations of key events. It highlights how events are depicted by a variety of media – literature, legal texts, the plastic arts. (Music has been strangely absent from the literature on the sociology of remembering, perhaps because of the technical knowledge thought to be needed for speaking about musical form?) Focus has also been directed to the often highly charged politics of rendering these representations, to the various interests and emotions involved in debate about what will be acceptable (e.g., Wagner-Pacifici and Schwartz 1991; Zolberg 1996). While this focus is indeed important, it by no means exhausts the subject. It also helps lead on to a number of additional questions. These questions centre on the issue of how memory is sustained. For inscriptions, representations of the past, are but one side of the equation of memory production. Memory also involves embodied, non-inscribed practices, through habitual and recurrent activities as performed by socially located actors. As Connerton put it (1989:4–5):

If there is such a thing as social memory, I shall argue, we are likely to find it in commemorative ceremonies; but commemorative ceremonies prove to be commemorative only in so far as they are performative; performativity cannot be thought without a concept of habit; and habit cannot be thought without a notion of bodily automatisms.

As John Urry has commented (Urry 1996:49), Connerton here points to the ways in which 'the past gets passed on to us not merely in what we think or do but literally in how we do it: how we sit when we write, how we stand, how we eat, how we travel and so on'. And while Urry lauds Connerton's focus on practice, he also observes that Connerton's perspective is too general; it is focused on how 'societies in general' (ibid.) pass on bodily memories. 'It remains', Urry says, 'at too general a level of analysis' (ibid.). (Note here an echo of my ongoing critique of Adorno's 'wrong level' of generality.) There are, Urry continues, 'various more localized processes to note' (ibid.) and he suggests that we lodge our studies of social memory within a Meadian 'philosophy of the present', by which he means a focus on how the past is continually a topic of recreation, both resource for, and artefact of, the ongoing and never-ending fabrication of social life.

This action-focus is useful and accords with the particular focus on Musical Events that I have been describing. It leads to a focus on the organisation and production of memory (as a form of cognition) within particular material cultural and aesthetic ecologies. It directs attention to, as Radley puts it, artefacts of memory and the ways that these artefacts impinge upon remembering in all its aspects ('in the very variability of objects, in the ordinariness of their consumption and in the sensory richness of relationships people enjoy through them, they are fitted to be later re-framed as material images for reflection and recall' (Radley 1990:57–8 as quoted in Urry 1996:50)). In short, this action perspective emphasises real-time memory praxis. This focus follows the production, via particular activities and performances, of recall and remembering. It examines this production as it transpires in relation to objects and cultural media.

The focus on non-inscribed memory practices leads to a second issue in the study of memory, one which a focus on music and Musical Events can help to highlight. This second issue returns us to Adorno's concern with music's link to styles of consciousness.

We remember, or are put in mind of, many things, only some of which are aspects of what we think of, in common-sense terms, as 'events' that 'happened' in the 'past'. Memory covers a much wider gamut than this. We do not simply remember *major* events 'in the past' – atrocities or special occasions, we also remember on a far more mundane level. In real time, on a given day, we 'remember' many aspects of what comes to stand as the furniture of consciousness. To be competent members of our social worlds, we are required to 'memorise' a variety of skills and passages of action. We remember 'types' of situations, generic scenarios, styles of being, posturing, or talking, stock gestures, manners, and conventions of action. We also remember – are able to recall if asked – things such as the names of current political leaders (the prime minister, or the president), our nationality, the 'news' and current cultural events and trends, our telephone number, or our workplace and our colleagues. Indeed, when we cannot recall these things with ease we may be thought to be 'a bit dull today' or, in more extreme cases, 'ill'. In mundane life, then, memory includes common-sense assumptions about – familiarity with – the 'contents' of social reality. And social consciousness consists of an awareness of these 'contents'. We may be *conscious of* things and we may be reminded of things by various materials that, as we say, 'jog' our memory. This is, in the parlance of common sense, 'normal' intelligence and those who do not demonstrate that they possess this intelligence (which includes non-cognitive memories such as – *pace* Connerton – comportment and table manners – such as remembering how to eat in public) are subject to censure and, at times, professional concern.

It is precisely this type of socialisation – the historically specific notion of consciousness as a reticule of remembering, remembering both major events and mundane matters – that Adorno subjected to critique. And it is here that we can begin to appreciate how and why Adorno criticised music in modern society for the ways it configured (appropriated) consciousness. It was possible, in Adorno's view, for music to over-furnish consciousness, to trigger the remembrance (consciousness of) a detritus of 'things' in a way that crowded out the capacity for non-identity. Consciousness – and intelligence – could be thus debased so that it was little more than a memory of 'what is', which, in other words, was also a kind of forgetting, a reification of social facts. Music, in short, could serve as a mnemonic device through which listeners were endlessly 'reminded' of particular configurations of the present. Indeed, this is why the respondents who were consulted for *Music and Everyday Life* frequently emphasised that if they were listening to music while doing mental work, they preferred music that was less familiar, that did not draw their minds to features and aspects of their daily lives (in ways that 'distracted' them from the tasks at hand). For Adorno, the form of the present to which popular music referred via convention and cliché was one that led to commodity fetishism, in the words of the poet Lawrence Ferlinghetti (written pre-Disneyland), in a *Coney Island of the Mind*:

> They are the same people
> Only further from home
> On freeways fifty lanes wide
> on a concrete continent/spaced with bland billboards
> illustrating imbecile illusions of happiness
>   (Ferlinghetti 1958:9)

In his critique of Stravinsky (and also via his criticisms of popular music), Adorno implied that music could afford a style of consciousness characterised by the presumption of a pre-given world, i.e., a world and a past that had, merely, to be remembered, recognised. Such a consciousness, according to Adorno presumed 'givens' (statements of fact and truths, whether at the level of scientific propositions or at the level of psycho-biographical *needs* or certainties (as in 'what I have always desired'; 'what I know for sure')). This consciousness was, in turn, the psychological prerequisite for social subjection, for subjugation to the rule of who or what ever proclaimed reality – elites such as experts or political leaders, and the media. When music (or cultural media more generally) afforded ontological security, they simultaneously drained consciousness of its critical faculty and ratified that 'which is' by affirming preconceived visions (remembrances) of 'reality'.

Music and memory as sensibility

In these ways, then, Adorno believed music could afford (channel) consciousness. But music is linked to a great deal more than the *cognitive* dimension of consciousness, and it is here that we need to broaden out the concept of memory once again. We have already seen how the sociological study of memory can be broadened from the remembrance of public events to the more mundane remembrance of everyday matters, and how memory study can shift from a focus on inscription practices to a focus on non-inscribed practices – acts – of meaning. At this stage, I suggest that memory studies can be broadened yet again.

Of particular interest in the study of culturally mediated and culturally instigated memory is how memories are fabricated in and through relation to cultural media, of which, of course, music is but one. It is possible, in other words, to speak of how remembering is also or may involve culturally mediated 'mis-remembering', as Celia Lury has described in her study of 'false memory syndrome' (Lury 1996). There, materials such as texts, photographs, or, though Lury does not mention it, music provide guidelines for remembering in ways that come to override experience. One recalls 'what happened' (or 'what is') in ways that are commensurate with the prosthetic technologies of remembering that are available. While 'false' memories of this kind are typically classified as pathological – as a syndrome – this type of mis-remembering is in fact not uncommon in everyday life, where it may feature both as a resource for the articulation of self-identity (how one aligns oneself with some sense of a 'norm') and as an effect of culture – i.e., of the individual adjustment of experience (cognitive experience of remembering) so that it is aligned with some collective representation of the shape and form of that experience (as when, for example, one remembers 'the war' or 'falling in love' in ways that reflect conventional techniques of representing those things).

Music as collective consciousness

So far, the examples offered in this chapter have been drawn from the individual's experience of culture. They have focused on music's role in relation to individual knowing and recognising/remembering. But is it possible to move from here to a concern with collective knowledge formation while still holding analysis at the 'right level' of the Musical Event? One way into this question is via attempts to follow the reception history of a song, style, performer, or genre within a particular community of use.

Two questions arise in relation to this project. The first concerns *how* individuals come to fixate on some songs or musical works rather than others – for at any one time there are many cultural materials within a field of social-psychological experience – why is it that only some of these come to have personal resonance? This question cannot be answered solely by considering the cultural forms in question – e.g., music's textual properties. It also requires empirical study of individual and collective 'use' – indeed, the pursuit of such an issue helps to ground the focus on trends and iconic cultural materials within eras. It includes, of course, the sociology of how some cultural materials may be positioned more prominently than others, thereby capturing attention. A second, and equally important, question concerns how the materials on to which actors fix themselves (e.g., the songs that become significant for them) then come to provide parameters of aesthetic action – conditions of action, feeling, and consciousness at a collective or interactive level for action's next iteration. This includes the various Musical Events where two or more individuals focus together on some music so as to produce a collaborative outcome of some kind (as, for example, when individuals fashion group identities, senses of 'belonging' via music, or when music is used to 'set the mood' (DeNora 2000:108–29)).

This issue has been broached by Eyerman and Jamieson (1998) in their study of music's link to collective movements. They describe social movement theory as overly cognitive and as failing to account for the non-cognitive dimensions of collective action. For example, they describe how movement theory tends to portray activists as 'motivated' by ideas and aims, beliefs, and policy-type agendas. By contrast, they suggest that there is a feeling component to movement activity and in this respect, their work overlaps with, and is augmented by, Kevin Hetherington's treatment of what he calls 'neo-Durkheimian' movement theory and its concern with the expressive character of social movement activity, the role of culture and the non-cognitive, and the way in which movement activity is simultaneously the 'expression of identity' (Hetherington 1998). While Hetherington does not examine music's role here, Eyerman and Jamieson do and their work is suggestive; they point to music as a paradigmatic resource, a medium that can be used for the constitution of exemplary action.

For example, they describe how Todd Gitlin, president of the Students for a Democratic Society (SDS) in the 1960s, described the SDS's identification with the music of Bob Dylan ('we followed his career as if he were singing our song; we got in the habit of asking where he was taking us next' (1998:116)). Here, then, musical motifs may provide a focal point for groups of actors across space and time, containers for what might otherwise pass as a momentary impulse to act, or a momentary identification of some kind. And they provide 'leadership' – they 'take' actors to the 'next phase' of social movement activity. In this sense music possesses, as was described above in the examples of Lucy and 'Ted'; music may serve, within the context of social activity, as a prescriptive device for conception and action. Within music's structures, its perceived connotations, and its sensual parameters (dynamics, sound envelopes, harmonies, textures, etc.), actors may 'find' things, among these things, themselves (both cognitively and emotionally), and their past and future trajectories.

This attempt to link music, memory, and collective action has been highly instructive. It has helped to illuminate some of the ways in which an aesthetic medium such as music may enter into the ways that we articulate and remember 'things'. At the same time, and despite its focus on the non-cognitive, it falls somewhat short of socio-musical studies' full potential in relation to music's role as a 'technology of memory'. This is because it does not actively invoke the embodied features of memory, a point on which Adorno was also tacit (though he does indeed discuss

Stravinsky's appeal to the body via music's pulse). For Adorno, however, when the body was invoked, it was virtually always in relation to some form of regression.

And yet, memory – and the act of remembering – is simultaneously an embodied, emotive activity. It also involves certain types of skill – such as the ability to reproduce, both in consciousness and in modes of action, past patterns (e.g., the ability to use language, to repeat motor actions as these are clustered into skills, such as baking a cake, the ability to repeat types of situations socially or to recall particular roles). While this point will be considered in further detail in the next two chapters, it is important, in the context of considering music as consciousness, to broach the subject of emotions here.

Memory as aesthetic calibration

As an artefact of memory, music has special status by virtue of its temporal and non-representational character (the very things that link it to embodied and emotional modes of being and the very things that make music's powers in relation to memory all the more elusive). As the above discussion of mundane remembering illustrated, remembering involves much more than recogntition. It involves, as Connerton suggested, a repositioning, sometimes literally as in the case of embodied postures and so forth. This is to say that to remember is to be repositioned aesthetically. When Elaine and Lucy above describe how music 'took them back', they are by no means describing a primarily *mental* process. On the contrary, as they tell it, being reminded involves the body; it involves tears, alteration in surface temperature, heartbeat, blood pressure, and mood. And to remember is to be emotionally and bodily *recalibrated*. To remember is thus simultaneously to engage in emotional work, to configure self as agent.

Where might the study of memory go next, and how can socio-musical studies help to advance it? It has examined, just like cultural studies of music, the forms memory uses, the struggles memory representation takes, the ways memory discourses crop up and are institutionalised. These issues are discussed in further depth in chapter 5. For now, however, they highlight how cognition consists of an aesthetic and emotional aspect, and how formulating knowledge and remembering things needs to be conceptualised at least in part as involving aesthetic materials. There is, in other words, an 'art' to knowing and a 'craft' to remembering.

Bloch's concept of visionary listening serves as a starting point here (Bloch:1988). This is the idea that music reception can, under some conditions, transfigure the conditions of human sensuous awareness. This point is important because it highlights a particular misconception of memory studies, namely, that remembering is not about how, within one frame of consciousness, one 'thinks about' the past. Rather, remembering is simultaneously a *repositioning* of consciousness and thus of the subject; to remember is to be transformed, to be susceptible to different stimuli, to be aware and alive in different ways. Memory – and remembering – involves sensibility and recall is, in fact, reorientation. This point is perhaps made most clearly in the most dramatic forms of memory retrieval – as described, for example, by Oliver Sacks.

In his various works over the years Sacks (1990) has described how music may 'awaken' victims of encephalitis lethargica, individuals who could not speak with any tone or force but who could sing loudly and with the normal range of tone and expression. Similarly, music could 'revive' Parkinson's Disease sufferers. For sufferers of strokes, when memory was so eroded that even the recognition of common objects was impossible ('the man who mistook his wife for a hat'), music could be employed as a mnemonic device, a medium that could entrain actions such as bathing or eating and so afford the reproduction of mundane action.

Sacks's examples from his case notes illustrate music's link to remembering *in extremis*. They are nonetheless useful for thinking about music and memory in more ordinary contexts because they highlight the ways in which remembering involves action, body, and emotion. And herein lies an important key to understanding Adorno's theory, in particular, for elaborating that theory in ways that are amenable to empirical investigation. If remembering is reorienting, and if music is a key to memory, then music can be understood as a device that structures agency. It can be understood in relation to 'control' in all the variants of that term: control over self, the shaping of self and others in mutually attuned and entrained ways; control of anonymous individuals and groups who are musically aligned (as in organisations and public spaces). To develop this issue I delve more deeply into one aspect of music and its link to the corporal – music's link to feeling and emotion. From there, in chapter 5, I attempt to consolidate the discussion through a more overt consideration of music and 'control'.

4   How does music 'channel' emotion?

Of all the arts, music is most typically associated with emotional experience. Claims within both the scholarly community and in everyday life on behalf of music's capacity to express and induce emotion in its listeners themselves testify to the idea of music as an emotional medium. In modern societies as in Bach's day, music is strongly associated with mood, feeling, emotion, and subjectivity.

Music's temporal feature – its unfolding over time – is often identified as the key to music's 'emotional' powers; unlike the plastic arts that portray nature and actors in arrested motion, music moves through time. Like the form of the novel, then, music can convey the mercurial dimension of emotional experience, the process of feeling. But unlike literature (though like theatre), music is a medium that unfolds across socially *shared* time. All actors involved in a particular music-producing and music-listening situation are involved for the same amount of time and are exposed to (or produce) the same 'parts' of music at the same time. This is so even for aleatoric or improvised music – even for a work such as 4′33″ (John Cage's 'silent' piece), which still positions listeners together within a time frame, one within which sounds happen.

Compared to theatre, moreover, music does something unique. It is (unless it involves text or libretto) *non-verbal*. And because of this, music is often experienced as the most emotionally direct medium, one with a capacity to appeal to the body and the emotions in ways that exceed other aesthetic media. As Susan Langer once memorably put it, music has the capacity to signify without simultaneously referencing directly aspects of the external world.

While not all music, composers, and music-stylistic eras are oriented to invoking emotion, and while (as will become clear presently) not all listeners orient to music as a medium that has impact upon emotion, the connections between music and emotion most discussed are most commonly traced back to music's temporal and abstract features. The thinking here is that music can 'describe' feeling without resort to explicit, visual, images and as such is closer to the experience of feeling *per se*. It will become clear momentarily that the concept of music versus emotion – the idea that music represents or otherwise 'captures' emotion – is not the most useful way of conceptualising music's link to feeling and emotion. Meanwhile, it is worth noting that a characteristic feature of thinking about music and emotion is that music is often posed as simultaneously both highly expressive and elusive of attempts to explain just how and why music provokes emotion. It is this paradox that makes the topic of music and emotion so intriguing.

There is a strong tradition of writing on music and emotion from Aristotle onwards. Much of this tradition has sought to answer the question – crudely posed – 'what music may induce which emotions?' Needless to say, much of the literature devoted to this topic is posed as speculation rather than as empirical enquiry. While one might reasonably expect to find the subject treated within music psychology, it has until recently been mostly ignored there. The social psychologists of music Patrik Juslin and John Sloboda (in 2001:4–5) have offered several reasons why the human sciences – psychology in particular – have been slow to consider the emotions in relation to music. First, emotions are difficult to examine under laboratory conditions, since emotions originate and take shape in relation to lived experience. In vitro studies of emotional responses to music may not be reliable indicators of how music and emotion interact outside the laboratory. Second – and, as I discuss below, this point relates to sociology as well as to social psychology – there has been a cognitive bias within psychology in general and music psychology in particular. This has been associated with an 'information processing' model of music perception. When emotions were studied in relation to music, the predominant focus was on how listeners matched emotional descriptors with musical excerpts. Third, the culture and ideology of music reception in Western societies, as analysed by Cook (1992) and Frith (1996), militated against a concern with emotion as part of the academic paradigm for music perception. There has been little reflection on the history of emotional listening as a part of reception history. And within music history writ large, listening is too often de-historicised in a way that imposes the model of the (historically specific) silent and respectful listener as a given. Within this assumption, the body of the listener is excised. And yet, such listening involves a high degree of bodily discipline (e.g., stillness, the suppression of coughing, talk, laughter). Indeed, the links between this mode of listening and the subjective experience of music raises further questions, for example, about the individuation of musical experience, its concentration as an 'internal' or subjective experience rather than as an experience that invokes the body, and about the history of how links between emotion, self, and other are made in relation to hearing music.

It is from within this set of conditions that Adorno's concern with music and emotion is perhaps best comprehended. There is no doubt that Adorno was one of the few music sociologists to be concerned with emotional responses to music. However, his approach to that topic was coloured both by (academic) cultural assumptions, and by a bias in favour of more cognitive modes of musical reception. This can be seen clearly in the hierarchical arrangement of his ideal types of musical conduct – the so-called 'types of musical conduct' he describes in the introduction to the *Sociology of Music* (1976 (1962)). The types are as follows:

1. *The expert*, who engages in 'structural hearing' – a 'fully conscious' listener (p. 4), one who recognises formal components of music as they occur and who is able to discern the overall architecture of the piece.

2. *The good listener*, who hears 'beyond musical details, makes connections spontaneously, and judges for good reasons, not just by categories of prestige and by an arbitrary taste' (p. 5). Unlike the expert, this listener is not fully conscious of music's structural form: '[h]aving unconsciously mastered its immanent logic, he understands music about the way we understand our own language even though virtually or wholly ignorant of its grammar and syntax' (p. 5). According to Adorno, this type was increasingly endangered, replaced by type 3, the 'culture consumer'.

3. *The culture consumer*, a 'copious, sometimes a voracious listener, well informed, a collector of records. He respects music as a cultural asset . . .' (p. 6). This type may have extensive knowledge of the music literature, but the type of knowledge that consists of an ability to name tunes and works. 'On the whole, his relation to music has a fetishistic touch' (p. 6). This type is very much the type of culture consumer described in the 1980s sociology of culture by Bourdieu, DiMaggio, and Peterson and Simkus in their respective studies of taste and social distinction. Music appreciation becomes, as it were, a social strategy.

4. *The emotional listener*, here, the listener is most unconscious of how music works – its architecture and compositional components, and, conversely, most susceptible to its influence. 'He is easily moved to tears, and his links with the culture consumer are continuous; the latter's arsenal too is rarely without an appeal to the emotional values of genuine music' (p. 8). Adorno believed this type of listener was most characteristic in Anglo-Saxon countries, 'where the stricter pressures of civilization necessitate evasions into uncontrollably introverted realms of feeling' (p. 8). Adorno identifies this type with 'notorious "tired businessmen" who seek, in a realm that will not affect their lives, to compensate for what they must deny themselves

otherwise' (p. 9). 'At times such people may use music as a vessel into which they pour their own anguished and, according to psychoanalytical theory, "free-flowing" emotions; at other times they will identify with the music, drawing from it the emotions they miss in themselves' (p. 9).

5. *The resentment listener*, this is the opposite of the previous type, those listeners who disallow themselves any emotional experience in relation to music (such as that illustrated by the staunch 'devotees' of Bach and those who police the performance of works for interpretive infidelities'. 'What this type wants is not only the counterpart of the romantic musicmaker; the wish is inspired by the most vehement affect against his imago' (p. 11). Related to this type is . . .

6. *The jazz listener*, who shares the resentment listener's aversion to the romantic conception of music as expression.

7. *The entertainment listener*, quantitatively the most significant type according to Adorno, 'the type the culture industry is made for, whether it adjusts to him in line with its own ideology, or whether it elicits or indeed creates the type' (p. 14). 'Socially, the entertainment listener type would have to be correlated with a widely noted phenomenon that can refer to none but a subjective consciousness . . .' (p. 14) ' . . . passive and fiercely opposed to the effort which a work of art demands' (p. 16)

8. *The musically indifferent, the unmusical, and the anti-musical*, this type, perhaps, Adorno suggests, due to early childhood experiences, consists of those who avoid music and who dislike it.

Adorno's typology highlights his concern with music's social and psycho-cultural function, its relation and ability to instigate modes of attention. In this respect, his work broached matters that then remained dormant until recently, as summarised by Antoine Hennion:

It is necessary, above all, to extract the social analysis of taste from the falsely objective perspective which makes it no more than the measure of differential consumption, according to predefined criteria. This type of objectivity has only the appearance of objectivity; measurement is possible only because music lovers have been reduced beforehand to nothing more than the vehicle of their socio-professional category, without that posing the slightest problem, and music to being nothing but a passive consumer good, whose only feature worthy of interest is the differential degree of education it requires. Music acts and moves, in relation to other mediations; it transforms those who take possession of it and do something else with it. Conversely it does not denote the same thing, depending on the situation and the time. This co-production, the co-formation of a music and of those who make it and listen to it (with other activities) can be the subject of a more balanced sociology of music, where sociology has as much to learn from music as vice versa (Hennion 1993). (Hennion 2001b:3)

In particular, Adorno was concerned – in all of his socio-musical work – with the breach that had been effected between music producer (composer) and music consumer (listener – indeed, as is evident from his description of type 3, Adorno had only disdain for the idea that music could be 'consumed'). As musical composition became, increasingly and, as he saw it, inevitably specialised, type-2 listeners – the good but unprofessional listening types – increasingly dwindled. For Adorno, this was nothing less than tragic in so far as it signalled a waning of music's capacity as an aid to cognition and therefore critical consciousness. Increasingly, as type 3, 4, and 7 forms of listening became 'normal', music ceased its function as a kind of mental exercise (and as a modelling of how 'things' or 'realities' could be 'contained') and instead came to provide either fetish, distraction, or stimulation. Moreover, as reason – instigated via music – dwindled, and as a new mode of orienting to the social world took over, the way was paved for social control. For Adorno, emotional listening was nothing less than an abdication of reason and thus of the resource upon which democratic participation was founded.

Adorno was certainly on to something when he suggested that the emotional and entertainment-type listeners provided clues to understanding how administration operates and I pursue this issue in chapter 5. Meanwhile, though, there are various problems with his theory – if theory it is – of listening. If they are to be of use in articulating a framework for the empirical exploration of music and emotion, Adorno's ideas require adaptation. Such adaptation will, moreover, make them far more amenable to empirical studies of music and its link to modes of control.

First, it is necessary to dispense with his cultural-evaluative stance. Although Adorno's suggestion that '. . . the lower stratum will surrender to unrationalized entertainment while the upper will dress it up idealistically, as spirit and culture, and will select it accordingly' (1976:14–15), the implication is nonetheless that emotional and entertainment listening is associated not only with particular strata but with particular musical genres. Second, the very typology assumed 'correct' modes of musical attention and in so doing failed to appreciate how music reception was often about 'doing' things to music – Adorno's typology not only pre-assumed types of listeners, it also presumed contexts of listening and thus, the social significance and consequences of emotional listening. Third, and related to these first two points, Adorno's conception of music reception was of *individual* listeners and of responses unconditioned by the interactional, temporal, and spatial contexts of particular listening occasions. In other words, Adorno – whose typology of listening was hampered by being 'merely theoretical' – failed to realise that actual listening need not be identical with the images of listening purveyed in the 'high-culture' concert hall. While one might no longer hear the cries of sausage-sellers during a Mozart opera, one might well hear one's friend or family member ask one to 'pass the cheese' while listening to a recording of Figaro – a possibility that was effectively blasphemous in Adorno's eyes! (This point has recently been raised within music education circles, where it has been noted that what 'counts' as musicality is often far removed from the actual 'musicking' – Small's terminology (Small 1998) of ordinary people, see also Cavicchi (2002); Green (2001).)

Finally, related to point three, Adorno's conception of music and its link to emotion was, in many respects, redolent of a stimulus–response model, as if, as it is sometimes phrased, 'the music itself' inculcated emotional responses in individuals. Adorno's consideration of music's mechanisms of operation, in other words, remained focused on musical texts and musical practices; he did not extend this focus to what in earlier work I have described as (somewhat inelegantly, but with a bow in the direction of technology studies) 'human–music interaction'. As I shall describe below, it is necessary to abandon the music–consumer dichotomy, namely, the idea that there are two entities, music and the subjective states of its consumers, and that one determines the other (and vice versa). By contrast, it is necessary to move to a paradigm that views both music and its subject as the object of mutual configuration, as a relation between what comes to be perceived and hailed as music (and as a type of music) and the 'response' on the part of music's beholders. Adorno's focus did not extend to this reflexive process and for this reason his explanation of music's link to emotion is constrained.

Adorno's perspective can be elaborated, however, and in ways that help to conjoin musicology and its social study. To do so, it is necessary to focus on emotions in-the-making, on particular Musical Events wherein emotions happen, where they take shape, change, and are stabilised. Such a focus is usefully developed in relation to sociological and psychological programmes of research. The groundwork is currently being laid within sociology for such a theory, while in the social psychology of music new work has begun to show how, in the minute uses of music, it is possible to see social structures and their accompanying dispositions as they are actually produced.

Emotion and social structure in (and as) action

Social bonds are built upon much more than shared knowledge, belief, and the respect of rules. There is a clear tradition within classic sociology that emphasises the realm of feeling and emotion. Best known perhaps are Tönnies's (1957) concepts of Gemeinschaft and Gessellschaft, terms used to distinguish between social bonds built upon communal, emotional, traditional, and personal grounds versus those produced via rational and administrative procedures. The distinction, and with it a concern with the 'feeling' bases of social organisation, has persisted and has established itself across a range of sociological perspectives. Max Weber's concern with the affective action (Weber 1978, vol 1:24–8), Max Scheler's concern with the emotional flashes of insight that lead to knowledge (Remmling 1967:33), Vilfredo Pareto's discussion of sentiments and non-logical action (Pareto 1963:161), the 'Human Relations Management' of Elton Mayo (Mayo 1933), Charles Horton Cooley's 'looking-glass self' and its focus on emotion as the outcome of imaginative co-operation with external images (Cooley 1902), and Randall Collins's treatment of emotion in relation to rational choice theory (Collins 1993) have all high-lighted emotion's role in relation to action and social structure.

And yet, despite this interest, the affective dimension of human social being was, throughout the 1980s, mostly relegated to sociology's periphery. Even now, when there is a substantial section of the American Sociological Association devoted to emotions, the bulk of emotion study within sociology is confined to specialised topics rather than integrated with core concerns. As one recent observer put it:

confined to micro studies and typically focussed on issues of emotional manage-ment. If work of the section is to draw the attention of sociologists more broadly then it is incumbent upon us to demonstrate the relevance of emotions to the full span of sociological work. This means both looking at the role of emotions in large-scale social processes and in areas of social activity in which emotions are not normally assumed to operate. (Barbalet 2002:3)

Within sociology's dominant disciplinary frameworks, phenomena such as revolution and war, diplomacy, occupations, social and class rivalry, political and economic activity, organisational and institutional behaviour, the rise and fall of social movements, and the exercise of social control were all portrayed as if they took place in passionless corridors, executed by agents who possessed reason but who did not *feel*. And yet, if an accompanying feature of emotion is the disposition to act, sociologists cannot afford to ignore the 'feeling component' of action and the role this plays in supra-individual movements and processes. Over the past five years or so, more sensitive sociological portraits of action have begun to emerge. With them, the status of the emotions as a topic has been elevated. From a number of sub-disciplinary directions has come a new concern with mood, emotion, and social action. This emphasis can be seen in current approaches to the sociological study of social and political movements and the emerging focus on the affective character of identification with a movement (Melucci 1996a; 1996b) and 'structures of feeling' as these are entered into, adopted, and adapted in the course of identity politics and movement activity (Hetherington 1998). This emotion renaissance is also evident in new work on political affiliation, for example, on the processes by which citizens transfer feelings of 'belonging' from nations to global entities (Berezin 2002). It has been further fuelled by a rapidly growing sociology of the body (Featherstone, Hepworth, and Turner 1991; Turner 1984) and embodied experience (Williams 2001). Thus sociology is now much more closely affiliated with concerns and topics traditionally lodged within the purview of social psychology.

A common thread running throughout nearly all of the recent focus on emotions within sociology has consisted of a focus on the interplay between emotions in lived experience and cultural forms. Inspired by the emphasis within post-structuralist and post-modernist theory on discourse, and by the concurrent emphasis on texts and artefacts as they imply readers, users, and 'subject positions' (i.e., particular and conventionally understood emotional stances, styles, or niches), sociologists across a wide range of specialist areas have devoted themselves to the question of how material cultural and aesthetic media may be understood to provide models or candidate structures for the production and achievement of emotion and feeling within specific social settings. This focus has been clear within areas such as gender and sexuality, and its concern with the cultural construction of desire and sexual practice (Jackson 1999), the study of spoken discourse in real-time encounters (Frazer and Cameron 1988), organisational behaviour (Witkin 1995), and the sociology of material culture (Akrich 1991; Latour 1991; Law 1994; Moore 1997; Woolgar 1997).

It is from within this framework that the sociology of music can be seen to interact with the broader sociological focus on emotion. Indeed, as I shall suggest below, emotion is the fulcrum and the pivot between consciousness and action, it is the topic through which access to the phenomenological and embodied character of social action can be explored, and through which the non-cognitive features of action, and, as I describe in chapter 6, 'control' (and its more neutral correlate, 'stability') can be examined in terms of how they are achieved. I suggest that this focus on the micro-sociological examination of emotion management (and emotion *attainment* as I describe via some studies below), also illuminates the process by which emotions are fashioned, how they come to be linked to action scenarios which are the building-blocks of social structure, and institutional and power-laden arrangements.

Music – key to emotion construction

Having undergone significant transformation in the past decade, socio-musical studies have moved from preoccupations with music's production and reception to concerns with how it is consumed and what it 'does' in social life. In this regard, developments within the sociology of music merge with developments in the sociology of the arts more widely (Bowler 1994). Recent developments within the field have examined connections between musical consumption and musical experience as a means for producing and sustaining social ordering in real time, over the life course, and with reference to organisational and collective spheres of action. These developments have helped to renew the sociology of music's emphasis on fundamental questions concerning music's role as the medium *par excellence* of emotion construction. In short, there is now a place at the top of sociology's table for the study of emotion – and music sociology can help to define this place. Such a project involves considerable sweep: it encompasses matters that are usually desegregated – a focus on systems of music production and distribution; on organisational ecology and management; and on subjective experience as it is configured in relation to musical media. I begin, as it were, from the 'outside' of emotion construction, with the focus – criticised by some (see above) as sociologically parochial – on emotion management in micro-sociological context, and on music's role as a resource for the production and self-production of emotional stances, styles, and states in daily life and for the remembering of emotional states. This work connects with recent and pioneering work in social psychology (De Las Heras 1997; Neilly 1995; Sloboda 1992; Sloboda and O'Neill 2001) focused on music and emotion in everyday listening. From within sociology, it converges with work on how actors produce themselves as identifiable agents, and how this production is achieved through 'aesthetic reflexive' practices (Lash and Urry 1994). In so far as these studies involve ethnographic methods, they interact with developments in the sociology of media and the arts (see, e.g., Press 1994; Radway 1988; Tota 1997).

Music and emotion work – producing feeling in daily life

Three studies can be used to illustrate this point: the first by Gomart and Hennion (1999), the second, my own (DeNora 1999; 2000); and the third, briefly (to be reconsidered in chapter 5) by Bull (2000). Methodologically, all three employed in-depth interviews focusing on music listening practices. They describe how actors can be seen to use music so as to prepare situations within which their emotional states undergo alteration.

In a piece that compares the love of music with the love of taking drugs, and which draws upon in-depth interviews with music lovers and with drug addicts, Gomart and Hennion (1999) follow actors as they engage in 'techniques of preparation' that produce forms of attachment so as to illuminate the mechanisms that produce 'dispositions'. In so doing, they shift the focus of their particular theoretical persuasion, 'actor network theory' from action (from the building of networks and the consolidation of alliances) to the study of interaction between people and things, and with this shift they make a concomitant move away from the overly general category of 'action' to the more specific concept of 'event', its phenomenological content and crafting. They place in the spotlight 'what happens' when, as part of the musical – or narcotic – experience, the self is 'abandoned' or given over to sensation and/or emotion. They are interested in no less than an ethnographic sociology of how musical 'passion' is produced.

Gomart and Hennion delineate how music lovers/addicts engage in a diverse array of practices that pave the way for the experience of being 'carried away'. This consists of priming situations and combining things so that particular effects are achievable. For example, interviewees describe becoming 'ready in one's head' for the ear to hear and the body to respond (1999:232), or how they employ particular listening strategies and rhythms so as to be ready to respond in preferred or expected ways. This process is akin to 'tuning in' or attempting to produce, through finely wrought practice, the power and clarity of a signal – its power to influence its recipients. Listeners, they suggest, like drug users, 'meticulously *establish conditions*: active work must be done in order to be moved' (1999:227, emphasis in original). Listeners are by no means simply 'affected' by music but are, rather, active in constructing their 'passivity' to music – their ability to be 'moved'. The music 'user' is thus deeply implicated as a producer of his/her own emotional response, is one who

strives tentatively to fulfil those conditions which will let him be seized and taken over by a potentially exogenous force. 'Passivity' then is not a moment of inaction – not a lack of will of the user who suddenly fails to be a full subject. Rather passivity adds to action, potentializes action (1999:243)

Gomart and Hennion were thus concerned with the question of how 'events' of musical passion and emotional response – the being 'taken over' by music – is reflexively accomplished by music lovers (DeNora 2000, see especially chapter 3). Similarly, my own research has dealt with music's role in the day-to-day lives of American and British women as they used music to regulate, enhance, and change qualities and levels of emotion. Nearly all of these women were explicit about music's role as an ordering device at the 'personal' level, as a means for creating, enhancing, sustaining, and changing subjective, cognitive, bodily, and self-conceptual states. Levels of musical training notwithstanding, the respondents exhibited considerable awareness about the music they 'needed' to hear in different situations and at different times, drawing upon elaborate repertoires of musical programming practice, and were sharply aware of how to mobilise music to arrive at, enhance, and alter aspects of themselves and their self-concepts. Part of their criteria for the 'right' music was how well it 'fitted' or was suitable for the purpose or situation they wished to achieve, or for achieving a particular emotional state (see the discussion of 'fit' in Sloboda and O'Neill 2001).

To return to the schematic framework of the Musical Event, respondents described how, so as to shift mood or feel particular emotions, such as joy or grief, they actively crafted particular Musical Events. Setting aside time to listen to music so as to calm oneself, or to grieve, or to become properly energised or upbeat prior to an evening out – all of these activities were routinely referred to by respondents for whom music was a technology of self. For example, respondents often chose music that reflected their moods and, in this example, they sometimes chose music that would intensify a particular feeling state so as to move beyond it. In this respect, music was a catalyst for reaching the climax of a particular (sad) mood state; it provided a medium through which that mood could be focused, amplified, and then dispelled. This sort of activity is, most definitely, emotional work, as the following respondent describes. She takes time out, sits on a settee to listen, follows the score as she listens, and works herself up into a particular emotional frame, and she knows which music to employ for which types of tasks:

It depends what mood you are in because if I feel like I want to do something jolly then I may listen to something jolly like Annie or Kiss Me Kate or something like that or Oklahoma say but then if I am feeling a bit more – see, when I listen to a musical I tend to just sit on the settee and listen and I usually look at the words and stuff as well and I just concentrate in the main on that. But . . . if I am sort of feeling a bit miserable I might listen to Les Miserables and then I quite often listen to Jesus Christ Superstar because that is very emotional . . . Sometimes you just want to sit there and just be miserable and my friend and I have this joke thing where, like you want to be miserable and you sort of look in the mirror at yourself being miserable to make yourself more miserable and that is what we always do (laughs).

These events were carefully crafted. Respondents made, in other words, articulations between music and desired emotional states. They used

TIME 1 – Before the Event (all prior history as meaningful to **A** Actor(s))

1. Preconditions
'stressed' 'Father's favourite' 'I remember . . . when I was little' 'my dad . . . played the piano when I was going to sleep' 'that music all my life has helped me, soothed me'

TIME 2 – 10 or 15 minutes before leaving for work

    A Actor(s) Lucy

    B Music Schubert, select short piano works

    C Act of Engagement with music she sits quietly and listens with aim of self-calming

    D Local conditions of C felt stressed, chose Schubert because 'I knew I wouldn't be disappointed'; chose particular bits she wanted to hear

    E Environment sitting room; rocking chair with speakers on either side where fireplace used to be; no one else at home

---

TIME 3 – After the Event

    3. Outcome She felt calmer, less stressed

    Fig. 5. Lucy and Schubert's Impromptus.

music as a reference point, model, or reminder of some emotional correlate and they thought about what music might, under different circumstances, 'work' for them. This practice was shaped by a range of proximal and distal factors, biographical associations and events associated with musical pieces or styles, conventional associations (e.g., 'romantic' or 'sad' music), music's physical properties (e.g., rhythms, pace, volume), and previous patterns of use (e.g., knowledge of what would 'work' on a particular occasion).

They involved pairing music with a variety of other materials, practices, and postures, for example, listening only at certain times of day, or in particular rooms or during particular events (e.g., during a bath but not in the kitchen), only with headphones, only played very loudly, heard only while sitting or while moving around doing the housework, paired with candlelight or with sunshine, and so forth. One of the most extensive examples of this type of activity comes from the respondent described in chapter 3, 'Lucy'. In *Music in Everyday Life* (DeNora 2000:16, 41–3), I presented Lucy, who described how, on the morning of the interview she was 'feeling very "stressed" . . . [because she was] in the throes of moving house'. She 'actively decided' to stop and to listen to some music. 'I needed it. It was only ten minutes or so, you know, I didn't listen to them all . . . just . . . to the bits I wanted . . .' (Lucy's experience can be diagrammed using the scheme for describing the details of a Musical Event, see figure 5).

As described in *Music in Everyday Life*, Lucy crafted a situation that enabled music to do its work 'on' her. It was significant, for example, that Lucy embedded this 'calming' music in the material cultural context of sitting, not on a stool or a typist's chair, for example, but in a rocking chair, the connotations of which include nurturing, being rocked like a baby in a cradle, and homeliness. These connotations then resonated with the meanings that these pieces held for Lucy, the ways they were linked to her personal history – they were pieces that her father played after dinner, pieces she would hear wafting up the stairwell when she was tucked into bed for the night, pieces that she would listen to with her parents by the fire, again in the evening before bedtime. Lucy thus embedded this music in a nurturing, domestic context, a context of listening that heightened the calming, nurturing, soothing qualities of this music – as she perceived them. These practices were, as described above, a way of fine-tuning the signal to which she then 'responded'.

These examples illustrate the ways in which emotional achievement involves a kind of practical knowledge, a form of knowledge and skill that both the French and the UK/US respondents exhibited repeatedly in their accounts of (often tacit) music practices. Through these practices, respondents produced themselves as coherent social and socially disciplined beings. All of the respondents routinely engaged in various practices of 'tuning in', of producing a Musical Event that would be capable of 'moving' them. This production of passivity in the face of music, and its subsequent emotional 'effects' was achieved through an assemblage of musical practices: the choice of specific recordings, volume levels, material cultural and temporal environments of listening (for example, choosing to listen in bed, in a rocking chair, in the bath in the evening, the morning, while preparing to go out), and the pairing and compiling of musical works, memories, previous and current contexts of hearing such that the respondents could often be conceived as – and spoke of themselves as – disc jockeys to themselves.

In short, recent studies of music in relation to the achievement of emotional states and events point to music's use, in real social settings, as a device that actors employ for entraining and structuring feeling trajectories. Music is a resource to which agents turn so as to regulate themselves as aesthetic agents, as feeling, thinking, and acting beings in their day-to-day lives. Achieving this regulation requires a high degree of practical reflexivity. And the respondents in both the French and the English/American case studies show how actors often perceive their 'need' for this regulation and know the techniques of auto-emotion work. These techniques may be found inadvertently (something is tried once and 'works' and so is later repeated and so becomes part of an individual repertoire), or they may be suggested through culture and the media (and so be, at least initially, imitative), or they may be handed down by associates (and so exist as part of group or family culture), or initially encountered in a social setting – all of these technique locations were mentioned by respondents. The natural history of the processes through which feeling states are identified and 'expressed' (i.e., enacted to self or other over time) is, moreover, a topic to be developed as it concerns the question of how aesthetic agency is configured in real time, as passion is choreographed and entrained. Holding on to this focus, but widening it from the individual experience of culture (and the social regulation of subjectivity in and through reference to cultural materials) to music's role in relation to the organisation of collective action and its emotional component is but the next step within this programme.

Music is a device for engaging in what the sociologist Arlie Hochschild (1983) calls 'emotional work', a term that references the various practices within a workplace, where workers were required to produce not only material goods or services but also to produce themselves as types of emotional agents acting under the organisational cultural auspices (and bearing strong resemblance to Cooley's conception of emotion constitution in his discussion of looking-glass self (see above)). Since its original use, the concept of emotional work has been adopted more widely within sociology, where emotion is conceived as a 'bodily co-operation with an image, a thought, a memory – a co-operation of which the individual is aware' (Hochschild 1979:551, quoted in Williams 1996:129). Respondents described how they used music both routinely and in exceptional circumstances to regulate moods and energy levels; to enhance and maintain desired states of feeling and bodily energy (e.g., relaxation, excitement); and to diminish or modify undesirable emotional states (e.g., stress, fatigue).

Respondents made, in other words, articulations between musical works, styles, and materials on the one hand, and desired modes of agency on the other, and then used music to presage, inspire, elaborate, or remind them of those modes of agency and their associated emotional forms. Music is, in other words, here conceived in Adorno's sense, as a device with which actors work themselves up and into particular subjective states and orientations. When respondents chose music as part of this care of self, they often engaged in self-conscious articulation work, thinking ahead about the music that might 'work' for them. And their articulations were made on the basis of what *they* perceived the music to afford. This perception was in turn shaped by a range of matters. Among these are previous associations that respondents have made between particular musical materials and other things (biographical, situational); their understandings of the emotional implications of conventional musical devices, genres, and styles; and their perceived parallels (articulations/homologies) between musical materials/processes and social or physical materials/processes.

A third study, by Michael Bull (2000), that examined the use of personal stereos helps to amplify these points and connects them to a theory of the subject as he/she negotiates public space. In this respect Bull's work can be seen as pivotal, shifting the focus from emotion to ordering activity. Respondents from roughly sixty in-depth interviews describe how personal stereo use covers myriad purposes: music is used among other things to control 'unwanted' feelings and otherwise regulate mood in ways that are similar to the strategies described in the French and US/UK studies. Bull describes how private music listening in public is part of the skill-set of urban dwelling. Individuals use music played on personal stereos to manage their daily patterns of existence in urban environments, in particular the buffeting and strain of travel on public transport, and the maintenance of mood and self-identity in anonymous and crowded environments.

Bull's study is unique in terms of its focus on the role played by music technology in these processes. As such, it further illuminates the way in which music's ability to 'channel emotion', as Adorno put it, is linked to the material cultural accoutrements of music hearing.

In this respect, his work overlaps with work by the French music sociologist Sophie Maisonneuve, who has also been concerned with the musical configuration of subjectivity, perceived from a historical angle, one concerned with the reconfiguration of the musical subject over time. Maisonneuve examines adaptations in recording technology and their interaction with modes of musical attention – she does not mention Adorno's work on music technology (e.g., Adorno 2002: 271–83) explicitly, though her work can be read as complementing and extending Adorno's. She shows how the introduction of the phonograph and its adjacent concept, the record collection, came to have an impact upon the possibilities for the experience of music consumption, in particular how these artefacts made way for new and more intensely personal modes of experiencing both music and the amateur 'love for music'.

In particular, Maisonneuve argues, they facilitated an aesthetically reflexive user, that is, a listener actively engaged in constructing her/his tastes and, simultaneously, in the self-monitoring of self-response. Maisonneuve compares the two 'technological revolutions' in music distribution during the twentieth century to describe how, during each, the social practices and concepts of listener, listening, and the music-listening subject were transformed. For Maisonneuve, the subject is configured in relation to what she terms the listening 'set-up', a concept that fits very well into the scheme for the analysis of Musical Events so far developed. The 'set-up' is a conglomerate of technological devices, material cultural environment in which listening occurs and the various material and textual artefacts that make up the instruments of listening – liner notes, music reviews, the phonograph or CD player, and so on. The listener is thus conceived as a node within a network of people and artefacts. And one of the most significant results of the transformation of this network during the two revolutions, then, was how the listener came to be positioned in relation to the musical canon of 'great' composers and works. As Maisonneuve puts it:

We thus see that 'classical music' is not a steady monument of works immutable in their essence: music exists thanks to the objects and practices which let it happen every time anew, in a set-up which is always reconfigured over time, and according to the objects and agents which participate in its production and enjoyment . . . It is important to realise the fact that the relationship to music is rooted in a material culture which evolves according to techniques, objects and agents by which it exists. The very material reality of music, and hence also its aesthetic potential, are defined and modified by this material set-up. (2001:105)

Maisonneuve's work brings the study of music and subjectivity firmly onto the ground level of situated occasions of hearing. For her, music is both configured by, and helps to configure, these settings, and the subjective responses of listeners may be conceived as artefactual of those settings, that is, as taking shape in, and with reference to, the properties of these settings. This is not to suggest that music's materials – such as compositional properties, tone colours, or conventional devices – play no part in how it comes to be linked to emotion. On the contrary – indeed, to make that suggestion would be to abandon the concern with music's materiality, a move that forfeits the crux of what should conjoin music scholars and social scientists. Rather, it is to point to how music is not 'the same' – is not an objective 'stimulus' that affects its subjects in pre-determined ways. This issue requires further consideration, both in the abstract and via some examples. And this consideration includes a focus on what it might be about music – as opposed to other things – that comes to afford emotion. For it is important not to overlook the fact that it was to *music* – not poetry, not painting, not drama – to which these individuals turned when engaging in emotion management. What, then, is it about music that may make it particularly conducive to, as Adorno put it, 'channelling emotion'? The section that follows offers by no means an exhaustive list, and the arrangement of topics is ad hoc. Indeed, there is no point in attempting to systematise the list since, ultimately, the only *empirically* significant features of music in relation to the evocation of emotion in its hearer are those made, and recognised, by actual hearers, within specific Musical Events. As the philosopher Stephen Davies puts it:

It will not do to attempt to reduce music's expressiveness to a catalogue of technicalities and compositional devices. Even if it is true that all, and only, music in minor keys sounds sad, it cannot be that 'sounds sad' *means* 'is in a minor key' . . . Musical features ground music's expressiveness, and it is interesting to discover what features those are, but identifying them is, at best, only an initial step toward an informative theory of musical expressiveness. (2001:28)

Everything else is mere anticipation of just what some of those links might be (perhaps many of which can be anticipated with some degree of accuracy, since listening is not an individual and idiosyncratic activity but, inevitably, a *cultural* activity). The point is simply to reflect upon some aspects of music's musical character that may provide leads to music's link with emotion, its role as a device for eliciting, evoking, channelling, representing, and/or inducing emotional response.

What might it be about *music* that gives rise to emotional response?

While music's actual links to emotion can only be specified from within the Musical Event, that is from within particular contexts of musical practice and music consumption/use, there are a number of factors that may be suggested, hypothetically, as aspects of music's emotion-inducing capacity. These include the following.

Materiality

Perhaps the most obvious place to begin is with music's materiality, both as an aural medium and in relation to the materiality of its hearers. For music has physical properties; it is sound, including ultra- and infrasound. It is fast or slow, regular or erratic. It is loud or soft. Its tones may be produced by a variety of means and these tones may be organised so that they cluster closely together (and thus may be perceived as 'clashing' or as 'tightly textured') or so that only one tone is heard at a time. These tones may be produced by a variety of means. If we consider only those means available to the standard Western orchestra and chorus, they may involve different physical and material techniques – strings, vocal chords, reeds, whistles.

All of these physical properties involve human bodily action and – at least potentially – reaction. With regard to the latter, as John Shepherd and Peter Wicke have suggested (Shepherd and Wicke 1997) and Shepherd has observed more recently (see Shepherd 2002, and DeNora 2002a), the physical medium of music (sound) should be thought of in terms of its internal impact (and potential impact) on the body. For example, one may feel the 'force' of a tutti 'wall' of sound; one may feel sympathetically a constriction of the throat when hearing a voice eke out the uppermost limits of her or his range.

So, too, music involves the body as it is externalised so as to perform music or to dance to it. The playing of brass instruments involves a vibration of lips in conjunction with a mouthpiece. To sing a high note involves certain muscular and breathing techniques. To play for a long time on a string instrument may result in a sore right arm, and so on. To double tongue while playing the flute involves again certain minute skills of co-ordination, as does producing vibrato on the violin. These are all bodily techniques and they in turn may be responsible for how they are perceived and – perhaps more importantly, to move away from the 'information processing' model described at the outset to this chapter – responded to by those who hear these things. Moreover, as Richard Leppert has observed, these techniques also involve in many cases a 'sight of sound' – one may observe the violinist 'sawing away' and so on (and even when listening to a recording one may 'see' in one's mind's eye many of the images that normally attend the production of the types of sounds one is hearing). So, for example, one may feel something like sheer joy on hearing a performance where, say, a soprano is able to reach and sustain a very high pianissimo note with ease and grace, *and* at the end of a phrase, because one 'knows', bodily, what is involved in this labour.

These sounds, the sheer texture and colour of particular instruments, may connote and perhaps evoke a sense of *what it is like to be* within specific material and corporal aspects of situations and settings – the sound of the horn, for example, may connote the out-of-doors and the hunt. Indeed, that instrument was used for this purpose in part because it was one that was audible from distances and one that could be played with one hand (while holding on to reins with the other). The reed family of woodwinds may connote water environments (e.g., the opening to *Swan Lake*) – again, note that there is a physical link between reeds and water. The lower brass, string basses, and bass voices may evoke a sense of strength and gravity, heaviness, solidity, in part because in Western cultures we associate low pitches with depth. But also because of the kind of sounds that they afford easily (steady movement and volume, for example, where we think of such concepts as 'the heavy brass') and the kinds of sound they afford only with difficulty (e.g., we are delighted with what the tuba can do in, say, the Vaughan Williams Concerto where it may seem to be 'so light on its feet' and contradict expectations, expectations based upon what that instrument normally performs, which is in turn based upon what that instrument affords). In short, and while it would be fruitless to attempt a taxonomy of these things a priori to how they are experienced (though a music therapist might wish to do just that in relation to a particular client and a potential strategy of healing), there are nonetheless associations between the production of sounds and bodily processes, perhaps particularly modes of touch and bodily comportment. The very illnesses to which different types of musicians are prone helps to highlight this. And listeners may often respond to these processes, often *sympathetically*, as they might to the sound of a deep bass voice at the bottom of its range. They may also respond *involuntarily*, as some listeners do to the sound of fingernails on a chalkboard, for example (or even to the suggestion of such a sound – as on this page now).

The capacity for these responses rests on the fact that the human body is (or can itself be thought of as) a musical instrument, and in ways that far exceed the capacity to sing or otherwise make music in the common-sense meaning of the term. And as an instrument, the body 'tunes in', 'clashes', and 'resonates with' the sound environment. The 'music' of the body includes pulse (heart rate), tempo (speeded or slowed heart rate), fluctuation (a sudden quickening of the pulse). It includes the sounds we make, involuntarily and voluntarily, in the course of simply being: the crying infant and the cooing mother; the rattling of a chest infection; the sounds of conversation – its pitches, rhythms, volumes, and tempos. These things and more are important, if neglected, matters linked to the hearing of music because any sound external to a given human body is in some form of relationship to it. To offer just one, and somewhat bald, example of this potential, consider how fast-paced dance music 'shows' the body of its hearer a mode of being that moves at a tempo well beyond the 60–70 heartbeats per minute of its listener; or how music marked 'adagio' (slow and relaxed) proposes a quite different set of bodily opportunities to its hearer. Any consideration of music's link to emotion can benefit greatly from thinking about how music shows or provides temporal opportunities and configurations and in this showing, music provides a structure against which individual and collective embodiment may be discovered/constructed.

Iconicity

Music often shares structural features with the things it is seen to represent. So, for example, Dowland's lachrymose pieces flow, melodically, downward, *like* the tears they describe, like the tears they may invoke.

Example 3. J. Dowland, *Flow my Tears*

It is this resource that was developed by baroque composers, such as J. S. Bach, concerned with the 'doctrine of the affections' (see chapter 5).

As a listener encountering music's iconicity, one may feel, virtually and sympathetically, an emotion parallel to some musical-iconic process. For example, in the study of aerobics, reported in DeNora (2000), this was illustrated time and time again, as when, for example, one might suddenly 'feel' and move more 'strongly' when the 'heavy' brass took over a theme (the exercise of strength) or when the theme modulated 'upwards' (a cranking up of energy). Here we can see music not only entering into the composition of feeling and emotion, we can also see how music is a medium that facilitates social consciousness. One may 'recognise' in music parallels to emotional and embodied processes.

Convention

Here, we move to the realm of music's symbolic meanings. This realm is by no means discrete from the previous two aspects discussed (materiality and iconicity), however, but it is used to refer the uses to which different types of sounds and sound-combination have been put in the past. Here is where the music-historical notions of style, genre, and other category-laden concepts come to the fore. Dirges and laments, the previous conventional handlings of, say, particular keys, tempos, textures, melodic styles – all of these things accumulate meanings. The Crucifixus of the B Minor Mass, for example, is composed in the key of E minor, which for Bach was the key associated with matters of the cross. Here, long experience – particularly on the part of listeners steeped within a particular tradition – may lead to listener habits, patterns of response to symbolic associations that music may conjure, as when one hears a choral number 'in the style' of Mozart, or a guitar riff, 'in the style' of Jimi Hendrix.

Temporality

Music is a form that moves through time. Its corporality and its iconicity are linked to this feature. Perhaps music's power in relation to emotion derives in part from its mercurial qualities, its ability to portray, ironically, symbolically, or materially, subjective processes rather than states. For example, when music moves 'upwards' to a 'climax' and feeling is intensified and then dispelled. Shepherd and Wicke (1997:159–68) have discussed this aspect of music in relation to Zuckerkandl's concept of the 'sonic saddle'. By this, Zuckerkandl means the tactile dimension of sound as it is presented to its hearers in a continually unfolding present (Shepherd and Wicke 1997:159). While it would be a mistake to accept that an analyst is able to define the various musical-syntactical 'moments' of the saddle in ways that would be isomorphic with how they come to be perceived (responded to) by listeners (an erroneous return to music-analytic priority), the concept nonetheless highlights music's unfolding character – and thus its explicitly temporal dimension – as a characteristic linked to its capacity as an emotional medium.

Expectancy

Leonard Meyer developed this theory, that emotions are aroused when the listener's response is inhibited, as with unresolved harmonies or other musical postponements. This perspective has recently come under criticism (Cook and Dibben 2001:58–9) on the grounds that it explains undifferentiated feeling but not specific feelings, such as joy versus grief, and that it over-emphasises the role of the unpredictable over the predictable (e.g., the conventional features of music as discussed, above) as generative of emotion.

Non-representativeness

Music's capacity to elide representation is also a feature that may afford emotional response. This is because it may provide a structure of feeling over time, one with which listeners may identify, corporally or cognitively, and so find 'expressions' or representation of 'their own' feelings. In DeNora (2000), I described how 'Lucy' (cf. chapter 3 of this book) found joy in hearing 'juicy' chords because within these moments she was able to 'see herself' or her role in life. So too, as Adorno put it with reference to Schoenberg, 'passions are no longer simulated . . . [but] . . . are registered without disguise' (1973:38–9).

Bits and pieces

In *Music in Everyday Life* I described how minute aspects of music were often emotionally significant. A 'cha-cha' rhythm, for example, or the moment when the violin line soared into the sonic stratosphere, or when voices coalesced into a major triad at the end of a section, or particular figures – what Philip Tagg refers to as *musemes* (Tagg 1991) – may trigger emotional and embodied responses in their hearers.

Music in context – listening and its frames

These, then, are but a few of many potential and specifically *musical* reasons why music may come to be linked to emotional response. How they feature, and how listener attention comes to be focused on them – i.e., in Maisonneuve's terms, the particular set-ups within which music may be framed – must also be considered. Here, another aspect from Leonard

Meyer's work, this time from his book, *Music, the Arts and Ideas* (Meyer 1967), is useful. Meyer describes how music listening – he writes of the concert hall, but his points are easily adaptable to any listening setting (I discuss this point in DeNora (1986b)) – is typically accompanied by various materials, such as programme notes, knowledge about the reputations of performers and the composer, expectations, critics' reports. These he refers to as part of the 'preparatory set' of music perception, those things that may dispose the listener to hear and thus respond in one way rather than another.

For example, when Felicity Lott's rendition of Richard Strauss's last songs is described, in the BBC Radio 3 programme, *Building a Library*, as 'golden', while another soprano's voice (viewed as a near-equal favourite) is described as 'silver' in character, one may not be able to avoid importing this framing into how one then perceives what is heard. It is precisely this that is at fault with any musical analysis when it seeks to deduce what music may cause to happen when it is heard or what it represents or signifies. For music offers so many possibilities for response and interpretation that there is no guarantee that a particular response will be forthcoming upon a particular hearing. This point harks back to Stephen Davies's warning that it is not possible to catalogue in advance just what emotions music may 'cause'.

Indeed, part of the preparatory set is the very ideology of listening, the work concept as discussed in chapter 1, and, indeed, the very idea that music is expressive or evocative of emotion. One has to work backwards, from Musical Events since music's semiotic and emotive force is produced from within these Events and from within the alchemical process of music's interaction with the set-ups within which it is produced. In responding to music we are not only performing, simultaneously, ourselves as feeling subjects and music as a medium capable of inducing feeling in us; we are also clustering music, interpretive devices and technologies, and ourselves in ways that can best be conceived as concoction, a pulling together of things so as to produce something (e.g., response, music's value, and effects) in situated time and space.

What else?

Until now, this discussion has centred on two key topics. The first of these is emotion construction, understood so far as individual emotion management. The second, and more abstract concern, has been with what it is about music that may be conducive to emotion on the part of those who hear it. There is, however, a good deal more to consider, and in the next section I take up three further topics. First, I clarify the concept of emotion. Second, I describe how and why a consideration of these matters needs to be drawn from the individual to the supra-individual level, and from a focus on what individuals and groups feel, to a focus on how these feeling forms come to be linked to action. I develop this third point through another case study of a Musical Event. Third, I consider how to explore the interface of emotion's 'inside' (i.e., the phenomenological *experience* of emotion in relation to music) with its 'outside' (i.e., the crafting of emotional experience for self/other via emotion management).

Emotion – some varieties

So far emotion has implicitly been conceptualised as *mood*. It is time now for more precision. Psychologists, when they refer to emotion, typically distinguish it from 'feeling' and from 'mood', and highlight how emotion and mood are typically linked to *valence*, by which is meant 'the tendency to attach differing degrees of positivity or negativity to whatever is being experienced or processed' (Juslin and Sloboda 2001:4), which is, in turn, linked to an individual's response capacities. These distinctions help in thinking about the different ways in which music may 'channel emotion'.

As Parkinson *et al.* describe in their study of 'Changing Mood' (1996), the term 'mood' is used to describe relatively stable feeling states that tend not to be directed to any particular object or incident and which can be understood as the background to an individual's ongoing being. So, for example, one might go to work in a 'good' or 'bad' mood; one might feel 'cheerful' or 'sad' throughout the morning, or afternoon, or week. Mood can be understood as the subjective backdrop or colour of action and being. Emotions, on the other hand, are typically object-directed and characterised by a shorter temporal trajectory. The onset of an emotion is more abrupt, and its trajectory is characterised by an intense onset and a rapid dissipation. An emotion is, as it were, a flare-up of feeling and may be accompanied by rapid shifts in physiological features – such as breathing rate, heart rate, blood pressure, neurological function, muscle tone and temperature, as well as facial and bodily posture. Parkinson *et al.* (1992) suggest that if one were to plot the intensity of feeling over time, the curve for emotions would look like figure 6, whereas moods are more stable over time and less intense. See figure 7.

Stephen Davies (Davies 2001:27) has suggested that emotions may be characterised by degrees of primitiveness – disgust, for example, may be more basic (and more involuntary) than a surge of patriotic feeling. Sloboda and Juslin suggest further that emotions are linked to adaptive behaviours, while moods are linked to modes of information processing

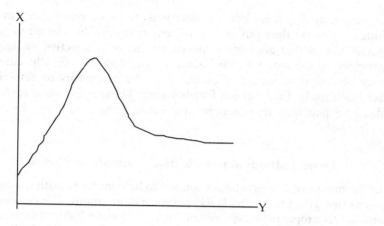

X = Time
Y = Intensity of emotion

Fig. 6. The intensity of emotion over time.

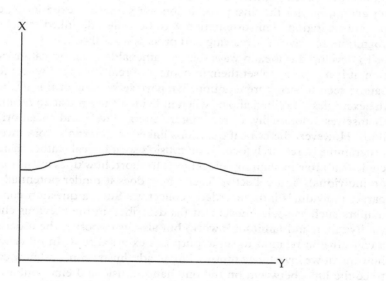

X = Time
Y = Intensity of mood

Fig. 7. The intensity of mood over time.

in ways that may influence our decisions, what we remember, and our judgements. As they put it: '[t]hus, emotions can be viewed as phasic perturbations that are superimposed on the *tonic*, affective background provided by the mood' (Sloboda and Juslin 2000: 75). Finally, emotions may be linked to modes of *arousal* – to the propensity to act (and to act impulsively, i.e., without forethought). These concepts are, in turn, distinguished from mere sensation – feeling (which may vary by degree of intensity).

From individual to collective, 'outside' to 'inside'

In the main, psychologists have tended to be concerned with the mechanisms that affect the *individual* experience of emotions. For sociologists, emotion is a topic to be explored in terms of its socio-cultural structuring, and this often means a focus on the forms of emotion and their allocation to specific social settings. In this respect, Adorno was a typical sociologist. It was his critical focus on the psycho-cultural bases of action that distinguished him (and his Frankfurt School colleagues) from what was then, in the USA, 'mainstream' sociology. Adorno was in this respect a pioneer; his work pointed to culture as a structure, as a matrix not just for action, but for the 'inside' of action, for subjective experience, emotional orientation. This orientation was, he believed, linked to habits of cognition, to ways of perceiving and processing reality.

To develop this idea in ways that are amenable to empirical investigation, it is necessary to set them in context of real situations where music can be seen to structure emotion. We have seen some of this already in the examples described above, when individuals use music to recalibrate themselves emotionally, to reconfigure energy levels and social orientations. However, the critical questions linked to Adorno's work involve a programme of research focused on music's sociological (rather than psychological) role in aligning subjectivity. In short, how does music operate on individuals at a collective level – how does it render potentially disparate individuals into an orderly collective? Such a question concerns matters such as social movement (as described in the previous chapter via Eyerman and Jamieson's work) but also its opposite, the ordering of a collective in relation to some purposes external to it. In other words, how might we investigate music's link to administration, and how can we trace the links between, on the one hand, music and emotion; and, on the other, administrative agendas? This topic is explored in detail in the following chapter. There are, however, some methodological and theoretical issues that are best taken up here, in the context of considering music and its link to emotion. Specifically, the next section seeks to underline, via a case study, the need for alternative methods for the study of this subject, in particular, the need for a scrupulously 'micro' interactive lens.

In *Music in Everyday Life*, I suggested that managers within organisations often use cultural devices to condition in-house conduct. What follows returns to the scene of that work to illustrate some methodological strategies for the exploration of cultural (musical) management. These methods combine fine-grained analysis of talk, researcher reflexivity (i.e., the researcher's reflection on what it 'felt like' to be involved in that event), and real-time recording of a phase of action. In what follows I present some new methods for socio-musical analysis in rudimentary form. The actual 'data' used in this example and the descriptions of it are used here for heuristic purposes, to describe the kind of research that might be able to tease out some of the real-time intersections of music and emotional action.

Some serendipitous features of micro-observation: 'Annette' and 'Tia'

Early on in the retail study (DeNora 2000) we employed a methodological strategy we referred to as the 'shadowing technique'. Working with volunteer shoppers (who were wired for sound – they had small microphones clipped to their collars and carried cassette recorders), we asked these volunteers to 'just think aloud' into the microphone while going about the business of retail browsing. Meanwhile, we – the investigators (myself and Sophie Belcher, research assistant for the project) were also wired for sound. The idea was that we would trail our volunteers at a respectful distance, commenting all the while on how they behaved. The two tapes, in so far as they shared the same soundtrack, could thus be synchronised for transcription, enabling the volunteer's comments and our own comments on the 'external' attributes of that volunteer's behaviour to be collated. The hope was that this would provide some access to the 'inside' of in-store activity, while simultaneously providing data on what it looked like, from a distance of twenty paces. Far less obtrusive than a video camera (using a camera would have required us to trail the respondent at a much closer distance, reminding the respondent all the while that she was 'being filmed'), the cassette recorder (usually slipped into a bag) and microphone (clipped onto a collar) were easily forgotten.

I initially embarked on these excursions with all the zeal of a private eye in the making. I went out with the intention of reporting in full on my volunteer's *every move*, in the style of, say, Sarah Peretsky's hard-boiled female detective (V. I. Warshowsky). (At the time I had recently heard

1. Volunteer 'shopper' and researcher both carry tape recorders with microphone attached to clothing.

2. Volunteer shopper is asked to 'think out loud' as s/he ventures through shops.

3. Volunteer shopper is 'shadowed' by researcher who is also linked to a tape recorder and comments on shopper's activities – what s/he is examining, how fast she is walking, how long she spends on examining an item, how long she spends in a given shop or area.

4. Tapes are synchronised through reference to common musical soundtrack.

5. Any number of shopper/researcher dyads can be located within one spatial/temporal setting, space permitting.

Fig. 8. Shadow technique, as envisioned prior to trial.

24 January 1998 (Friday)	Small City, UK	12.30pm, upmarket chain store
Time in seconds	Shopper (Annette, age 24)	Shadower (Tia)
0	It's quite relaxing	. . . perhaps not.
2		
4	These are nice	
6		
8	Too much lolly though	
10		
12		
14	Too long	
16		
18		
20		
22	**Oh that's a YUMMY**	**Certainly, *I* would**
24	**jumper!**	**like to come back**
26		**here later!**
28		
30		
32	Mmm. Sixty five pounds.	
34		
36		
38	A black one as well.	
40		
42		
44	Mmm. It's definitely	
46	George Michael.	

Fig. 9. Excerpt of Enigma transcript, January 1998.

a BBC Radio broadcast of a Peretsky story with a deep and somewhat gruff-voiced Kathleen Turner in the leading role.) But plans often go awry and this plan did. In retrospect, the technique was more useful for what its failure illuminated than for its success as an investigative tool.

Transcribing the tapes, I was initially dismayed to discover at times quite a lot of blank space, such as in the snippet of collated transcript shown in figure 9, which occurred during a visit to a shop with the pseudonym, 'Enigma'.

Perhaps more surprising was the level of 'researcher failure', given my commitment to the role of observant 'private eye'. In what follows, however, I suggest that, at the core of this failure was something socio-musically interesting, namely, an example of how I (who was meant to be functioning as the researcher rather than the researched), came to be enlisted into a stylistic and, at one point, specifically musically generated emotional response to the retail space.

On the uses of autobiography – the researcher as researched

What went 'wrong' in Enigma then? I believe that my own failure as 'observer' on the occasion of this shopping experiment was linked to how I, the researcher, reverted to being 'yet another' research subject. I shifted in and out of role, sometimes reporting on Annette, sometimes engaging in reverie. It was only during the analysis phase of research, after the event, that I realised this 'failure' was in fact opening a door to some interesting issues.

In contrast with the previous shops we had visited on this occasion (which neither of us cared for – they tended to cater to young women), when we arrived at Enigma, both I and Annette engaged with the shop, with its environment and its goods. This engagement can be heard, overtly, in Annette's positive comments on store ambience and goods (she describes it as relaxing, she comments positively on specific goods). Moreover, I can recall my own response to the shop (occasionally referenced on the tape): I found it a pleasant contrast to the previous shops. Indeed, I can be seen in figure 9 to comment that I would like to revisit the shop!

Producing adaptation, music and 'fit'

Enigma is an 'artful' space. Brand managers there are seriously concerned with environmental factors in-store, far more committed to 'atmospherics' than the average high-street chain. And this costs money. Any Enigma outlet features wooden – never utilitarian plastic – clothes hangers, hard wood floors, an enormous vase filled with lilies, a 5×6 foot gilt-framed mirror, a lack of clutter (there are rarely sale racks groaning with jumbled items, and then only in some of the smaller outposts of the outlet – never at its main and flagship branches), and, on the occasion of our visit, well-spaced displays of clothes in colours (and this too is significant) such as pink and raspberry (which were then in-vogue – note, too, we were two weeks away from St Valentine's Day). All of these objects and their properties carry *potential* meaning (e.g., the gilt on the mirror; the pink, 'feminine' colours) and most of them perhaps also imply modes of embodied conduct modes.

Now, what did the shop sound like when we entered it? The music, for the duration of our visit consisted of one song followed by silence. The song, by George Michael, was 'Waiting (Reprise)', and on the day of our visit I was hearing it for the first time. A ballad that might be heard as reminiscent of Elton John's work, the song's lyrics lament lost love and consider the possibility of reprise, of resumption of a former relationship. The singer tells the song's recipient that there is a year of his life in the songs he sings, and that some of those songs are about the recipient. He continues by requesting that they 'try again', stating at the song's close, simply, 'here I am'.

The song moves at an unhurried pace; the accompaniment includes acoustic guitar and *sotto voce* chorus. Musically, it 'does' waiting through repetition. The build-up to a climax is slow (see below). Heard in context of a previous diet, in the shops we had visited earlier, of Top 40 music, I listened gratefully (far more gratefully in that context, it should be added, then I might have done in a concert hall!). Taken in context of what had come before, this music seemed 'relaxing'; a very welcome antidote to the earlier, more up-tempo sounds of the other shops. Annette was familiar with the music (but could not quite remember what it was), and she made comments on and off about how she thought she recognised the artist (she finally gets there in the end). Both of us comment that we found the music, and the atmosphere more generally, relaxing. Both of us, on that occasion – and at a semi-conscious level – became engaged by, were drawn into the setting. I think our engagement can be accounted for by a variety of factors.

The space struck us both as carefully designed, and both of us noted this on tape. We found, I think it is safe to suggest, a kind of aesthetic 'logic' there. Things – goods, décor, music – seemed to 'fit' together. Even the sensuous detail of the music seemed to 'work' here – for example, the sound of the guitarist's hand gliding along the fingerboard, the breath, and, in Barthes's sense, the *grain*, of the singer's voice, Michael's aspirated hs, for example – all this seemed to 'go with' the natural 'grain' of the other materials (including the literal 'grain' of the wood floors and hangers) and uncrowded space of the setting. It is worth underlining that I am not attempting to make a general statement about 'what' this musical-material setting will 'make happen'. Rather, I am seeking to describe the responses of *two people* to this music, my own and Annette's (which is not to suggest that others might not share some or all of these responses with us).

Whether or not one 'liked' these things, they seemed compelling, for both Annette and myself, *at that time and in that space (e.g., as against the context of what preceded it)*.

Some years ago, Michele Callon coined the term 'interessment' (Callon 1986) to describe how actors may be interposed between two subjective trajectories and drawn into one or the other – how they may become 'interested' in spaces, scenes, situations, or plans. I think this concept is useful in understanding what happened to me in this example. I – in this case, 'the researcher' – can be understood as interposed between two modes of acting: the first which I brought with me to the setting (detective, observer), the second, which I embarked upon *after* I entered the setting and became *interested* in the shop environment. I engaged in (and this will be important in the context of chapter 5) adaptive behaviour in relation to the space, in relation to what modes of conduct were implied/afforded by that space.

One aspect of this adaptation was my style of speaking – and this was captured on the audio-tape. In Enigma my voice took on (and unbeknownst to me at the time) new qualities. Though I was saying little more than, 'she's looking at a yellow jumper', the voice that said these things was softer, more highly pitched, more stereotypically feminine than the dull, clipped and gruff ('V. I. Warshowsky'?) monotone that I had employed up until arriving at Enigma. It began, moreover, to linger on words and trail off or upwards in pitch on the ends of phrases. In short, it adapted, I suggest, to the tenor of a particular aesthetic space, and here I would like to suggest that micro-analysis of speech and bodily style may help us to understand better what it means to speak, in Arlie Hochschild's words, of 'emotional work'. Here, in other words, I can point to a specific and grounded moment when an actor's (my own) conduct shifted in 'co-operation' with an aesthetic space.

In other words, here, an actor (me on this occasion) arrived on a scene with a quasi-conscious aim (to describe in detail Annette's movements) and, associated with that aim, a role or style of action (private detective). Within moments after entering the setting, both of these prior action commitments were abandoned. The 'detective' became silent, the detective's voice took on new and different parameters, indeed stylistic parameters not usually associated with being a detective.

There is a long tradition within socio-linguistics devoted to the idea of conversational style (e.g., Tannen). This tradition highlights how actors may, within particular situations and settings, and with different conversational partners, assume voices or communicative styles – a telephone voice, a voice with which to meet personages or talk to children,

TIME 1 – Before the Event

1. Preconditions
negative or neutral evaluation of previous shops, evaluation of Enigma as more 'up-market' and oriented to thirty-something women; the 'feminine' window display of pink clothes; understanding of shop décor and Enigma's place in this spectrum.

TIME 2 – During the Event (the event may be of any duration, seconds to years)

2. Features of the Event

    A Actor(s) The Researcher

    B Music George Michael's 'Waiting (Reprise)'

    C Act of Engagement with music moving around the shop, shadowing the volunteer shopper, examining the shop, other customers, goods, aware of 'relaxing' or 'romantic' music in background

    D Local conditions of C on research trip; explicitly oriented to music's role in-store; intention to comment about volunteer shopper, playing role of 'private eye'; had never heard this music before but 'liked' it *in situ*

    E Environment shop décor consists of wood floors, wood hangers, carefully displayed goods, flowers, room fragrance, more expensive items than in stores nearby on high street

---

TIME 3 – After the event

3. Outcome became interested in revisiting the shop; enjoyed in-store time; vocal speech style shifted (became more 'feminine'?); felt more positive mood, perhaps more relaxed and more energised than prior to shop visit

Fig. 10. At Enigma, with George Michael on the tannoy.

an intimate voice, and so on – the labels are less relevant here than the idea of *modulated* speech: babyish, commanding, stentorian, confidential, sympathetic, efficient, intimate, whatever. To speak of styles is to speak of actors' employment of different cultural repertoires of action and this idea is discussed in chapter 5.

In sum, I suggest that in this space at this time it was possible to hear in my voice and in the words I uttered on tape, my taking pleasure in, and adapting to, a spatially aesthetically implied persona – a more 'feminine' type of actor (and jettisoning a prior role commitment). I suggest on this occasion that I was able to reflect on myself as I engaged in the emotional work of 'doing' a type of being, in this case, stereotypical femininity – a style of emotionally charged, embodied action congruent with retailer aims. I suggest that this enactment was facilitated (induced?) by the way in which I came to attend and respond to the space in question. This event can be diagrammed following the schema for the Musical Event introduced in chapter 2 (see figure 10).

Getting to the 'purchase moment' – music and emotion

In one respect, music is just another aesthetic material within a space. But in another respect, it is not 'like' other spatial 'furnishings', lighting or climate control, because music *moves* through time. First, music – electronically reproduced music at least – can be added, or removed, or changed with the flick of a switch. Second, as discussed above in terms of what it is specifically about music that is conducive to emotion, music moves, and this movement is itself a medium that may afford being 'moved' in an emotional sense (that is, experiencing emotive change over time). This is, perhaps, one of the most difficult topics to explore through socio-musical studies' more conventional methodologies.

On the tape of our visit to Enigma, there was an interesting moment of synchrony between Annette and myself (remember we were separated in-store). In this moment, we each uttered what were undoubtedly the most enthusiastic comments made by either of us during the entire exercise (see again figure 9, bold section). I exclaimed that I would like to return to the shop in future and Annette's voice rose in pitch and volume as she exclaimed, 'that's a *yummy* jumper!' These utterances coincided with a melodic phrase and a particular structural phase of the song – the point at which a reasonably socialised listener would 'know' that the song is moving toward its 'climax', a climax in which George Michael's voice breaks slightly on a high note. (Because the song participates in song conventions, one would – if familiar with these conventions – 'know' that a climax was imminent even if one had never heard the music before.)

It is in the lead-up to that climax that Annette makes the comment about the 'yummy' jumper and I exclaim that I should like to return to the shop. These were, for both of us, moments when we experienced a kind of energy boost, an emotional surge. I think that these separate but synchronised moments *may* be attributable to the music at that point. Both of us were certainly attending to the music, the shop was uncrowded and quiet, we were moving, in desultory fashion from section to section, I following Annette. Returning to the distinction between mood and emotion discussed earlier, I suggest that we experienced a musically instigated surge of *emotion* here that, in turn, came to be objectified as an enthusiasm for the shop and, in Annette's case, for one of its goods for sale. In other words, an indefinite emotion, musically generated, came to be situationally specified in relation to where we were and what 'objects' were available to us there. I had made a mental commitment to return to the shop and Annette was poised on the brink of a purchase decision. (Which

TIME 1 – Before the Event – feeling relaxed and enjoying shop environment

1. Preconditions
shop environment as explored over previous minutes, tuning in to shop ambience, the music prior to this moment (i.e., earlier sections of 'Waiting (Reprise)'.)

TIME 2 – During the Event (the event may be of any duration, seconds to years)

2. Features of the Event

    A **Actor(s)** The researcher, the volunteer shopper

    B **Music** George Michael's 'Waiting (Reprise)'

    C **Act of Engagement with music** (known only for the researcher): feeling of pleasure and emotion as the music moves towards melodic climax

    D **Local conditions of C** had 'liked' music up until this point because it was relaxing and 'fit' the setting, it was 'romantic' and fit the feminine space/clothes; there seemed to be a 'logic' to the space and aural environment

    E **Environment** shop décor consists of wood floors, wood hangers, carefully displayed goods, flowers, room fragrance, more expensive items than in stores nearby on high street

---

TIME 3 - After the Event

3. **Outcome** surge of emotion and enthusiasm for shop, expressed as commitment to return in future

Fig. 11. An emotional moment (in musical time).

she then rejects when the cost is considered – a 'decision' that occurs *after* the musical climax.) Perhaps unsurprisingly shops wish to instigate emotional surges in consumers, surges that may come to be configured as a desire for an object (e.g, shop goods).

Thinking about this issue opens up a somewhat new way of thinking about music and emotion. It points towards the analysis of particular musical figures, gestures, techniques, and other micro-musical phenomena as relevant within the moment-to-moment constitution of subjectivity, within the 'sonic saddle' as Shepherd and Wicke put it (Shepherd and Wicke, 1997:159–68). These figures may or may not be significant in relation to their location within a wider musical logic. They may also be free-standing or iconic, such as a hunting call played on a horn. In either case, we can speak about music in time and its link to subjectivity in time. Music, in other words, is not just related to emotional 'states' (in other words, stable patterns of feeling, being, and doing) and how we shift from one to another state, but is implicated in the constant *fluctuation* of subjectivity, in the heightening and diminishing of feeling and in the mercurial character of subjectivity in time. Music is, in short, linked to the embodied features of experience and to the flux of their social organisation. In conjunction with other features of space, it may be linked to particular identifiable modes of action.

Subjectivity and administration

Seen in this light, the study of music's links to emotion, situated within social settings, spaces, and scenes, moves consideration well on from the so-called 'private' realm of individual subjectivity. It highlights by contrast how the topic of music and emotion is, in turn, linked to a basic topic within sociology: how social reality, and with it forms and relations of feeling, is produced in real time and within specific social milieux. Critical here is the issue that preoccupied Adorno and which concerns music's role in modern societies: the matter of how the aesthetic environments that come to afford agency's production are themselves produced. And so the study of consumption returns full circle to the study of production and dissemination as complementary enterprises. Especially with regard to the public spaces where agency is produced, music's role here has grown massively over the past two decades. And if music is a device of social ordering, if – in and through its manner of appropriation – it is a resource against which holding forms, templates, and parameters of action and experience are forged, if it can be seen to have 'effects' upon bodies, hearts, and minds, *then* the matter of music in the social space is of critical importance to studies of social control and social resistance, and this is the topic of the next chapter.

5   Music and 'control'

Popular music is objectively untrue and helps to maim the consciousness
of those exposed to it.   (Adorno 1976:37–8)

Because it is so crudely simple, however, the standardization of that music should be interpreted not so much intramusically as sociologically. It
aims at standardized reactions, and its success – notably its adherents'
fierce aversion to anything different – proves that it has gained its end. It
is not only the interested parties, the producers and distributors of pop
music, who manipulate the way it will be heard; it is the music itself,
so to speak, its immanent character. It sets up a system of conditioned
reflexes in its victim, and the crux is not even the antithesis of primitivity
and differentiation. Simplicity in itself is neither an asset nor a shortcom-
ing. But in all music that deserves the name of art, every detail, even the
simplest, would be itself; none would be arbitrarily interchangeable . . .
                                                          (Adorno 1976:29)

When Adorno speaks about music's link to 'standardized reactions', as he
puts it, and suggests that music 'sets up a system of conditioned reflexes
in its victim', he is talking about what, for him, is the 'wrong' kind of
music – popular music writ large and also all those 'classical' composers
and works (Rachmaninov, Tchaikovsky, Stravinsky – the list could easily
be expanded) of whom he disapproves. In his view, these forms of music
inculcate conformism; they are nothing less than a mechanism of social
control. The 'victims', as Adorno calls them, of bad music are taught, via
musical example (indeed, as Adorno puts it here, *conditioning*), to respond
in automatic ways. More specifically, at the heart of this 'wrong' mode of
response is a capacity for, as Adorno puts it, 'arbitrary interchangeability',
the loss of the particular, detailed feeling for 'difference', the feeling for
specificity. From Adorno's viewpoint, popular music inculcates a psycho-
cultural collapse of the particular into the generic and, via some form of
conditioning process, simultaneously induces consciousness to collapse
into, as he puts it elsewhere, 'that which simply exists'.

The problem with Adorno's vocabulary, apart from its value-laden
character (as described in chapter 1), is that it asserts but does not specify

how music's structuring powers might actually operate in real time and space within the Musical Event. It would be wrong to lapse into a discourse of musical determinism. Indeed, to do so would be to fall back upon one of the two unsatisfactory forms of determinism, namely, describing music's power as either fully determined by its social uses or as fully determining social uses and responses. These are equally crude and I have rehearsed the arguments against them in earlier work (DeNora 2000, ch. 2).

If we do not attempt to transcend Adorno's deterministic discourse on the matter of music and social 'control' (a term that should be qualified since the very idea of control itself requires further specification), it is simply not possible to open the 'black box' of music's effects. In this chapter I shall suggest that there may be new ways of thinking about 'control' that draw upon Adorno's pioneering studies so as to develop our understanding not only of how music may come to structure action but more broadly how agency may be conceptualised in relation to culture. One way into this complex terrain can be found through the recent focus within cultural sociology on 'cultural repertoires'. This new work shifts cultural theory away from static 'readings' of cultural media (and from culture as a marker of social structural location) and towards a concern with action and performance. It focuses in particular on how any social performance mobilises (available) resources, both socially distributed and locally available (situated), such as action-strategies and action-repertoires.

To return to the topic of music, the concern with repertoires leads away from thinking about music in isolation from other features of social situations and settings – the traditional way in which music is conceptualised by musicology. On the contrary, most music perception occurs well away from the concert hall. It is integrated into the fabric of social settings and ongoing interactions. By turning attention to these necessarily grounded topics and their focus on social performance, it is possible to pose the question of music as a technology of 'control' in terms of its mechanisms in real time and space. This last term – space – is critical for what follows.

Social 'order' and the idea of 'culture in action'

Music – its production and its reception – is inevitably located somewhere. That 'somewhere' – musically configured space – is where we can begin to situate music as a technology of 'control'. To do so brings the topic within the remit of the Musical Event paradigm described in chapter 2. As cultural geographers and others concerned with space have helped to remind us in recent years, space plays an important role in the production of identity. Space can be understood as providing materials through which action – and agency, understood as capacities for action – is produced. If this is so, then it is possible to speak of space in terms of how it may inform or structure action, as affording actors with possibilities for action, types and styles of action. What role, then, does music play in the configuration of space and, therefore, situated action?

The focus on situated action leads on to a concern with social performances. In recent years within American sociology there has been a growing interest in making connections between the study of interaction and identity performance with a more structural focus on the social distribution of cultural media and cultural strategies.

Known as the Cultural Repertoires (CR) perspective, this focus on the nexus of culture and agency has illuminated how, in the words of one of its founders, Ann Swidler (1986), culture can be seen, 'in action'. Swidler's original article posed culture as a 'tool kit' for action. Culture provided, in other words, the means for producing action and for filling in aspects of institutional relations – structures – that were left otherwise unspecified or that posed problems to actors. The CR paradigm took further inspiration from William Sewell's seminal work (drawing on Bourdieu and Giddens) on the structural and schematic properties of culture, that is to say, the logical and, thus, causal implications culture holds in relation to action, for example, patterns or principles of thought that may guide action.

To take a simple example, and one that harks back to the socio-linguistic issues described in the previous chapter (in the section on autobiography), one draws upon cultural-linguistic tools in speaking to different types of actors, for example, conventional communicative styles and patterns for different types of social actors (roles) one encounters in daily life (e.g., how one might typically speak to children or occupational superiors). One draws upon a gamut of strategies one has observed and, in various mediated ways, imitated (think of learning courtship practices). (This point is illustrated, perhaps most painfully, by those discussion-chat television shows where 'ordinary people' are encouraged to 'tell' about themselves and those closest to them in ways that are, at times, excruciatingly generic. For a discussion of how actors draw upon conventional strands of discourse in real-time interaction, and how these may be triggered by the interrogative strategies, see Frazer and Cameron 1988). These strategies may be adapted and honed over time to the point that they become repertoires, for the production of all types of action. In this sense, cultural repertoires can be understood as the means through which social structures are both expressed and renewed. This is a highly useful perspective, since it converts the concept of structure into something dynamic and performed (it becomes something one mobilises to do and get through social interaction), thus dispensing with the otherwise cumbersome agency–structure dichotomy. In recent years this perspective has been developed, both by Swidler herself and by others, mostly within American sociology.

Swidler's original (1986) formulation has since been criticised on two main grounds. First, it did not characterise cultural 'tool kits' in terms of their internal structuring or external distribution. It did not deal with the question of how the tools provided by culture could be understood to be related to each other and therefore *structure* their uptake. For example, one might suggest that 'eggs go with ham but not with chocolate sauce and that one should eat the eggs and/or ham *before* turning to the chocolate'. To do so is to purport that there is a culinary classification system (what goes with what), a grammar (what comes first, second, third), and a sensibility (particular culinary arrangements may carry connotations and may resonate with aesthetic inclinations). To be sure, no system is hard and fast, and exceptions are not only 'allowed' according to convention, practice, and orientation; they are often *sought and cultivated*. Indeed, it is precisely the handling of exceptions that enables change. One may, in other words, produce a meal that combines eggs with chocolate (e.g., eggs in a chocolate molé sauce, a chocolate mousse, or a haphazard meal where the chocolate may be eaten before or with the main course), and these innovations may be secured over time as 'normal' practices.

Related to this, the second ground on which Swidler's original theory has been criticised is that it did not deal with the question of how cultural tools may be socially *distributed* in ways that, again, structure use. To return to the egg and chocolate example, culinary skills and knowledge (and the uptake of particular cooking and meal planning styles) has long been associated with position in the social space, a point famously underlined by Bourdieu's *Distinction* (1984).

More recently, these critical omissions have been addressed by Swidler herself (Swidler 2002:10). She has suggested that the key task for cultural sociologists concerned with culture's causal properties is now to identify the hierarchical relations that may adhere to cultural practices, for example to search for core or *anchoring practices*, around which other domains of practice/discourse may revolve. So, for example, under some conditions – e.g., a Wall Street executive breakfast, a protest rally – the very concept of that event may 'anchor' associated practices – how one speaks, what one eats, and what one wears, to name a few.

The concept of anchoring practice is highly promising for sociology in so far as it points to the idea that a situation – and more dynamically the tone and stylistic parameters of interaction – can be defined through some key practice – and in particular through the practical deployment of objects or aesthetic media. This issue has been discussed within critical management theory. For example, in a study of the British academic managerial sector, Prichard (2000) describes a case in which a new (and female) vice-chancellor brought cookies to her first senior management board meeting and with that practice managed to alter the culture of future meetings (the cookies stood on behalf of, and implied, a more homely and informal action style).

Additional elaboration of Swidler's 1986 tool-kit theory has been provided by Lamont (2000). Lamont suggests that it is possible to think about cultural repertoires in terms of two 'tiers' – macro-, or distal, repertoires, and proximate tool-kits. The first category is then seen to shape the second, rather as, in Bourdieu's work, the *habitus* – an individual's horizon of expectations and the almost tacit dispositions governing the 'choice' of (read access to) particular tools or strategies – is the proximal version of the more distal social space (social distribution) of cultural practices, tastes, and habits that accumulate as cultural capital. There are precedents here in the work of Robert Wuthnow, who has long been concerned with the interrelationships between (rather than meanings of) cultural elements, an emphasis that seeks to retain the sociological impetus within cultural studies.

As Wuthnow has observed, meanings emerge from cultural systems and fields that provide 'categories in which formal thinking about ourselves' may occur. This perspective would, at least implicitly, call for a focus upon actors as they engage with, and mobilise, cultural materials, as they move through particular cultural fields and so configure themselves as conscious agents. In principle, then, the concern with cultural repertoires is one within which the concept of action – in particular of the structure, process, and consequences of culture mobilisation – is preserved. And in this respect, the notion of cultural repertoires complements the focus, within organisational studies, on structuration and agency – work such as DiMaggio's (1982) focuses on agents as the producers and reproducers of organisations. As DiMaggio has observed, the shift to 'how people use culture' (1997:392) provides a means for exploring culture's causal properties in and for action.

With regard to music – a topic that, apart from DiMaggio's early work, has been left mostly unexplored in relation to action – we shall see that this 'culture in action' perspective is highly useful. Its utility is linked to the ways in which it shifts attention from culture-as-meaning and culture-as-text (an object to be decoded and received – and thus a programme of research reduced to semiotic readings and/or reception studies) to a programme focused upon culture as a structuring medium of action and, in particular, to music as providing a set of 'cues' for different cultural frames as they may be invoked within situations. This latter focus leads to a strong cultural sociology that not only contributes to the study of institutions, power, and structuration but also leads such study.

The work on tool kits and repertoires is, viewed within the context of American sociology, a breakthrough in the sense that it advances the status of *cultural* sociology within the American Sociological Association. This is due to the way it seeks to demonstrate culture's capacity to 'enable and constrain' action – to structure action in and through the ways that it serves to elaborate or fill in relational matters. (Swidler's example here is how cultural configurations of 'love' are used to enact the often problematic institution of marriage, such that the action trajectories taken within the marriage institution may be understood as culturally 'caused'). To put this differently, her work suggests that institutions are not reproduced through norms and rules alone, particularly since those rules are often insufficient or ineffective for the purpose of enacting/reproducing institutions, but through the use of cultural devices and through the ways actors draw upon cultural repertoires.

Despite these obvious strengths, there are areas that the CR paradigm could develop, areas the full potential of which has not yet been explored. One obstacle to this exploration has been, as described in the next section, the CR focus's implicit commitment to cognitive and structural questions, and its tendency to sidestep the non-cognitive and aesthetic dimension of action. Exploring the non-cognitive, however, greatly enhances the explanatory value of CR theory. In particular, it highlights the quasi-conscious use of (and orientation to) cultural repertoires (a theme that is already implicit in the CR approach). And for this task, music is an excellent medium with which to think.

Two modifications of CR

Consider the following statement from Swidler:

If we look at culture by trying to understand what is in individuals' heads, we discover that people 'know' much more culture than they use . . . People make selections from their repertoire based on problems of action. Because they face many different kinds of problems with differing structures, they keep on tap multiple, sometimes discordant, skills, capacities and habits . . . Like a library that holds more books than any one person could ever read, a 'culture' contains an array of resources that people can draw on in different ways. (Swidler 2002:7)

There is no mistaking here a poetics of 'information processing'. 'Heads', 'knowing', 'selections', 'books', 'reading' 'problems', and the idea of culture as a resource to be mobilised – these are the linguistic components of a sociology oriented to a model of action-as-consciousness and action-as-choice – in the face of 'problems' and 'differing structures'. And yet, many 'decisions' (e.g., 'what to wear?' 'what food to serve?' 'what to say under difficult or sensitive circumstances?') are accomplished by feel or intuition, and as such are not well described by terms such as 'strategies', or 'skills', or 'selections'. Rather, many such so-called 'decisions' are made at an embodied or emotional (rather than conscious) level. (Indeed, there is a social stratification to the ability to mobilise arrays of cultural resources – a point beautifully captured by Peterson and Simkus's (1992) concepts of the omnivore and the univore modes of cultural consumption/skill in late twentieth-century American society.) In short, cultural action is not necessarily deliberate, problem-solving activity – one may be bound to cultural forms with varying degrees of tightness; one may not be able to 'select'; and one may respond or deploy culture in ways that elide cognition, deliberation. This point is nicely illustrated when we turn to the topic of music as cultural tool, in particular when we consider music's role on-location of action.

So much of music is consumed and 'acts' in ways that are at best semi-conscious and often tacit. The point so far has been that while the CR model is useful in highlighting culture's 'causal' connection to action, it simultaneously evades consideration of one of culture's key properties – its *aesthetic* (i.e., non-cognitive) dimension. Aesthetics, in other words, need to be rescued from their subservient role in relation of norms, roles, and institutions – to what is conventionally termed social structure.

The cultural repertoires focus has so far been employed to deal with the question of how actors set out to enact *institutional* arrangements, when they are presented with 'problems', the question of how to make those arrangements 'work' in practice – how, in ethnomethodology's vocabulary, actors 'get through' or 'pass' in and as certain 'types' of situations and agencies. Drawing upon Swidler's key example for illustration here, the CR approach would examine how actors draw upon socially distributed cultural tools so as to make a 'marriage' work, or to 'do' employer–employee or doctor–patient interaction, or otherwise to accomplish recognisable forms of situated action. Here, to paraphrase Swidler's 1986 article, we follow culture 'in action', that is, how culture becomes or provides action's schemas or scripts, ways of proceeding, lines of action, ways of *furnishing* or fleshing out scenarios and institutionalised relations. Culture, here, is both the medium through which these relations are performed (and so sustained) and also the medium through which these relations are specified; it is the 'accompaniment' or entailment (Swidler 2002:7) to – it is implied – rational or quasi-rational action.

For example, Swidler describes how, unlike the social construct, 'love', which has been portrayed in myriad guises via the media, literature, and popular discourse, the idea of 'marriage' has enjoyed relatively little cultural elaboration historically. In our own era, however, when marriage 'becomes more problematic' (2002:7) the relationship is subject to cultural elaboration (as, for example, via notions of communication, compromise, and commitment). Swidler's point is that the culture 'that organizes individual action emerges in the gaps institutions leave' (ibid.). The enactment of structure becomes, in other words, the act of problem-solving and resource allocation.

This statement implies that *structure* – relations and patterns of action and the norms associated with these patterns – remains, within the CR model, the ultimate quarry (and determinant) of action. By that logic, culture is the *means through which structures are worked out*. And this, in turn, implies that culture is not itself a medium through which structures are created. But does this view too quickly, albeit unintentionally, belittle culture's powers?

The CR model posits structure (e.g., the institution of marriage) implicitly as a given, while simultaneously seeking to show how structures are performed. To speak of structures as performed is to define structure as the retrospective accumulation of action, constantly renewed even when repeated. Structure is, in other words, merely a historical phenomenon. It is achieved through accumulated patterns of action which may provide a resource for the reconstitution of the present.

Consider Swidler's example of marriage. While the state and legal machinery, and the religious institutions of marriage, are all involved in stabilising that institution (as, for example, when bigamy is discovered or when divorce necessitates the division of property), these factors are not in the foreground of most marriages as experienced day-to-day. Even Giddens, who has himself been accused of reifying structure (King 1999; forthcoming) has observed that 'the structural properties of social systems exist only in so far as forms of social conduct are reproduced chronically across time and space' (1984:xxi).

So, culture is not merely a medium with which to realise pre-given structures and, a related point, culture is often an *end* of action – one does not simply use culture to 'do' (i.e., realise, reproduce) pre-existing or assumed structures (such as one's assumption of family or relationship norms), one may also tinker with what one takes to be 'given' structures, so as to achieve certain cultural ends, aspirations, and aims. (For example, an alternative aesthetic may drive innovatory social or institutional arrangements – including the organisation of intimacy.) For this reason, cultural media require exploration as media, not just instrumentalities, of action. That is, cultural media (such as music, but also culinary conventions, fashion, and any other material cultural practice) are not just the 'means' ('tools') to structural ends. Indeed, it is precisely on this topic that the CR model reveals its greatest promise for cultural sociology: with it we may be able to identify events, eras, scenes, or situations where *culture takes the lead* – think, for example, of the reaction to rock 'n' roll in the 1960s, or to the 'new look' for women after the Second World War, or to cubism in the early twentieth century – all of these things arguably permitted (i.e., afforded) actors new ways of being and new social arrangements – which was why reactions to all of these things were so widely polarised.

In short, the CR perspective, particularly when it is allowed to encompass the non-cognitive, takes culture seriously – as a tool that uses its user, a medium that mediates. Such a perspective helps to highlight how culture 'gets into' action; how what we do, imagine, and feel takes shape in and through cultural media. And this, in turn, permits a culturally bullish position wherein the study of cultural media provides an avenue into sociology's core concern with the origin and maintenance of social structures. (Indeed, this cultural bullishness is aimed at in the original CR formulations.) To posit cultural as 'causal' is to connect with neo-Durkheimian perspectives as outlined by a range of theorists who highlight the importance of theorising action as inhabiting and taking shape within a cultural matrix (e.g., Hetherington 1998; Hennion 1992). And, in that connection, a place is re-established for theorising the non-cognitive and the aesthetic dimensions of action. And it is here that we can begin to collect neo-Durkheimianism, CR theory, and Adorno into a common project, one that can now be illustrated through a discussion of music as an aesthetic medium of action. Adorno was concerned with how culture (music) could draw actors onto lines and trajectories of conduct, and how, in aligning particular, specific actors with generic and non-specific modalities of action, it was possible to see music providing a technology of control (one might more neutrally speak here of 'ordering', but to do so would be to erase Adorno's critical and historically informed analytical edge).

To speak of these issues is to speak of how culture (music) may configure its users/consumers. This issue gains *critical* saliency when music's users enter into musically mediated settings that have been framed by a sub-set of participants who may aim overtly to mediate conduct in particular (e.g., organisationally, institutionally, or politically congruent) ways. So, too, the converse – the focus on individuals or groups as they resist musically configured settings so as to resist the social implications of those settings, as, for example, in the case of Pipedown, the anti-muzak organisation discussed below.

When 'control' over others is sought through musical means, it is possible to speak of music as providing an 'anchoring' medium, one that may provide a centre of gravity around which other cultural repertoires/practices may come to be aligned. This point has been discussed in passing by Lanza (1994:11), where he describes Schopenhauer's notion of the 'deep relation which music has to the true nature of all things . . .', which, according to Schopenhauer, also explains the fact that '. . . suitable music played to any scene, action, event or surrounding seems to disclose to us its most secret meaning, and appears as the most accurate and distinct commentary upon it' (Schopenhauer, quoted in Lanza).

The issue to which Lanza (via Schopenhauer) points is that music may function as a contextualising device; it may frame social and environmental space. To speak of such framing is to say that music becomes, in the language of cultural repertoire theory, an anchoring device. How music comes to provide such anchors is then precisely what needs to be explored. Is it possible, in other words, to speak of putting a musical construction on a setting or space in ways that may provide a gravitational 'pull' – that have structuring properties – within that space?

A further addition to the CR paradigm

While actors may well deploy particular musical devices so as to accomplish particular institutional arrangements, and while I have described in the previous chapter actors as they mobilise music so as to perform emotional work in their personal lives (see also DeNora (2002b) for a discussion of how actors involved in 'love' relations may use music to fill in or establish the aesthetic parameters of a particular scene, whether via 'our song' music or through the choice of music for tête-à-tête interactions in a particular style), there is no explicit exploration, within the CR paradigm, of a non-strategic actor or of an actor who *happens upon* a particular scene where she confronts (perhaps at best semi-consciously) cultural media already established as the 'tools' of the setting. (Moreover, actors may 'know' that others are seeking to 'control' their action trajectories, comment upon this reflexively, and still fall into patterns of conduct that are congruent with musically implied styles. This is precisely what happened to me, as described in chapter 4, when I became musically 'interested' in a particular retail scene.)

In short, to the extent that the CR model remains a *cognitive* sociological model, assuming an agent who searches for and chooses certain 'tools', it elides one of the most obdurate features of interaction, namely, that most of interaction's settings are not unfurnished but come, by contrast, equipped with pre-existing ambient, atmospheric and pragmatic features and that in these situations, one may be compelled to 'do the job' with situation-specific, spatially and organisationally stipulated tools. Moreover, one may well act in ways that do not fully invoke or require deliberate thought. If anything, public spaces are often aesthetically over-determined. To examine the uptake of spatially provided aesthetic media is thus a task of the critical organisational study of 'control'. And it is here that the study of music in relation to such topics as the management of collective behaviour comes into its own. In what follows, I suggest that the study of music as a type of cultural material and the study of Adorno as a type of theorist both help to redress certain gaps and elisions in the CR model. Both highlight the often unconscious or semi-conscious dimension of action – its non-cognitive and often emotive dimensions, and the ways that it is often through these dimensions that action is 'structured'.

Sonic spaces and action as performance

As cultural geographers and others concerned with space have reminded us, space plays an important role in the production of identity (Hetherington 1998; Bennett 2000). This focus on space as a matrix for action is sociologically powerful because it is simultaneously a move away from individualist conceptions of action and – at least in part – also from cognitive-based, information-processing models of how action takes shape in real time.

There is a level on which the impact of cultural space – its 'causal' character – on action is obvious. Think, for example, of how there are probably certain types of action one might feel constrained or compelled to perform within different types of spaces – even when those spaces might not be furnished with actors. 'Public' versus 'private' spaces; 'sacred' versus 'profane' ones; spaces where one might automatically roll up one's sleeves or loosen one's necktie; spaces where one might speak formally rather than informally; and so on. At an experiential level, actors are often aware of space and its implications – its presence in relation to action – even if only at an embodied level.

In his study of the personal stereo in everyday use, Michael Bull has called attention to these points through the work of Henri Lefebvre's spatial analysis of urban experience:

Directly lived through its associated images and symbols, and hence the space of 'inhabiters' and 'users' . . . Representational space is alive: it speaks . . . bed, bedroom, dwelling house; or square, church, graveyard. It embraces the loci of passion, of action and lived situations . . . It . . . is essentially qualitative, fluid and dynamic. (Lefebvre, quoted in Bull, 2000:126)

In some life realms, such as with regard to the constitution of personal or intimate space (Wilson-Kovacs 2000) we may have a high degree of control over space and its impact on action. Wilson-Kovacs's research shows how actors are deeply involved in the crafting of time–space environments, which then become platforms for intimate conduct and intimate culture (including memories), configured in particular styles. In that work we see clearly the importance, and leading role played by, culture 'in action' as it is part of the matrix for the socio-cultural-physiological activities associated with intimacy. In other situations, however, actors may be constrained to 'make do' with the 'aesthetic' (sometimes perceived as 'anti-aesthetic') furniture of space, where options for its modification are minimal.

Lefebvre's work has been an inspiration for cultural-spatial studies in so far as it has called attention to *the idea* of spatial organisation as enfolding occupants into rhythms and trajectories of action. At the same time, it does not provide a means for empirical exploration of these issues, indeed, as critics have rightly suggested (Bull 2000), it tends to 'drift' towards determinism. How, then, may we illuminate aesthetic and symbolic space as it impinges upon the production of action, and how are we to account for the mechanisms of this operation? In what follows, I begin with two key senses in which space and action are linked. In the first sense (and one that is still congruent with Swidler's 'information-processing' metaphor, but which takes that model to cases where information processing and interpretive orientation to space may not involve deliberation or conscious awareness), spaces may foster the use of particular cultural repertoires through the materials they place on offer, through atmosphere, objects, and other scenic features and through the ways that these materials may provide information that allows user-occupants to make 'appropriate' behavioural responses within those spaces. In the second, moving beyond the information-processing connotations of cultural repertoires, spaces may also afford less rational forms of adaptive action through the ways they appeal to memory, the body, and the senses. With regard to both of these, *music* and more broadly *sound* is key. For space – aesthetic space – is often, probably always aural (cf. John Cage's experience in an anechoic chamber (Cage 1961:8)).

An invisible source of information?

Social psychologists of music have been concerned with the empirical documentation of sound and action, mainly through experimental and quasi-experimental methods of investigation. One of the most common 'spaces' to be explored in this context is the retail space, where music is deliberately deployed so as to influence purchase and browsing behaviour (see DeNora 2000, ch. 5).

The retail space is heuristically useful as a case-in-point. A setting linked to clear organisational aims and sub-aims – the purveyance of goods and the accumulation of profit; the accumulation of symbolic capital in the form of reputation (e.g., as 'cool', or 'trendy', or 'reliable') – it allows for the assessment of whether it is possible to structure space so as to afford particular – and organisationally preferred – forms of action. For example, in a study conducted in a wine cellar (Areni and Kim 1993), music was linked to purchase behaviour – not to the quantity of bottles sold but rather to the cost of individual purchases. When classical music was played, customers bought more expensive wines than they did when Top 40 music was played. Picking up on earlier work by MacInnis and Park (1991), which focused on music and advertisements, the authors suggested that customers adapted their purchase behaviour so as to 'fit' it to perceived ambience, more specifically, they reacted to the situational cues provided by the music. Music, in other words, provided resources for sense-making within the social setting; it helped to configure the space as a space fit for particular action strategies and trajectories and in this capacity, music's structuring powers 'showed up' in conduct. With Mozart playing in the background of a wine shop, so the reasoning goes, one is likely to feel out of place asking a sales assistant for a large bottle of 'Mad Dog 20/20'! Music can, if actors acknowledge and connect to it in certain ways, enable and constrain behaviour in so far as that behaviour is 'action' – meaningfully oriented in its course.

The concept of 'fit' is one that helps to highlight how cultural repertoires come to be invoked as actors hone in on particular cues and adjust their conduct according to what seems appropriate. In this respect, music is again special because, unlike objects that are localised in particular regions of a given space, music, like ambient temperature, lighting, or fragrance, is diffused through space. Music, then, to the extent that it remains audible, is a *global* condition of space.

In this sense, music may help to frame the perception of that space, as it did in the study described above by Areni and Kim. Music may *prime* the ways that actors attend to other initially less obvious features of a space, in the case of retail spaces, for example, the goods distributed for display and purchase across space such that music with 'high culture' connotations may 'announce' the space and the goods as 'up-market'. The aesthetic configuration of space thus provides information; it offers cues about types and styles of acts, and the various social-psychological experiments that have been conducted in shops and supermarkets seem to show how human beings orient to these cues, often in subliminal ways, as they engage in patterns of behaviour that involve choices or rival lines of conduct.

Musical styles and genres provide cues about the spaces within which they are aired. To the extent that such cues are interpreted and can be seen to be linked to the modification or formulation of conduct, it is possible to speak of music as a condition of action. Examples of modification or formulation of conduct here include interrelated things such as the alteration of *conduct style* (e.g., hushed or sombre versus boisterous, exuberant); *behavioural modification* (an actor who enters a room shouting and quickly modifies the volume of her speech, for example); or *personal roles*, as when an actor who implies through her behaviour certain promissory or identifiable information about who s/he is or is likely to 'be' over the duration of the interaction (e.g., a physician shifts from a 'friendly' or 'caring' persona during consultation to a 'clinical' persona while conducting the actual examination).

Simultaneously the study of this modification/formulation illuminates behaviour *as conduct*, as, in Max Weber's sense, social action, that is meaningfully oriented action, action that takes shape with reference to things that the actor perceives, consciously or in some non-cognitive way, as lying outside of her/himself. So, for example, the wine consumers described by Areni and Kim and by North, Hargreaves, and McKendrick (1997) establish 'fit' between their purchase behaviour and what they perceive (with varying degrees of conscious awareness) as ambience. Critically, in that case, the 'fit' that is established is achieved through a one-way modification – the actor, upon entering the retail space, modified his/her behaviour to fit the perceived context. It is thus possible here then to speak of musical space as 'configuring' (and indeed 'controlling') the actor's social response, to see aesthetic environment as it becomes a constitutive, structuring factor of action. The implications of this point are worth further development here, because the concept of 'fit' as developed by social psychologists is, I suggest, just the tip of the sociological iceberg.

Sympathy in C major

Humans seem to have a tendency to fall in with the aesthetic tenor of situations and not necessarily consciously, as one does when one makes, for example, 'an effort to be cheerful'. Often we find ourselves falling into emotional and embodied modes that 'fit' with settings and without any conscious effort. One might be tempted to posit a human capacity for co-operation – co-operation not only with other humans but also with the action-implications of ambience. Such a capacity extends well beyond the more critical notion initially described by Riesman of other-directedness. This propensity for co-operation is part of our social skill, part of what enables us to collaborate and act in concert so as to achieve collective endeavours. This capacity extends well beyond sense-making and also beyond the ability to do what has been verbally or rationally stipulated (e.g., 'you hold that end and I'll hold this end'). It extends to more embodied and tacit matters (e.g., how we may have a feeling that the load is too heavy for the other person) and to aesthetic/stylistic matters (e.g., how are we to play this? softly or shall we 'come over heavy?'). It is this capacity for co-operation that organisations such as retail outlets use to their advantage. What is sought – and sometimes achieved – is nothing less than to induce us to engage in emotional work, to engage co-operatively and bodily in the co-operation with a cultural representation or mode of being/doing (see chapter 4). We seek to 'fit' ourselves into situations and spaces as we perceive them. True, we do not always do this – we may resist particular scenic implications and we may seek to modify what can be done in particular spaces. But – and especially when we are tired, uncertain, marginalised, or unmindful – we often fall into repertoires that are anchored by particular cultural materials, such as music.

The research conducted by social psychologists North and Hargraeves (1997) underlines music's power to provide a structured environment within which purchase behaviour is constructed – in the face of uncertainty. Their work shows how two different types of music may (as Lanza describes via Schopenhauer in the passage quoted earlier) frame perception and desirability of products displayed. In the presence of stereotypical French music (accordion/Parisian bistro), an actor may, without conscious awareness of the sources of her action, choose French wine rather than German from a foregrounded display. Conversely, when German 'um-pa' music plays, the same actor may opt for the German produce, the point being that action is fitted to ambience and ambience is anchored through music. As North and Hargreaves have observed, music is more likely to function effectively here when the consumer is not knowledgeable or uncertain about which product to buy, that is, when she has not already anchored her action in terms of some idea(s), plan, or some aesthetic orientation she brings with her to the purchase environment.

In this situation, a musically foregrounded line of action is further structured by the spatial distribution of that suggestion. The physical environment has also been engineered so as to structure 'choice'. And 'choice' here is better conceived as a kind of sub-logical, aesthetic, if not emotional, form of action, a form of action, moreover, that is coherent and that makes sense within the highly structured aesthetic-material environment of the supermarket wine section. 'Choice' here is the co-operation, quasi-consciously, with a mode of conduct environmentally implied. Alternatively, the music may 'remind' the consumer, in a highly prepositional way, of the pleasures of one product over another. Here, then, music becomes information (albeit not prepositional information) and as such it may 'suggest' a line of conduct (e.g., 'remember: German wine').

In either of these cases, music may help to frame perception of some things rather than others; that is, music may be a condition of perception and/or information-processing; it may highlight or suppress the recognition of some features of a setting. So, for example, the German wine may 'seem' foregrounded due to the ways the German music may 'point' to it. Or – when things go wrong – music may serve to underline certain deficiencies of a setting. To take a purely hypothetical example (harking back once more to Schopenhauer), Chopin's Funeral March played in, say, a busy fast-food burger bar, *might* put consumers off their food because its connotations (sombre, funereal, slow) run in contrast to conventional ideas of the fast-food aesthetic, with its synthetic cheeriness and brisk service/consumption. Less hypothetical examples – in relation to in-flight music – are described in DeNora (2000): certain songs are simply banned from in-flight entertainment because they reframe or anchor the meaning of that (airborne) space in ways that disturb. In anything, these issues in relation to air travel are heightened as air travel has become more intensely associated with terrorism.

Even after the music stops (e.g., when consumers get home with their purchases), the aesthetic environment and its structuring capacities may be consequential for conduct, specifically for the ways in which in-store purchase decisions come to be integrated into later conduct at the time of product consumption (e.g., what one then cooks or chooses to eat; how one dresses for dinner; or the spirit into which one enters when engaging in these things). Indeed, this point raises the question of how actors translate themselves from one space, situation, and scene to the next; how they may reflexively incorporate earlier performances or attitudes into later settings and scenes; and how they may attempt to thread together different times and scenes into larger structures. To speak of this issue is to speak of how action or 'choice' on occasion A may provide repertoire or *modus operandi* for occasions B, C, and D. Actors may also pick up or learn new strategies from the spaces through which they move over the course of a day, week, or lifetime, such that the modification of action within scene A may lead to a raft of modifications in other scenes as a new style or conduct option is either learned or rediscovered.

Critical here is that the deployment of a conduct option or style (e.g., 'let's go with the German style tonight rather than the French') is dependent upon the actor's recognition of something familiar, generic, conventional. To the extent, then, that 'fit' is established between music and conduct, we may speak of music's recognisably semiotic content, and in particular its ability to reference other things (in this case, a style of being/choosing that is different from another style of being/choosing – 'German' versus 'French'). It is this *familiarity* that is responsible, then, for music's capacity to structure (or help to structure) conduct – actors recognise something that they perceive, consciously or not, as suggesting a familiar line of conduct or a familiar style of being, and they in turn act upon that familiarity. This is nothing less than action, conventionally facilitated. Here, then, music is one of the cues for tuning in to at least a semblance of what is socially shared.

We have come a long way from Adorno's notion that music simply 'conditions' or, in some deterministic way, 'controls' its hearers. By contrast, music is a medium to which agents may turn as they engage in their routine, full-time sense-making procedures in real-time daily life. Music structures action, but only reflexively, in so far as it is acted upon, i.e., recognised as a condition of action by participants. That we do, often, orient our conduct (and emotions) to musical settings may be due to our tendency to process music in ways that elide consciousness. Music is perhaps a highly insidious medium in the spaces of daily life and, for this reason, it is of critical concern to pose questions about how music is deployed within spaces, particularly public and quasi-public spaces (see DeNora (1986b) for a more detailed discussion of 'work' in relation to musical sense-making).

It is here that the notion of 'fit' can be considered in relation to Adorno's work, in particular where his analysis of the 'pseudo-individualism' of popular music makes most sense. Adorno suggested that pop songs had to be both familiar and unfamiliar, that is they had to conform to formulas while still providing surface differences from each other, rather as groups of individuals following a particular fashion (e.g., formal evening dresses, hair styled or coloured in current mode) seek both to conform well to a particular image but also show distance from it – a kind of personalised conformity. Richard Middleton alludes to this process and how it inculcates a prefabricated realm of musical genera:

Because of popular music's ubiquity and vast scale of production, it has been possible to establish in the collective mind a set of conventional musical 'colours' – 'Spanish', 'pastoral', 'cowboy', 'blue', 'hippie', 'punk', and so on – and arrangers and producers can simply lift the technical devices needed for these ready-made veneers off the shelf when needed . . . In a sense, anything – even 'modernist' dissonance or punk 'anti-vocal' singing – can become clichéd and pseudo-individual, as many TV commercials testify. But does what is an un-doubted tendency justify Adorno's extrapolation of a monolithic law, today or in respect of the 1930s? (1990:50)

Middleton frames his answer to this question in the negative. The more intensely one looks at popular music, the more differentiated it appears. In part, Middleton argues, popular music only seemed monolithic, ho-mogeneous to Adorno given the distance from which Adorno chose to observe it, given his 'abstractionism' (Middleton 1990:54):

The lack of analysis of specific songs in Adorno's writings means that it is impos-sible to know whether he is talking about real pieces or, more likely, ideal types. In fact, there seems to be a kind of Ur-pop song in Adorno's mind – to which no actual song, however standardized, could totally conform. (ibid.)

By contrast, Middleton suggests that the 'standardization' so disdained by Adorno may, in the context of 'world music' be better, and less pe-joratively, conceived as 'formulaic' (1990:55). As Middleton notes (and as has been discussed in chapter 1), not only does a good deal of folk music follow predictable patterns, so too does a good deal of Western art music. Adorno's analysis, Middleton goes on to suggest, is coloured by a post-Beethovenian musical system of value, one that lauds individ-ual 'genius' and in which transformative aesthetics (the idea of breaking formulas) are enshrined. What is missed by such a value system is an emphasis on socially shared and facilitated co-ordination, on collectively shared ways of doing – the value of conventions as enabling – not only as constraining. Following this critique of Adorno by Middleton, and applying it to the issue of music's role within organisational-managerial cultures, one might suggest that it is not formulas *per se* that are prob-lematic (there may be as many ways of responding to French accordion music as there are French cheeses). Rather, the ways in which the generic *formulas* come to be used and lodged within social spaces/times such that their reception and use comes to be structured in particular ways is at issue. Within the supermarket, for example, it is irrelevant whether there are a thousand responses to 'French-style' music; it is irrelevant just what individuals may remember or feel when they hear this music; only rele-vant is that these myriad responses come to be expressed in the uniform manner of a purchase decision *here and now* in favour of French wine. And that shaping of action, via the aesthetic environment, helps to illu-minate music as it comes to be lodged within a wider network of objects and symbolic meanings, how it may serve as an anchoring medium and how more generally it is part of a scenic space.

Contingency and micro-meaning

So far the issue of music and 'control' has dealt with music as a 'global' constant, a condition to which actors may orient as they formulate and engage in action. This is an appropriate way to think about music within confined space, in indoor environments, where music 'fills the space' – for example, when it is relayed via speakers and amplifiers throughout a space.

At the same time, music is not a global 'constant'. Unlike lighting (particularly within an indoor shopping mall, where individual stores have no shop-front mirrors), thermostatically controlled temperature or – to a lesser extent – in-store fragrance (e.g., the various smells of the clothes, incense, room 'freshener'), music is a temporal medium and this aspect of music – one of its specifically musical properties – must not be ignored.

Most of the time, and in music from a wide range of cultures and times, music is understood through its production of sonic *variation* – change – over time. In this sense, music is arguably one of the most dynamic global conditions of (indoor) space. Indeed, all the other conditions of space that are characterised by the same degree of temporal flux – conversation and the movement of bodies, an individual's free association of thought or shifting centres of attention, for example – are produced interactively. Music is arguably the only pre-ordained aesthetic material of space that is intrinsically temporal in character. And, because of this, music may be referred to by actors as a medium against which the temporal flow of activity or attention is constituted.

For example, within a musically temporalised space, it is possible to follow subject-bodies as they interact and are entrained with music – not just finger snapping, toe tapping, or dance movements, but the mundane choreography of movement style as this includes such things as posture, degree of flowing or disjointed movement, pace and rhythm of movement, level of arousal (e.g., degree of muscle tension, energy, focus, and, in some cases, physiological matters such as pulse and blood pressure, breathing, temperature). Various social psychological and consumer research studies have emphasised the links between music and levels of arousal, albeit only in the broad brush strokes of statistical correlations between time spent in a shop or other commercial setting and the tempo of ambient music (Milliman 1982; 1986; Smith and Curnow 1966; for discussions of this work see DeNora 2000 and North and Hargreaves 1997). What remains, as I describe below, is to attempt to map musical-experiential time spent within a particular setting; to investigate the specific fluctuations that may occur there and then to link these fluctuations to the formation of subjectivity and agency in real time.

Within different musical environments (and within environments as they are musically modified over time), one may be and become different types of being. This being is linked to and may provide a basis for one's subjective sense of self and occasion. One may happen upon oneself, for example, with racing heart and identify the process as, variously, a feeling of love, fear, or exhilaration. One may, in other words, engage in cultural interpretation by attributing meanings to the states within which one finds oneself as an embodied actor. And, in this sense, the body may lead social action in that it may serve as one of the resources with which the situation in which it finds itself is defined, in which meaningful trajectories for action are executed. 'This comes from the heart', we may say, to allude to how our emotional, embodied being may have led us to make a particular action move. As it plays through time, music may provide a culturally connotative referent against which real-time embodied subjectivity takes shape. And those bodily manifestations themselves take shape and come to be known to their subject-owners in interaction with cultural-material (e.g., musical) environments. Here, again, we are some distance from Adorno's initially deterministic conception of music and its effects: we may investigate links between ambient music, embodiment, self perception, and action style/action trajectory in real time and social-material-cultural-technical space. Indeed, it is precisely this set of links that providers of ambient music exploit, though typically fail to theorise.

Music over time/music and temporal–spatial experience

In earlier work (DeNora 2000), I described how changing patterns of music over time and the musical presentation of specific musical features in time could be used to create particular musical contexts within which some forms of action, emotion, and embodiment came to be heightened (enabled/afforded) while others were suppressed (constrained/ not afforded). In these examples of aerobic music 'consumption', music was not, for most of the time, attended to as if it were information or a 'meaningful' medium. Rather, it was a medium that recipients perceived in more bodily ways, as bodies responding to its properties – as 'users' of (or those used by) music. The songs used for aerobics were not songs that exercise-class participants consumed or recognised as aesthetic objects (for example, most class participants did not actually recall or recognise the songs outside the context of the exercise classes). Rather, the music was consumed and responded to in ways that were peripheral to focused consciousness. Joseph Lanza's description of muzak's role in relation to perception captures this point nicely. He says (1994:3), 'mood music shifts music from figure to ground, to encourage peripheral hearing.

Psychoanalysts might say that it displaces our attention from music's manifest content to its more surreal latent content', one that may shift or proceed 'with a rhythm and logic indifferent to our own'.

For example, within aerobic activity, rhythm and modulation often worked to 'chunk' or package time in ways that enlisted participants to keep moving, that minimised the self-perception of fatigue, and that created a virtual sense of moving through space, e.g., 'upwards' (nearing the top), downwards (gliding easily), or into 'open space' versus 'closed space'. I described how music did this by enlisting the body, by entraining bodily activity, such that embodied conduct came to be synchronised with musical structures. In these ways, and others, music offers a medium that – according always to listener orientation – is capable of drawing its recipients into particular trajectories, by which I mean modes, styles, and forms of agency. To speak of 'drawing recipients into particular trajectories' is, of course, also to speak of modifying recipients' current trajectories, their current modes of embodied and subjective being, and I shall return to this point below when I turn to an example from music therapy.

As we saw in chapters 3 and 4, music may remind listeners of past events and more generic, social ways of being. It may also serve as a referent against which feeling states are constituted and embodied activity organised, comported. The aerobics research found that that music could be used to facilitate bodily recalibration, and that this process occurred when embodied listeners became entrained with music's rhythms or otherwise tuned in to music's structural and sometimes connotative features (always only in so far as they perceived/oriented to these features). The research found that it was possible, using music, to 'trick' the body (and the self-perception of bodily states), something that was clearly visible in the context of a 45-minute exercise session. Music provides, in other words, frames against which corporeal-subjective being takes shape and is reflected upon by subjects in real time, from moment to moment. Music is thus an instrument of corporeal-emotional change in real time, and the overall patterns of mood, emotion, and bodily conduct that it facilitates may be linked to trajectories of behaviour, conduct, and social action. The real time 'unit' of musically facilitated activity may be only a moment, even a few seconds, as was described in chapter 4 ('*un moment musical*'). It may be an hour or two between friends or intimates (DeNora 2002b). Or it may be an entire work day on the factory floor, an example of which I shall consider below.

The point is simply this: *music, as it moves through time and changes over time, provides a device with which subject-bodies orient to and configure themselves within the environments within which music plays. In this respect, music is a powerful means for reconfiguring ambience, and for doing so in ways that have the power to shift subjective orientation to space in real time. And to the extent that this is so, music may serve as a device of social ordering and social control.*

At a practical level, music workers know these things well. Music providers of all persuasions, from all types of taste communities and musical-spatial environments, not only provide music but also think hard about how the music they provide should be *arranged so as to produce an evaluative-affective response of some kind.* J. S. Bach employed various musical devices, 'to organise the congregation through music' as he put it. A crucial feature of this organisation was the concept of affection, the link between music and affect, music and feeling and the means for binding humankind, for gathering disparate individuals into a fold, a social rhythm of affective states.

Leo Shrade, in his famous essay *Bach: The Conflict Between the Sacred and the Secular*, describes this desire for 'organisation' as follows:

Affection was to the man of the baroque age perhaps the deepest secret of life. It was like an inexhaustible force always striving from within outward to find expression in human gestures; we are not able to say whence it comes, or what it is that continually renews it. This force retained its mysterious character in the music of the baroque. Men of the age were spontaneous in their understanding of the affections, because they felt in themselves their power. They thought of them as the various states through which man manifests his life in relation to the world. The succession of these states would form a dynamic rhythm rising and falling like a tide though his whole being, stirring body and soul alike. It is this rhythm that controlled the baroque conception of art. (Shrade 1955:133–4)

After Bach, composers no longer spoke of music's effects in these terms. And yet, the concern with 'organising' the listener was by so no means set aside in classical music. It can be found equally in the conventions and practices of Haydn and his contemporaries as it can in Beethoven, though the discourses within which that desire is couched change over time. Nineteenth-century composers of symphonic music provided different types of music for beginnings and endings (a slow second movement but a rousing finale) not just because this ordering is conventional but because the convention is itself linked to a conventional occupational objective, the desire for hearty applause, for a 'roused' audience. Implicitly, 'ending' music is oriented to reconfiguring the listener (the same listener who heard the slow second movement, moreover) so that s/he is aroused in a particular way at the close of the work. The pyrotechnical displays of the nineteenth-century virtuosi similarly sought to stir listener-observers, at times to fill them with terror or awe. Eighteenth-century composers, by contrast, felt constrained by convention to include a minuet, the favoured dance of aristocrats.

So, too, popular music draws upon conventional materials and patterns of arranging music to 'organise' its recipients, not only via genre, but via the generic patterning of feeling structure in real time. Conceived in this way, music may be posed as a medium within which subjectivity may be understood as a process; music offers external models of feeling patterning, models that may become, for particular individuals, exemplars of their own feeling states (as described in chapter 4). A particular type of song – a ballad versus an up-tempo, high-energy number – offers itself as a candidate within a generic slot, that it will 'work' in a particular way upon its listener(s) not only to suggest general attitudes, moods, and lines of conduct that are 'fitting', but also to provide structures of feeling. Music provides a grammar of emotion – it shows us feeling's structures, how the peaks and troughs of emotion might interrelate, how, when, and with what intensity feeling may climax or crystallise. This concern with configuring the listener applies equally to disc jockeys who attempt to manipulate energy levels over the course of an evening. And it applies in workplace settings where muzak is paced so as to bolster productivity and prevent 'worker fatigue' – slower-paced music in the mornings, more 'up-beat' music after lunch as energies start to flag.

There is still a long way to go if we are to open up the black box of just how music functions as a device of social ordering (and 'control'). As North and Hargreaves noted in their survey of research devoted to the topic of music and consumer behaviour (1997:282):

. . . the many commercial uses to which music is put, and the amount of money spent on these, far out-weigh the extent to which empirical research has provided clear guidance for commercial practitioners [one might add, and also for those who remain critical of the commercial and organisational uses to which music is put]. Although the number of studies has grown over the past two decades, there is still a clear need for research that replicates earlier investigations (Hubbard 1994); that refines and extends the tentative empirical modes described above; and that investigates severely neglected areas such as the effect of music on employees . . .

Note their terminology: 'the effect of music on . . .': the investigative lens needs to be widened here from studies of consumer behaviour in relation to, or arising from, exposure to music. We need to examine music's role as a medium of social organisation – and 'control' – far more generally. To do this, it is necessary to study actual Musical Events, occasions in which music comes to be linked to modes of embodied, emotional, and aesthetic agency that are not only congruent with but desired by actors, institutions, or organisations who deploy particular types of music so as to draw individuals or groups more closely towards those modes of agency. Perhaps the most obvious case in point here is the music therapeutic event.

Music as a medium of therapeutic 'control'

Consider this extended quote from an interview with a music therapist (DeNora and Belcher n.d.):

This is a little boy that I worked with who . . . has got no sight . . . I worked with him for a long time and when we first started it was very obvious that music was the only thing he related to. He would often be found banging his head in a classroom very disturbed . . . if they put a music tape on he would calm down and in sessions he would bite me on the way to the room but when we were in the room as soon as I started playing it was alright. So what you will notice about this session is that I am playing incessantly and it does feel like incessant. When we first started I would play in the middle of the piano and what I would do is that he would walk around the room feeling his way around the room tapping rhythms on things and I would be following all his rhythms very much like [she names another client where she uses a similar practice]. Just taking out what he gave me and following that. And then gradually he started, you will see that there is a much more two way interaction and that . . . if we played the piano together he would be right up one end and nowhere near me and now he is actually coming right over to me and he is asking me for physical touch as well which is, in autistic people, often they can be frightened of physical touch. So he is actually asking for that but he won't let me volunteer it. His rules are quite rigid about that. And also when I first started he was very, very frustrated and had very loud banging on the drum and I accompanied with very discordant music most of the time so it is quite a different sort of little boy really that we are seeing here. Another thing is he used to get in a real state when the session came to the end. He would start screaming and banging . . . so what I wanted to do was to make sure that the beginning and the end were really clear so that he has always the same hello song at the beginning and then it was because the end was a problem I needed to do what I do in the beginning. I ignore any rhythms he is doing when I am doing the hello song; I am in charge then. The middle section is I am following him mostly and then when it comes to the end I am taking control again and not listening to his, well I am listening but not responding to his [music], so I play the tune of his hello song this sounds a bit sort of a strange way of doing it but I play the tune of his hello song to signify that I have taken control again and then I play the goodbye song so you will hear that at the end.

In this passage, a music therapist describes some of the mechanisms through which, on that and on other occasions with her client, music (conceived in its broadest terms as organised sound) provides a medium of 'control'. First, the simple presence of music ('playing incessantly') mediated the client's behaviour. It captured his attention in some way that diverted him from his previous train of activity and so drew him in or *interested* him in its properties, unfolding over time. Second, the therapist describes how, in the beginning of their sessions together, as the boy walked around the room, exploring his therapeutic environment, she simply 'followed' all his musical utterances ('feeling his way around the room tapping rhythms on things'). In this way she was providing, through a medium that had managed to capture his attention, a way of performing an environment that was capable to reflecting, via music, the client's presence to himself. Through her musical mirroring activities ('Just taking out what he gave me and following that'), she was able to 'show' the client to himself, to draw him on to a plane on which he would be able to recognise himself, musically, through the echo of his utterances. Another way of putting this is to suggest that the client was able to identify with the sounds made by his environment, eventually recognising those sounds as made not by the 'environment' but by another person in that environment, and it is at precisely that point that the client becomes a (musically) empowered, social actor. And as he is drawn into the social activity of making music together he gradually begins to forget his earlier fear of physical proximity and thus overcome his autistic tendencies ('if we played the piano together he would be right up one end and nowhere near me and now he is actually coming right over to me and he is asking me for physical touch'). Finally, music becomes the medium within which time is defined and packaged and the purpose of that time stipulated:

I ignore any rhythms he is doing when I am doing the hello song; I am in charge then. The middle section is I am following him mostly and then when it comes to the end I am taking control again and not listening to his, well I am listening but not responding to his [music], so I play the tune of his hello song this sounds a bit sort of a strange way of doing it but I play the tune of his hello song to signify that I have taken control again and then I play the goodbye song so you will hear that at the end.

Gradually, as the client grows secure in his musical environment, as he learns that he can manipulate it, as he hears his own musical utterances mirrored back to him, he is drawn into the fold of a socio-musical frame; he begins to interact within that frame, responding in turn to things that are offered to him. He becomes, over time, receptive to a musical form of interaction and is thus drawn out of himself.

A musical-social plane for action

In the example above, we saw how a music therapy client was drawn out of or away from a mode of action that was uncoordinated with the social world of others. The point of his music therapy was to provide him with an alternative basis for action, a medium that, while it provided him with a means for expression, simultaneously disciplined him through its objective properties (e.g., when he was playing the piano he could not also engage in biting or self-destructive physical behaviour patterns, simply

TIME 1 – Before the Event (all prior history as meaningful to **A** Actor(s))

1. Preconditions
musical associations are gradually established by the therapist through repetition over time

---

TIME 2 – a particular music therapy session

2. Features of the Event

    A Actor(s) music therapist and client

    B Music 'hello song' versus improvisational middle section

    C Act of Engagement with music client's musical 'utterances' are supported by therapist in middle section. Client is unable to affect what therapist does during the opening and closing performance of the 'hello song'

    D Local conditions of C therapy sought to build up pattern over time of music as scheduling device so as to enlist client in co-ordination activity

    E Environment music therapy room. In what setting does engagement with music take place (material cultural features, interpretive frames provided on site [e.g., programme notes, comments of other listeners];

TIME 3 – After the Event

3. Outcome The client 'learns' which form of conduct 'go with' different types of musical material. He cannot alter the 'hello song', despite attempts. Over time, he decreases his attempts to play his own music when the 'hello song' is being played by the therapist. Musical material comes to be associated with behavioural 'material'. The client has achieved a co-ordination task.

Fig. 12. Musical material establishes mutual orientation to the temporal organisation of a situation.

because, to make music, he had to divert his physical activities to the task at hand). This diversion is, simultaneously, a conversion with others similarly diverted – music-making, in so far as it requires certain bodily discipline and bodily entrainment (co-ordination, turn taking, imitation, mutual recognition), simultaneously draws its participants onto a plane or basis for action that is shared. In this respect, at this basic pragmatic level so well described by Schutz in his essay 'Making Music Together', actors are controlled: they control themselves so as to make music; and the making of music in turn controls them, renders them similar. While they make music, their differences are momentarily obliterated: they act 'in concert'.

    While there is a world of difference between this music therapy client and a consumer in an ambient retail environment, the similarities are also worth exploring since, in both cases, attempts are made (albeit for quite different types of ends) by music therapist/managers to 'control' conduct. In both cases, music is used to divert clients, to draw them onto a plane above or outside of that upon which their trajectories of activity would otherwise occur. So, for example, just as the music therapist seeks to draw her client into mutual (musical) engagement, retail outlets seek to draw consumers into engagement with goods. In both cases there is an instrumental, managerial aim, though in the first case that aim is considered legitimately congruent with the client's 'interests', whereas in the second it is above all congruent with the organisation's. Also in both cases, music can be used to reinforce particular senses of things. In the music therapeutic sessions, music is used interactively and flexibly to 'mirror' the client's real-time utterances and thus 'show' him to himself via a kind of mirroring. In stores, as I have discussed above in relation to the concept of 'fit', music may be used to signal particular generic and typical social contexts and so 'remind' consumers of themselves as *types* of beings, and to provide soundscapes in which aspects of their being that are not congruent with the objectives of the setting/event are ignored (for example, just as the client could not 'get anywhere' musically interactively when his therapist was playing his 'hello' song, so, too, consumers in store may not be able to 'get' to or invoke particular cultural repertoires or aspects of self-identity while particular types of music sound). This is to say that music may provide parameters for, and indeed on occasion trigger, cultural practice, identity work, and thus, action. Once reminded, and without conscious reflection, actors may then fall into 'role', they may 'fit' themselves to the musically implied situation – that is, to their readings of that situation. And, in both cases, music may instigate emotional fluctuations in real time, as such serving as a device for regulating arousal, as we have seen in the example here of music therapy, and in the aerobics example, and in the example of a surge of emotion in real time. Finally, music may – often very subtly – imply information about the scheduling of action, about, for example, when something is beginning or ending, or when a particular phase (e.g., a high point, a low point) is being approached. In a shop, then, soundtracks may provide a resource through which consumer attention and subjectivity are recalibrated, and through which the temporal structure of that subjectivity – its shape and intensity over time – varies.

Different musical formats may, then, prove more or less useful according to their settings of use. Within the retail clothing sector (and in relation to musically untrained or uneducated consumers), shorter musical works may be most useful in so far as 2–3-minute selections may provide a matrix where emotional shifts and fluctuations may occur more rapidly than in longer works, where logics and build-ups may be extensive and thus less likely to induce the kind of emotional fluctuations conducive to a locally generated, short-term *desire for* goods, the consummation of which constitutes a 'point of purchase' ('impulse') buy, a connection between organisational aim (to sell) and consumer behaviour (to buy). Moreover, in so far as shorter selections facilitate rapid shift between different stylistic poses that a retail space offers its visitors, they dynamise that space; that is, musical selections – and the changes between selections – may highlight first one and then another facet of the retail space, like a revolving set, in which first one and then another cluster of attitudes may be implied (e.g., a sentimental ballad versus an up-beat dance number may call one to attention/action in quite different ways, may invoke, within a particular Musical Event, different aspects, orientations, and feelings in a particular listener or group of listeners). To imply such attitudes is simultaneously to highlight some aspects of the space, aspects which may be 'read' by consumers as 'going with' ('fitting') that space and thus logical purchase items (e.g., French not German wine). Within retail settings, in other words, the organisational aim may be to encourage consumers to 'try on' as many personae as possible during their (usually brief) visit to the space, a strategy that increases the engagement with goods and thus the likelihood that some sort of connection will be made between ambience, disposition, display, and purchase.

Putting music to work

Seen from the perspectives outlined so far, it is easy to understand why employers would ban certain music from the workplace. Music is a resource to which subject-bodies may appeal; in this appeal, levels of arousal are constituted, some of which may not be commensurate with organisational-cultural commitments. Music may imply 'information' about appropriate modes of conduct and social roles; it may remind hearers of styles of activity and situations. In these ways, music is an instrument of 'control', part of the environmental apparatus that highlights some modes of being and, in so doing, suppresses others. In the workplace, then, music may highlight potential lines of conduct and attitudes, it may sketch particular modes of subjectivity. Simultaneously, it may suppress others, just as particular modes of workplace dress (company uniforms, whether of the suit-and-tie variety or the name-badge overall) or décor may (Witkin 1995).

In a recent study of the history of music in the workplace (Korczynski 2003), this issue has been highlighted. Korczynski traces the shift from music's role as a tool for the self-pacing and self-regulation of work under pre-industrial work relations to music's role in relation to machine-paced and management-regulated work pace and its attendant, 'passive consent'. He suggests, rightly, that insufficient attention has so far been devoted to the question of how music in the workplace may be subliminally pacing productivity while simultaneously buoying mood. There is much more to such research, as Korcznski suggests, than can be gleaned by examining workplace music via the 'coffins of their text' (Korczynski here quotes Michael Pickering (1982:2)). Workplace music, thus understood, is a tool, part of a repertoire of social action on-site.

For these reasons actors may try to renegotiate or resist organisational ambience. The various organisations against piped music attest to this. On its website, for example, the British (and increasingly international) organisation against piped music, Pipedown, decries:

Cows, when being milked, are supposedly more productive if lulled by piped music; the same principle is used to stupefy us into mindlessness before parting us from our money, votes, wits
(Pipedown web site: http://www.btinternet.com/~pipedown/about.htm)

Pipedown has so far been successful in persuading Gatwick Airport and some UK supermarkets to withdraw piped music from its sites. It has also managed to achieve successful media coverage after a range of colourful protest activities (e.g., a bagpiper and Pipedown group who marched through one of London's large department stores in 1999). So, too, it has acquired high-level support from UK media personalities (e.g., Spike Milligan, John Humphreys).

At an individual level, too, aural environments may be resisted, and in exploring the nature of that resistance we can see yet more clearly just what it means to speak of music as a medium of 'control'. This issue is well illustrated by Michael Bull's study (as described briefly in chapter 4) of personal stereo use (2000), where in-depth interview respondents describe how the personal stereo is a device with which they manage (redefine, resist) the phenomenological aspects of space, time, and occasion. By changing the music (via headphones and personal stereo), in other words, one is able to change the nature of the spatial and scenic terrain within which one must function. Bull's respondents describe how, through programming their own aural environments, they are able to construct narratives that help them to find coherence in spaces that otherwise they would perceive as 'bereft of interest' (2000:39). In this way, the use of the personal stereo permits, as Bull puts it, 'biographical travelling' (ibid.):

The narrative quality that users attach to music permits them to reconstruct these narrative memories at will in places where they would otherwise have difficulty in summoning them up. These memories provide the user with a feeling of being wrapped up in their own significance whist existing in the perceived narrative anonymity or invisibility of their spatial present. (2000:39–40)

As with the music therapy example described above, personal stereo use allows Bull's respondents to cope with contingency (and the potential anxiety associated with uncertainty and an unpredictable life environment). Bull suggests that this private music listening is a means of recalibrating the relationship between intention, thought, and orientation. This process is two-pronged: it consists of music's use in relation to mood regulation and emotion (a topic I have explored in this chapter); and in relation to users' attempts to structure the content of their thoughts. Bull (like DeNora 2000, ch. 3) shows how respondents use music to hold on to moods, to alter energy levels, and generally to 'escape' from a current environment.

These uses in turn permit users to reappropriate the phenomenological features of time. Listening may reclaim time, convert it into time 'for self'. But, more profoundly, personal stereo use may provide a means of reconfiguring the perception of time's passing. Describing a respondent who listened every day on his journey to work, Bull shows how the journey 'becomes a function of the sequence of music listened to on the personal stereo' (2000:63). In these ways, Bull argues, the personal stereo is 'technologically empowering' such that, 'the headphones enclose the ears and substitute chosen and specific sound for the . . . sounds of the street' (2000:119).

Bull's approach is typical of the 'new' focus, within music sociology, upon consumption and use. This focus moves well beyond the earlier empirical concern with how musical 'meaning' was received. That perspective took as its end point listeners' evaluations or interpretations of music – what was thought of music as opposed to what people do with music. In all of this, Bull's study extends socio-musical paradigms. And, as discussed above, it shows just how important a material music is for the constitution of social experience.

There is, however, a gap in this perspective and that is that, in its prioritisation of consumption and use, it leaves in shadow the question of how specific musical materials may play a role in the processes Bull describes. One of the most obvious places this emerges is in the discussion of how time and time's perception are managed. For music's form, its internal contrasts and specifically musical parameters, may themselves package or bunch time, albeit not in deterministic ways. In my own study of music in aerobic exercise classes, this point was very clear: different types of musical materials could be used to facilitate particular courses and styles of exercise movement and motivation level. Thus, music is not only a tool used by individuals for self-determination and self-control; it is also used by individuals and organisations as a tool for the 'control' of others, as we saw above in the music therapy example.

Bull's study recognises this in so far as there are particular aspects of public space that individuals wish to resist. Some of these aspects involve negative features such as contingency, uncertainty, and the general buffeting characteristic of life in public spaces. Others involve resisting more intentional features of public space, and these features include aesthetic ecologies, often designed, as in the case of retail spaces, to control the inhabitants of those spaces.

It is here that we return to the germ of Adorno's critical focus, one which, in my view, Bull quite rightly criticises for its over-determination:

Adorno's analysis of auditory experience, in which structural imperatives take precedence in the constitution of an 'imaginary', appears to be similar to Lefebvre's. This potential weakness in their work needs to be addressed in order to gain a more dynamic understanding of personal-stereo use. I argue, somewhat generously perhaps, that their understanding of the colonization of experience that manifests itself in aspects of their work goes against the grain of their own theoretical frameworks in which there can be no mimetic, one-to-one relationship between subject and object, as this would reflect a collapse of the dialectical nature of experience. This drift into determinism I see as a consequence of insufficient attention to empirical study. This is particularly true of Adorno who has an incipient theory of oppositional experience contained in fragmentary form throughout his work to which he nevertheless pays very little attention. (2000:127)

'Empirical study': just how should this be configured if we are to explore the question of 'control'? Most recent music sociology has focused on consumption. It has done so from the point of view of what music can 'do' for those who appropriate it. This focus has centred on identity (music as a resource for affirming self, or group, or location-based identity, for example) and, as Bull's research illustrates, individual renegotiations of the public and personal parameters of time and space. This focus on musical activity – a position taken to extreme by Christopher Small in *Musicking* (1998) – is, as I have argued throughout this book, the right line of focus, albeit with a theory of music-as-affordance. The development of the scheme for exploring the Musical Event has been concerned with just this issue, with the individual experience of culture, and with the precise points at which music 'gets into' action. A critical difference, however, between the scheme for exploring Musical Events and most other concerns with consumption is that the Musical-Event paradigm maintains a space for musical material, for the ways in which music may be seen to inform consciousness, action, subjectivity. Music here is much more than a space into which the social is projected; music may provide a mediator through which the social is formulated; it is, in short, nothing less than a medium of social construction and, conversely, much more than a socially constructed medium. And it is here, in this focus on musical material, that it is possible to return, methodologically wiser perhaps, to Adorno's original concern. The focus on music as a potential technology of 'control' – part of Adorno's original critical project – draws the Musical-Event paradigm strongly in the direction of interdisciplinary research. It draws together musicology's abiding concern with musical structures; music education's focus on musical learning, that is learning both about and via music; ethnomusicology's focus on musical practices; sociology's traditional concern with structures, power, and agency; and popular music studies' eschewal of a priori value distinctions. The interdisciplinary focus on music's capacity to structure or mediate action (individual and/or collective) is precisely a focus that highlights music's dynamic powers. Such a focus leads back to some of the most inspirational writing in the music-sociology/ethnomusicology fields – John Blacking's focus on the musical environment and Raymond Williams's notion of 'structures of feeling':

> For what we are defining is a particular quality of social experience and relationship, historically distinct from other particular qualities, which gives the sense of a generation or of a period. The relations between this quality and the other specifying historical marks of changing institutions, formations, and beliefs, and beyond these the changing social and economic relations between and within classes, are again an open question: that is to say, a set of specific historical questions . . . We are talking about characteristic elements of impulse, restraint, and tone; specifically affective elements of consciousness and relationships: not feeling against thought, but thought as felt and feeling as thought: practical consciousness of a present kind, in a living and interrelating continuity. (1965: 131–2)

Here is the nub of a critical sociology of culture ('characteristic elements of impulse, restraint, and tone; specifically affective elements of consciousness and relationships'). We need to think about how to reveal the individual uses of culture/music, the deployments of particular cultural tools and repertoires, and, within that focus, *music*'s mediating capacities as themselves mediated by convention, learning, proximity, habit, and the history and social distribution of these things. For, because humans need to co-ordinate in order to survive, and because culture is about providing publicly available modes of doing and being, modes which are shared, which come to be evaluated, imported, exported, cultural materials do often come to be associated with regularities of response – with 'effects' – and in this respect music is no different from any other form of culture or way of making social life.

It is for this reason that culture is associated with patterns of collective conduct, with regulation and thus with 'control'. Here, then, we are returned to Adorno, namely to his focus on the dialectical relationship between subject and object. The object – in this case music – accumulates meaning and use historically; these, in turn, may give it the illusion of objectivity. But it is the subject who initiates and reproduces these uses (affordances) over time, inevitably, however, in relation to the objects which stand 'outside' of her making or 'control'. We draw upon and use the cultural tools that stand within our reach and these tools may be afforded from habit, proximity, serendipity, or chance, as well as due to often arduous or heroic forms of appropriation and creation. In real time, and through the course of everyday interaction, we may draw upon cultural tools in highly routine, predictable ways, and we may respond to culture in ways that are not only learned but habituated. Here, then, is the social basis for music's role as a technology of 'control': music may be employed to structure time (both time as externally represented and internally experienced) and space (ambience, bodily co-ordination) in particular ways, not all of them congruent with the more general liberation of consciousness and action.

6   After Adorno: rethinking music sociology

To speak of the sociology *of* music to is to perpetuate a notion of music and society as separate entities. It is also to imply that the task of socio-musical studies consists of various attempts to see the social in music – as influence on musical shape and style, and as ideology to be revealed in music's content. In all of this effort there is too much stasis, too much thinking 'about' music and what it says, what it does, what makes it take the forms that it assumes. There is, one might suggest, too much of an *academic* attitude to music here and too little interrogative focus on music as a medium of living and being.

With respect to the latter, Adorno's work is unparalleled as a serious alternative to the otherwise rather scholastic focus on music's social meanings and social shapings: it exceeds both semiotic and the now-traditional sociological focus on music's social production. Adorno focused on music's role in relation to consciousness, to the psycho-cultural foundations of social life. In that focus, he implicitly rejected the dualism of music and society.

Music *as* society – a summary of Adorno's view

To speak, in this way, of music as causative is to excise the 'and' from the phrase 'music and society'. It is instead to view music as a manifestation of the social, and the social, likewise, a manifestation of music. The difference between the two then becomes merely analytical – dependent upon temporal or spatial priority (such as whether one is interested in an extra-musical outcome of a Musical Event or in a musical outcome of a Social Event), and dependent upon where one begins in an analytical exercise. Music is thus not about, or caused by, the social; it is part of whatever we take to be the social writ large. Music is a constitutive ingredient of social life.

Adorno's recognition of this idea was, I suggest, the single most important aspect of his enormous contribution – and it was not a contribution to the field of music sociology, but to the much greater project of thinking about how we operate as human social beings. It is worth, at this stage, reviewing the features of that contribution.

Adorno was the first theorist of modern times to take seriously the classic, Platonic, concern with music's causative properties. This focus, otherwise abandoned by twentieth-century socio-musical scholarship, had been made all the more difficult because music – due to its so-called 'abstract' features (its involvement of neither images nor words) – was seen as distinct from social realities and thus impervious to social analysis. Adorno's great contribution was to eschew a focus on what music might mean or represent, and to concern himself instead with musical procedures and musical formal patterns. His focus centred on the compositional *handling* of music (music composition's procedural features). It implied that these features in turn structured listeners' patterns of responding to music – and thus to reality more generally.

In Adorno's eyes, musical procedures, the specific modes of music's material handling, were exemplary for praxis – for compositional praxis certainly (through the ways that musical compositions created sedimented history, a history with which subsequent composers had to grapple), but exemplary for thinking about the nature of reality. In Adorno's account of Schoenberg, for example, it is quite clear that music serves an almost allegorical function; it is a simulacrum of how one might seek to organise knowledge about the world. The fact that Schoenberg's music was shot through with dissonance was exemplary for a conception of reality revealed through contradiction. In this sense and via its exemplary or paradigmatic character, music served as an object lesson in how to think about, and attend to, material reality in extra-musical realms. Music, in this respect, held a didactic function in Adorno's scheme and Schoenberg's music provided a contrast structure against which 'all the darkness and inclarity of the world' (Adorno 1973) could be illuminated.

To speak of music as didactic in this sense is to move well beyond the idea of musical metaphor. It is not to point to structural similarities between music and some other activity or medium; rather, it is to observe that music shares basic procedural traits with extra-musical activities and that these traits will have consequences for the doing and handling of those extra-musical matters. It is here that we can begin to appreciate just how dynamic a medium music is in relation to extra-musical matters. And it is here, thanks to Adorno, that we can begin to see how music, in deciding how to handle, for example, the interrelationship between voice parts, is inevitably a moral medium: that morality is made manifest in and through music's handling of material.

These points could be made (and have, as I relate in chapters 1 and 3) in relation to textual as well as tonal praxis, and Adorno's own textual practices have helped to shed light on just this topic. Adorno's refusal to package his philosophy into formulaic statements, his delight in convolution and verbal 'dissonance', his use of exaggeration – all of these strategies resisted music's too-easy digestion, all perpetuated an almost limbic state of suspended recognition. This concern, with the moral and exemplary character of cultural praxis – whether textual or musical – in turn connects with a second aspect of music's didactic function. And it is here that we can begin to see how music's role in relation to cognitive orientation is, in turn, connected with music's more immediate appeal to the subjective and embodied features of music's audition.

This focus on music and cognition leads to Adorno's second major contribution to a theory of musical dynamism – that musical handling implies modes of listener response, an idea that is given play through Adorno's discourses on popular music and the music of which he disapproves (such as Stravinsky). According to Adorno, this music abetted 'darkness and inclarity' in so far as they inculcate reflex responses; they encourage the listener to give in to familiar pleasures and patterns. In this gratification is, simultaneously, pacification and, more insidiously yet, the reinforcement of standardisation. Through replication (through rehearing old favourites and through hearing generically similar music over time) there is, in other words, an autodidactic reinforcement of honed patterns of response and, thus, a draining away of the capacity for the listener's discernment of difference – in music or elsewhere. Through this process, music contributed to the standardisation and dulling of consciousness. From here it is not so far to a focus on how music may be used as an instrument of social control – in advertisement and marketing, in political campaigns, to configure conduct within physical spaces.

New methods, classic concerns

In the course of this book I have sought to take these ideas from Adorno and subject them to redevelopment. I have proposed new methods, in some cases more explicitly than in others and, perhaps inevitably, with varying degrees of success. The work in charting out this new terrain for music sociology is only just beginning; it is being conducted in a range of locations – ethnomusicology, music education, musicology, sociology, anthropology, geography, social psychology. The crux of my own criticism of Adorno's work has centred on the idea that, despite Adorno's concern with a philosophy of the actual, his work proceeded in an ungrounded manner, at a level that was too general and too abstract. I know this view will not be shared by everyone, in particular by many musicologists committed to the idea of music analysis as the analysis of musical discourse, i.e., as the observation of musical patterns and parameters articulated at the level prior to action – at the level of culture rather than culture-in-action.

As I have described in chapter 2, I believe there is a middle way that can be charted between the analysis of music-as-discourse and the analysis of music-as-action. This is via the concept of musical affordance. This notion allows us to maintain Adorno's concern with music's exemplary and didactic features, and with music's ability to configure its hearers' responses, while simultaneously removing these concerns from the sole purview of music analysis (music analysis becomes, as I tried to suggest in chapter 3, an important component, a means by which to generate investigative questions, not an explanatory resource in its own right). The focus on how music is drawn into action, how, within the Musical Event, music may be seen to participate, involves shifting from a concern with 'what' music does to a concern with 'how' music can be seen to afford specific actors resources for social-musical world building of any kind. This focus draws musicology and sociology more closely together into a new type of interdisciplinary project that transcends the traditional boundaries of both and there, I suggest, lie the makings of a very interesting adventure.

To put the key characteristic of this adventure somewhat cryptically, the project entails the following task: replacing what is currently too general with something more specific; and replacing what is currently too specific with something more general. In relation to the first half of this project, we need to move away from any attempt to arrive at general conclusions about what music does (e.g., the Mozart effect; music to drive in rush hour traffic; music for boosting purchases) to some very specific conclusions about how music is lodged within specific locations of use. From these specific studies it may, in time, then be possible to generate robust conclusions at a more general level about what music may be used to do. Conversely, it is necessary to move beyond the analysis of specific texts. We need to move fully away from the work concept to a far more general notion of how different types of musical materials may afford different actors different things at different times. Indeed, the work concept may itself provide a set of affordances for actors (imagine actors playing records for each other and saying 'this is a classic' – that may configure the listening situation in quite a different manner from a simple 'I like this one'). This, more general, focus on musical materials leads into the sociological concern with culture as providing a system of materials with which one may act, feel, do, and be. What is relinquished in terms of the focus on works and authors is gained at the level of thinking about cultural tools and cultural repertoires; it helps to highlight music as a medium of action and experience. In so doing, we chart a course between the notion that 'the music itself' is the author of music's effects (which would be linked to a paradigm consisting solely of music analysis) and the idea that music's effects derive from nothing more than what people say about music and its powers. We navigate towards, in other words, s symmetrical approach in which we pay equal attention to musical materials and to the circumstances in which these materials are heard and integrated into social experience in real time.

And it is here we arrive at the Musical Event. This concept is not without difficulty; to be sure, not everything that should be counted as part of the social world has actually 'happened'. And the concept of the Musical Event as discussed throughout this book tends to be biased in favour of transaction. That need not be the case – an event may occur in imagination, in a novel, and indeed the very term 'event' is merely a convenience to describe the conjunction of music and experience, real or imagined. In this respect, it has affinities with Max Weber's concept of action.

After Adorno?

Where is there to go after Adorno? Since his death, in 1969, we have seen many new directions within socio-musical study and I have described these in previous chapters: the production of culture or art worlds approach within sociology; semiotics and musical discourse analysis within musicology; the focus on music-making as activity within ethnomusicology; recent music sociology and social psychology of music. These last developments, with their focus on how people make and do things with music, have sought to move beyond the music/society dichotomy and it has been no secret within the pages of this book where my own particular sentiments lie. I have sought, in short, to highlight the ways in which Adorno's initial concerns may be advanced through a focus on particular, spatially, and temporally located instances of music's use and uptake, and to use these instances to try to capture the actual mechanisms through which doing music is simultaneously doing other things – thinking and remembering, feeling, moving/being, and co-operating, co-ordinating, and sometimes colluding with others. That project was described in chapter 2 and implemented in relation to a few of Adorno's key concerns in subsequent chapters. The aim of those chapters was indicative – to show but a few of the themes and possibilities that a grounded and overtly empirically oriented music sociology might help to develop. It is now time to draw together the strands pursued there. In the context of a Musical

Event, what can music do? And what can *music sociology* do to illuminate this process?

To answer the second question first: music sociology needs to follow Adorno's lead in taking on a holistic perspective. A key feature of this perspective, then, is to forgo attempting to divide the social-material-cultural world into 'parts' a priori (e.g., music, action, furnishings), but rather to look at how, within particular environments and temporal frames, people and things are put together – to look at the shifts, movements, and flows of people and things over time and space. To put this differently, it would behove music sociology to adopt a radical environmentalist position, one in which music is conceived as an environmental feature. From there, and without a priori assumptions about music and its role, we can follow actors as they orient to, invoke, mobilise, or otherwise engage with music – as they can be seen to be involved in Musical Events. (It is here understood that Musical Events can also be conceptualised, simultaneously, as other types of events – as conversational events, for example – the term 'Musical Event' is used here only as a device for highlighting and holding on to music's place in the crafting of action and experience, but it is but one medium of many and is only important only to the extent to which it is oriented by actors.)

So what can music do? We know that music is involved, that it is a participant in what happens over time and space. We have seen, for example, how music enters the production of knowledge; how it may serve as a mental switch, reminding actors of some things while simultaneously helping them to forget others. We have seen how music may provide templates for the shaping of ideas or representations about things, how it may come to exemplify a line or course of action or otherwise serve as a paradigm. We have seen how music may clutter the mind with reminders of givens and how this, at times, may serve as distraction from attempts to think. And we have seen how music may be an instrument of local memory production, a technology of memory in real time.

We have also considered music in relation to subjectivity, to the emotional and embodied flux that is experience. Here, music's material and physical properties, its iconicity and temporal features, are as vital as whatever musical convention may come to symbolise. And throughout all this, seen at both the individual level of practical musical consumption and at the collective levels upon which music consumption may be framed, we have seen the importance of music's link to other things: to discourses about music; to the material settings in which music is lodged; and to modes of musical attention.

Music acts, albeit only 'in concert' with the material, cultural, and social environments in which it is located. But because music is associated with effects, it may also lend itself to actors and organisations concerned with structuring the conduct (and subjectivities) of others, and it is here that music benefits from being considered in relation to humans' attempts to 'control' each other, in relation to institutional and organisational aims and objectives.

Music, stability, change

Music is implicated in social change – in large-scale change as seen in such things as social movement activity, but also in moment-to-moment transformation, as in changes of mood and social orientation. Music is a medium of change in so far as it may trigger memory, provide a model for thought or action, signal ambience, or provide parameters against which the body reorganises its processes of movement or energy. In this sense, music is a medium through which the social is temporally configured, through which difference takes shape from moment to moment.

It is thus possible to speak of the ways that music is a medium within and with which being is performed. It is a medium, in other words, of action. Music gives us modes and instrumentalities for doing social life. It is here that we can begin to see music as not distinct from 'society' but as a medium for doing what we then sometimes refer to as 'social' life. Music is, in this sense, social life, and socio-musical studies are not about how society can be found 'in' music at all but about how music is simply one way in which we do that which we end up *calling* social action. As John Cage put it, in relation to his famous 'silent' piece, 4'33" (which was anything but silent!):

Most people mistakenly think that when they hear a piece of music that they're not doing anything but that something's being done to them. Now this is not true and we must arrange our music, we must arrange our art, everything, I believe, so that people realise that they themselves are doing it and not that something is being done to them. (Nyman 1974:21)

Music sociology will have achieved its ultimate aim, in other words, when – in all realms of social life – we come to attend to the sounds that are all around us, to know these as our accomplices (and opponents) in the doing, being, and feeling that is social life. And in that knowing lies what Leonard Meyer once referred to as a radical empiricism and what Cage (Gena 1982:44) termed a 'demilitarisation of language; a serious musical concern'. In relation to the construction of a music sociology concerned with music's powers, then, we need to see how both we, as analytical agents, and those to whom we turn for examples of music-in-practice, can do no better than to take inspiration from Adorno's celebration of Schoenberg, in whose music he found his own adventurous exemplar:

Schoenberg's music demands from the very beginning active and concentrated participation, the most acute attention to simultaneous multiplicity, the renunciation of the customary crutches of a listening which always knows what to expect . . . it requires the listener to spontaneously compose its inner movement and demands of him not mere contemplation but praxis. (1967:149)

Bibliography

Adorno, T. 1973. *Philosophy of Modern Music.* (Trans. A. G. Mitchell and W. Blomster). New York: Continuum.
1976. *Introduction to the Sociology of Music.* (Trans. E. B. Ashton). New York: Continuum.
1981. *In Search of Wagner.* (Trans. R. Livingstone). London: Verso.
1981. *Prisms* (Trans. S. Weber and S. Weber). Cambridge, Mass.: MIT Press.
1992. *Mahler: A Musical Physiognomy.* (Trans. E. Jephcott). Cambridge: Polity.
1998. *Beethoven: The Philosophy of Music.* (Ed. R. Tiedemann, trans. E. Jephcott). Cambridge: Polity.
2002. *Essays on Music* (Trans. S. Gillespie, ed. with commentary R. Leppert). Berkeley, Los Angeles, and London: University of California Press.
Adorno, T. and M. Horkheimer. 1972. *Dialectic of Englightenment.* (Trans. J. Cumming). New York: Continuum.
Akrich, M. 1991. 'The Description of Technical Objects', in W. E. Bjiker and J. Law (eds.), *Shaping Technology/Building Society.* Cambridge, Mass.: MIT Press.
Areni, C. S. and D. Kim. 1993. 'The Influence of Background Music on Shopping Behaviour: Classical Versus Top-40 Music in a Wine Store', *Advances in Consumer Research* 20, 336–40.
Barbelet, J. M. 2002. 'Reflections on the Sociology of Emotions: the Section and the Discipline', *Emotions Section Newsletter*, American Sociological Association 16:1, 3–4.
Barnes, B. 1977. *Interests and the Growth of Knowledge.* London: Routledge.
1978. *T. S. Kuhn and Social Science.* London: Macmillan.
Barthes, R. 1990 [1977]. 'The Grain of the Voice', in S. Frith and A. Goodwin (eds.), *On Record: Rock, Pop and the Written Word.* London: Routledge, 293–301.
Becker, H. S. 1982. *Art Worlds.* Berkeley, Los Angeles, and London: University of California Press.
1989. 'Ethnomusicology and Sociology: A Letter to Charles Seeger', *Ethnomusicology*, 33, 275–85.
Bennett, A. 2000. *Popular Music and Youth Culture: Music, Identity and Place.* Basingstoke: Macmillan.

Benzon, W. 2000. *Beethoven's Anvil: Music in Mind and Culture*. New York: Basic Books.

Berezin, M. 2002. 'Secure States: Towards a Political Sociology of Emotion', in J. M. Barbalet (ed.), *Sociology and Emotions*. London: Basil Blackwell, 33–52.

Birke, L. . 'In Pursuit of Difference: Scientific Studies of Men and Women', in G. Kirkup and L. Smith Keller (eds.), *Knowing Women: Feminism and Knowledge*, Cambridge: Polity, 66–77.

Blau, J . 1989. 'High Culture as Mass Culture', in A. Foster and J. R. Blau (eds.), *Art and Society: Readings in the Sociology of the Arts*. Albany: State University of New York Press, 429–40.

Bloch, E. 1988. *The Utopian Function of Art in Literature*. Cambridge, Mass.: MIT Press.

Blomster, W. V. 1976. 'Sociology of Music: Adorno and Beyond', *Telos* 28 (summer), 81–112.

    1977. 'Adorno and his Critics: Adorno's Musico-Sociological Thought in the Decade Following His Death', *Musicology at the University of Colorado*, 200–17.

Born, G. and D. Hesmondhaugh. 2000. *Musicology and its Others*. Berkeley and London: University of California Press.

Bourdieu, P. 1984. *Distinction*. London: Routledge.

Bowler, A. 1994. 'Methodological Dilemmas in the Sociology of Art', in D. Crane (ed.), *The Sociology of Culture*. Oxford: Blackwells, 247–66.

Buck-Morss, S. 1978. *The Origin of Negative Dialectics*. New York: The Free Press.

Bull, M. 2000. *Sounding Out the City*. Oxford: Berg.

Burnham, S. 1995. *Beethoven Hero*. Princeton: Princeton University Press.

Butler, J. 1989. *Gender Trouble*. London: Routledge.

Cage, J. 1961. *Silence*. Middletown, Conn.: Wesleyan University Press.

Callon, M. 1986. 'Some Elements of a Sociology of Translation: Domestication of the Scallops and the Fishermen of St Beiene Bay' in J. Law (ed.), *Power, Action and Belief: A New Sociology of Knowledge*, 196–233.

Canetti, E. 1962. *Crowds and Power*. (Trans. C. Stewart). London: Gollancz.

Cavicchi, D. 2002. 'From the Bottom Up: Thinking About Tia DeNora's Everyday Life', *Action, Criticism and Thoery for Music Education* 1:2, 1–15. http://mas.siue.edu/ACT/v1/Cavicchi02.pdf

Citron, M. 1992. *Gender and the Musical Canon*. Cambridge: Cambridge University Press.

Clarke, E. and N. Cook (forthcoming). *Empirical Musicology*. Oxford: Oxford University Press.

Collins, H. 1983. 'An Empirical Relativist Programme in the Sociology of Scientific Knowledge', in K. Knorr-Cetina and M. Mulkay (eds.), *Science Observed: Perspectives on the Social Study of Science*. London: Sage, 85–114.

Collins, R. 1993. 'Emotional Energy as the Common Denominators of Rational Choice', *Rationality and Society* 5, 203–20.

Connerton, P. 1989. *How Societies Remember*. Cambridge: Cambridge University Press.

Cook, N. 1992. *Music, Imagination and Culture*. Oxford: Clarendon Press.

Cook, N. and Dibben. 2001. 'Musicological Approaches to Emotion', in P. Juslin and J. Sloboda (eds.), *Music and Emotion: Theory and Research*. Oxford: Oxford University Press, 45–71.

Cooley, C. H. 1902. *Human Nature and the Social Order*. New York: Charles Scribner's.

Davies, S. 2001. 'Philosophical Perspectives on Music's Expressiveness', in P. Juslin and J. Sloboda (eds.), *Music and Emotion: Theory and Research*. Oxford: Oxford University Press, 23–70.

De las Harras, V. 1997. '*What Does Music Collecting Add to our Knowledge of the Functions and Uses of Music?*, unpublished M.Sc. dissertation, Department of Psychology, University of Keele.

DeNora, T. 1986a. 'Structure, Chaos and Emancipation: Adorno's Philosophy of Modern Music and the Post-WW II Avant-garde', in R. Monk (ed.), *Structures of Knowing*. Lanham, New York, London: University Press of America, 293–322.

1986b. 'How is Extra-musical Meaning Possible? Music as a Place and Space for "Work"', *Sociological Theory* 4, 84–94.

1995a. *Beethoven and the Construction of Genius*. Berkeley, Los Angeles, and London: University of California Press.

1995b. 'Deconstructing Periodization: Sociological Methods and Historical Ethnography in Late Eighteenth-Century Vienna', *Beethoven Forum* 4, 1–15.

1996. 'From Physiology to Feminism: Reconfiguring Body, Gender and Expertise', *International Sociology* 11:3, 359–83.

1997. 'The Biology Lessons of Opera Buffa', in Mary Hunter and James Webster (eds.), *Opera Buffa in Mozart's Vienna*. Cambridge: Cambridge University Press, 146–64.

1999. 'Music as a Technology of the Self', *Poetics* 26, 31–56.

2000. *Music in Everyday Life*. Cambridge: Cambridge University Press.

2002a. 'Music into Action: Performing Gender on the Viennese Concert Stage, 1790–1810', *Poetics: Journal of Empirical Research on Literature, the Media and the Arts*, Special issue on 'New Directions in Sociology of Music' (guest ed. T. Dowd) 30:2 (May), 19–33.

2002b. 'The Role of Music in the Daily Lives of Women – the Case of Intimate Culture', *Feminism and Psychology*, Special issue on music and gender (guest ed. S. O'Neill) 12:2 (May), 176–81.

DeNora, T. and S. Belcher (n.d.). 'Interview with a Creative Music Therapist'. February 1998.

DiMaggio, P. 1982. 'Cultural Entrepreneurship in Nineteenth-century Boston', *Media, Culture and Society* 4, 35–50 and 303–22.

1997. 'Culture and Cognition', *Annual Review of Sociology* 23, 263–87.

Dowd, T. (forthcoming). 'The Mitigated Impact of Concentration on Diversity: New Performing Acts and New Firms in the Mainstream Recording Market, 1940–1990', *Social Forces*.

Durkheim, E. 1915. *The Elementary Forms of Religious Life*. New York: The Free Press.

Eco, U. with R. Rorty, J. Culler, and C. Brooke-Rose. 1992. *Interpretation and Overinterpretation*. Cambridge: Cambridge University Press.

Edström, O. 1997. 'Fr-a-g-me-n-ts: A Discussion on the Position of Critical Ethnomusicology in Contemporary Musicology', *Svensk Tidskrift for Musikforskning (Swedish Journal of Musicology)* 79:1, 9–68.

Etzkorn, P. 1973. 'Introduction', in *Music and Society: The Later Writings of Paul Honigsheim*. New York: John Wiley & Sons, 3–42.

Eyerman, R. and A. Jamieson. 1998. *Music and Social Movements*. Cambridge: Cambridge University Press.

Farrell, G . 1998. 'The Early Days of the Gramophone Industry in India', in A. Leyson, D. Matless, and G. Revill (eds.), *The Place of Music*. New York: The Guilford Press, 57–82.

Fauquet, J. M. and A. Hennion. 2002. *La grandeur de Bach*. Paris: Fayard.

Featherstone, M., M. Hepworth, and B. Turner. 1991. *The Body: Social Processes and Cultural Theory*. London: Sage.

Ferlinghetti, L. 1958. A Coney Island of the Mind. New York: New Directions.

Fox Keller, E. 1983. *A Feeling for the Organism*. New York: W. H. Freeman.

Frazer, E. and D. Cameron. 1988. 'On Knowing What to Say', in R. Grillo (ed.), *Social Anthropology and the Politics of Language*. London: Routledge, 25–40.

Frith, S. 1996. *Performing Rites: Evaluating Popular Music*. Oxford: Oxford University Press.

Frith, S. and A. Goodwin. 1990. *On Record: Rock, Pop and the Written Word*. London: Routledge.

Garfinkel, H. 1967. 'Passing and the Managed Achievement of Sexual Status as an Intersexed Person', 116–85, in *Studies in Ethnomethodology*. New York: The Free Press, 116–85.

Geena, P. 1982. *A John Cage Reader in Celebration of his 70th Birthday*. New York: C. F. Peters.

Gillespie, S. 1995. 'Translating Adorno: Language, Music, and Performance'. *Musical Quarterly* 79, 55–65.

2002. 'Translator's Note', in T. W. Adorno, *Essays on Music*. Berkeley, Los Angeles, and London: University of California Press, xiii–xv.

Goehr, L. 1992. *The Imaginary Museum of Musical Works: an Essay in the Philosophy of Music*. Oxford: Oxford University Press.

Goffman, E. 1961. *Asylums*. Garden City: Doubleday.

Gomart, E. and A. Hennion. 1999. 'A Sociology of Attachment: Music Amateurs, Drug Users', in J. Law and J. Hazzard (eds.), *Actor Network Theory and After*. Oxford: Blackwell, 220–47.

Green, L. 1997. *Music, Gender and Education*. Cambridge: Cambridge University Press.

2001. *How Popular Musicians Learn*. London: Ashgate.

Hanrahan, N. 2000. *Difference in Time*. New York: Praeger.

Hennion, A. 1992. *La passion musicale*. Paris: Metaille.

1995. 'The History of Art-lessons in Mediation', *Réseaux: The French Journal of Communication* 3:2, 233–62.

1997. 'Baroque and Rock: Music, Mediators and Musical Taste', *Poetics* 24, 415–25.

2001. 'Music Lovers: Taste as Performance', *Theory, Culture and Society* 18:5, 1–22.

Hennion, A . and J. M. Fauquet. 2001. 'Authority as Performance: the Love of Bach in Nineteenth-century France', *Poetics: Journal of Empirical Research on Culture, the Media and the Arts,* Special issue on 'Musical Consciousness', (ed. T. DeNora and R. Witkin), 29:2, 75–88.

Heritage, J. 1984. *Garfinkel and Ethnomethodology.* Cambridge: Polity.

Hetherington, K. 1998. *Expressions of Identity.* London: Sage.

Hochschild, A. 1983. *The Managed Heart.* Berkeley and Los Angeles: University of California Press.

Hoppin, R. 1978. *Medieval Music.* New York: W. W. Norton.

Husch, J. 'A Music of the Workplace: A Study of Muzak Culture', Ph.D. diss., University of Massachusetts 1984.

Huxley, A. 1932. *Brave New World.* London: Chatto.

Jackson, S. 1999. *Questioning Heterosexuality.* London Sage.

Jay, M. 1973. *The Dialectical Imagination.* Boston, Mass.: Little, Brown and Co. 1984. *Adorno.* London: Fontana.

Johnson, J. 1995. *Listening in Paris: A Cultural History.* Berkeley, Los Angeles, and London: University of California Press.

King, A. 1999. 'Against Structure: a Critique of Morphogenetic Social Theory', *Sociological Review,* 47:2, 198–222.

(forthcoming). *Against Structure.* London: Routledge.

Kingsbury, H. 1991. 'Sociological Factors in Musicological Poetics', *Ethnomusicology* 35, 195–219.

Knorr-Cetina, K . 1983. 'Introduction', in K. Knorr-Cetina and M. Mulkay (eds.), *Science in Context.* London: Sage, 1–18.

Korczynski, M. (2003). 'Music at Work: Toward an Historical Overview'. *Folk Music Journal* 3.

Kuhn, T. 1962. *The Structure of Scientific Revolutions.* Chicago: University of Chicago Press.

Lamont, M. 2000. *The Dignity of Working Men.* Cambridge, Mass.: Harvard University Press.

Lanza, J. 1994. *Elevator Music: a Surreal History of Muzak, Easy-listening and Other Moodsong.* London: Quartet Books.

Lash, S. and J. Urry. 1994. *Economies of Signs and Space.* London: Sage.

Latour, B. 1987. *Science in Action.* Cambridge, Mass.: Harvard University Press. 1989. *The Pasteurization of France.* Cambridge, Mass.: Harvard University Press. 1991. 'Where Are the Missing Masses? A Sociology of a Few Mundane Artefacts', in W. E. Bijker and J. Law (eds.), *Shaping Technology/Building Society: Studies in Sociotechnical Change.* Cambridge, Mass.: MIT Press, 225–58.

Law, J. 1994. *Organising Modernity.* Cambridge: Polity.

Law, J. and J. Hassard (eds.). 1999. *Actor Network Theory and Beyond.* London: Sage.

Leppert, R. 1993. *The Sight of Sound.* Berkeley, Los Angeles, and London: University of California Press.

2002 'Commentary and Notes', in, Adorno, *Essays on Music.* Berkeley, Los Angeles, and London: University of California Press.

Leppert, R. and McClary, S. (eds.). 1987. *Music and Society*. Cambridge: Cambridge University Press.

Leyshon, A., D. Matless, and G. Revell. 1999. *The Place of Music*. Surrey. The Guildford Press.

Lury, C. 1996. *Prosthetic Culture: Photography, Memory and Identity*. London: Routledge.

MacInnes, D. and C. Park. 1991. 'The Differential Roles of Charateristics of Music on High- and Low-Investment Customers' Processing of Ads', *Journal of Consumer Research* 18, 161–73.

Maisonneuve, S. 2001. 'Between History and Commodity: the Production of a Musical Patrimony Through the Record in the 1920–1930s', *Poetics* 29:2, 89–108.

Martin, E. 1989. *The Woman in the Body*. Milton Keynes: Open University Press.
1991. 'The Egg and the Sperm', *Signs* 16, 485–501.

Martin, P. 1995. *Sounds and Society: Themes in the Sociology of Music*. Manchester: Manchester University Press.

Mayo, E. 1933. *The Human Problems of an Industrial Civilization*. New York: Macmillan.

McClary, S. 1987. 'On Talking Politics During the Bach Year', in R. Leppert and S. McClary (eds.). *Music and Society*.

McNeill, W. 1995. *Keeping Together in Time*. Cambridge, Mass.: Harvard University Press.

Melucci, A. 1996a. *Challenging Codes*. Cambridge: Cambridge University Press.
1996b. *The Playing Self*. Cambridge: Cambridge University Press.

Merquior, J. G. 1986. *Western Marxism*. London: Paladin.

Meyer, L. 1967. *Music, the Arts and Ideas*. Chicago: Univeristy of Chicago Press.

Middleton, R. 1990. *Studying Popular Music*. Milton Keynes: Open University Press.

Milliman, R. 'Using Background Music to Affect the Behaviour of Supermarket Shoppers', *Journal of Marketing* 46, 86–91.

Moore, L. J. 1997. 'It's Like You Use Pots and Pans to Cook With', *Science, Knowledge and Human Values* 22:4, 434–71.

Moores, S. 1990. *Interpreting Audiences*. London: Sage.

Murdoch, I. 1985. *The Good Apprentice*. London: Chatto and Windus.

Negus, K. 1992. *Producing Pop: Culture and Conflict in the Popular Music Industry*. London: Edward Arnold.

Neilly, L. 1995. 'The Uses of Music in People's Everyday Lives', unpublished undergraduate diss., Department of Psychology, University of Keele.

Nersessian, N. 1984. *Faraday to Einstein: Constructing Meaning in Scientific Theories*. Bostin: Martinus Nijhoff.

North, A. and D. Hagreaves. 1997. 'Music and Consumer Behaviour', in D. Hargreaves and A. North (eds.), *The Social Psychology of Music*. Oxford: Oxford University Press, 268–89.

North, A., D. Hargreaves, and J. McKendrick. 1997. 'In-store Music Affects Product Choice', *Nature* 390, 132.

Nyman, M. 1974. *Experimental Music: Cage and Beyond*. Cambridge: Cambridge University Press.

O'Neill, S. 1997. 'Gender and Music', in D. Hargreaves and A. North (eds.), *The Social Psychology of Music*. Oxford: Oxford University Press, 46–66.

Orwell, G. 1961. *1984*. New York: American Library.

Paddison, M. 1982. *Adorno's Aesthetics of Music*. Cambridge: Cambridge University Press.

Pareto, W. 1963. *The Mind and Society*. New York: Dover.

Parkinson, B., P. Totterdell, R. Brier, and S. Reynolds. 1992. *Changing Moods: The Psychology of Mood and Mood Regulation*. London: Longman.

Peterson, R. (ed.). 1976. *The Production of Culture*. Los Angeles: Sage.

1997. *Creating Country Music*. Chicago: University of Chicago Press.

Peterson, R. and D. Berger. 1990 [1975]. 'Cycles in Symbol Production: the case of popular music', ed. S. Frith and A. Goodwin (eds.), *On Record: Rock, Pop and the Written Word*. London: Routledge.

Peterson, R. and A. Simkus. 1992. 'How Musical Tastes Mark Occupational Status Groups', in M. Lamont and M. Fournier (eds.), *Cultivating Differences: Symbolic Boundaries and the Making of Inequality*. Chicago: University of Chicago Press, 152–86.

Pickering, Michael. 1982. *Village Song and Culture*. London: Croom-Helm.

Plato. 1966. *The Republic*. (Ed. and trans. by A. I. Richards). Cambridge: Cambridge University Press.

Pollner, M. 1987. *Mundane Reason*. Cambridge: Cambridge University Press.

Press, A. 1994. 'The Sociology of Cultural Reception: Notes Toward an Emerging Paradigm', in D. Crane (ed.) *The Sociology of Culture*, 221–46.

Prichard, C. 2000. *Making Managers in Universities and Colleges*. Milton Keynes: Open University Press.

Radley, A. 1990. 'Artefacts, Memory and a Sense of the Past', in D. Middleton and D. Edwards (eds.), *Collective Remembering*. London: Sage.

Radway, J. 1988. 'Reception Study: Ethnography and the Problems of Dispersed Audiences and Nomadic Subjects', *Cultural Studies* 2, 59–76.

Randel, D. 1992. 'The Canon in the Musicological Toolbox', in K. Bergeron and P. Bohlman (eds.), *Disciplining Music: Musicology and its Canons*. Chicago: University of Chicago Press, 10–23.

Remmling, G. 1967. *The Road to Suspicion*. New York: Appleton Century Crofts.

Riesmany, D. 1950. *The Lonely Crowd*. New Haven: Yale University Press.

Ritzer, G. 1993. *The McDonaldization of Society*. London: Sage.

Sacks, O. 1990. *Awakenings* (rev. edn). London: Palgrave.

Schrade, L. 1955. *Bach: The Conflict Between the Sacred and the Secular*. New York: Merlin.

Schutz, A. 1964. 'Making Music Together', in *Collected Papers Vol. 2*. The Hague: Martinus Nijhoff.

Shepherd, J. 2001. 'Sociology of Music', in S. Sadie *et al.* (eds.), *The New Grove Dictionary of Music and Musicians*, 603–14.

2002. 'How Music Works – Beyond the Immanent and the Arbitrary', *Action, Criticism and Theory for Music Education* 1:2.

Shepherd, J. and P. Wicke. 1997. *Music and Cultural Theory*. Cambridge: Polity.

Sloboda, J. 1992. 'Empirical Studies of Emotional Response to Music', in M. Riess-Jones and S. Holleran (eds.), *Cognitive Bases of Musial Communication*. Washington, DC: American Psychological Association.

2000. 'Everday Uses of Music Listening', *Proceedings of the 5th International Conference on Music Perception and Cognition.* Seoul National University.

Sloboda, J. and S. O'Neil 2001. 'Emotions in Everyday Listening to Music', in P. Juslin and J. Sloboda (eds.), *Music and Emotion: Theory and Research.* Oxford: Oxford University Press.

Small, C. 1998. Musicking: *The Meaning of Performing and Listening.* Hanover and London: Wesleyan University Press.

Smith, P. C. and R. Curnow. 1966. '"Arousal Hypothesis" and the Effects of Music on Purchasing Behaviour', *Journal of Applied Psychology* 50, 255–6.

Steward, S. and S. Carratt. 1984. *Signed Sealed and Delivered: True Life Stories of Women in Pop.* London: Pluto.

Stockfelt, Ola . 1997. 'Adequate Modes of Listening' (trans. Anahid Kassabian and Leo G. Svendsen), in D. Schwarz, A Kassabian, and L. Siegel (eds.), *Keeping Score: Music, Disciplinarity, Culture.* Charlottesville: University Press of Virginia, 129–46.

Subotnik, R. R. 1976. 'Adorno's Diagnosis of Beethoven's Late Style', *Journal of the American Musicological Society,* 29.

1991. *Developing Variations: Style and Ideology in Western Music.* Minneapolis: University of Minnesota Press.

1996. *Deconstructive Variations: Music and Reason in Western Society.* Minneapolis: University of Minnesota Press.

Swidler, A. 1986. 'Culture in Action: Symbols and Strategies', *American Sociological Review* 51, 273–86.

2001. *Talk of Love: How Culture Matters.* Chicago: University of Chicago Press.

2002. *Culture: The Newsletter of the Culture Section of the American Sociological Association* (winter), 6–8.

Tagg, P. 1991. *Fernando the Flute: Analysis of Musical Meaning is an ABBA Mega-Hit.* Liverpool: The Institute of Popular Music, University of Liverpool.

Tönnies, F. 1957. *Community and Society.* (Trans. and ed. C. Looms). Ann Arbor: Michigan State University Press.

Tota, A. L. 1997. *Etnografia dell'arte: Per una sociologia dei contesti artistici.* Rome: Logia University Press.

2001a. *La memoria contesa. Studi sulla comunicazione sociale del passato.* Milan: Angeli.

2001b. 'Homeless Memories: How Societies Forget their Past', *Studies in Communication Sciences* 1:2, 193–214.

2001c. 'When Orff Meets Guinness: Music in Advertising as a Form of Cultural Hybrid', *Poetics* 29:2, 109–24.

Turner, B. S. 1984. *The Body and Society.* London: Sage.

Urry, J . 1996. 'How Societies Remember the Past', in S. Macdonald and G. Fyfe (eds.), *Theorizing Museums. Representing Identity and Diversity in a Changing World.* Oxford: Blackwell, 45–61.

Van Rees, C. J. 1987. 'How Reviewers Reach Consensus on the Value of Literary Works', *Poetics* 16, 275–94.

Wagner-Pacifici, R. 1996. 'Memories in the Making: the Shapes of Things that Went', *Qualitative Sociology* 19, 301–21.

Wagner-Pacifici, R. and B. Schwartz . 1991. 'The Vietnam Veterans Memorial: Commemorating a Difficult Past', *American Journal of Sociology* 97, 376–420.

Weber, M. 1958 [1921]. *On the Rational and Social Foundations of Music*. Carbondale: Southern Illinois University Press.

— 1978. *Economy and Society*. (Ed. G. Roth and C. Wittich). Berkeley and Los Angeles: University of California Press.

Weber, W. 1975. *Music and the Middle Class*. London: Croom Helm.

— 1992. *The Rise of Musical Classics in Eighteenth-century England*. Oxford: Clarendon Press.

Webster, J. 1994. 'The Concept of Beethoven's "Early" Period in the Context of Periodizations in General', *Beethoven Forum* 3, 1–27.

Williams, R. 1965. *The Long Revolution*. Harmondsworth: Penguin.

Williams, S. 1996. 'The Emotional Body', *Body & Society* 2:3, 125–39.

Williams, S. J. 2001. *Emotions and Social Theory: Corporal Reflections on the (Ir)rational*. London: Sage.

Wilson-Koves, D. 2000. 'The theatrical coherence of intimacy'. Paper given to International Conference on States of the Arts, Department of Sociology, University of Exeter.

Witkin, R, W. 1995. *Art and Social Structure*. Cambridge: Polity.

— 1998. *Adorno on Music*. London: Routledge.

— 2002. *Adorno on Popular Culture*. London: Routledge.

Woolgar, S. 1997. 'Configuring the User: Inventing New Technologies', in K. Grint and S. Woolgar (eds.), *The Machine at Work*. Cambridge: Polity, 65–94.

Zolberg, V. 1990. *Constructing a Sociology of the Arts*. Cambridge: Cambridge University Press.

— 1996. 'Museums as Contested Sites of Remembrance: The Enola Gay Affair', in G. Fyfe and S. MacDonald (eds.), *Theorising Musicians*. London: Sage.

Index

Printed in the United States
By Bookmasters